NORTH AMERICAN ELDERS

NORTH AMERICAN ELDERS

United States and Canadian Perspectives

EDITED BY
ELOISE RATHBONE-McCUAN
AND BETTY HAVENS

CONTRIBUTIONS TO THE STUDY OF AGING, NUMBER 8

Greenwood Press

NEW YORK • WESTPORT, CONNECTICUT • LONDON

Library of Congress Cataloging-in-Publication Data

North American elders.

(Contributions to the study of aging, ISSN 0732-085X ;
no. 8)
  Bibliography: p.
  Includes indexes.
  1. Aged—United States—Social conditions. 2. Aged—
Canada—Social conditions. 3. Aged—Care—United
States. 4. Aged—Care—Canada. 5. Gerontology—
Cross-cultural studies. I. Rathbone-McCuan, Eloise.
II. Havens, Betty, 1936– . III. Series.
HQ1064.U5N595   1988   305.2'6'0973   87-15048
ISBN 0-313-25484-2 (lib. bdg. : alk. paper)

British Library Cataloguing in Publication Data is available.

Library of Congress Catalog Card Number: 87-15048
ISBN: 0-313-25484-2
ISSN: 0732-085X

First published in 1988

Greenwood Press, Inc.
88 Post Road West, Westport, Connecticut 06881

Printed in the United States of America

The paper used in this book complies with the
Permanent Paper Standard issued by the National
Information Standards Organization (Z39.48-1984).

10 9 8 7 6 5 4 3 2 1

Contents

71

Illustrations

TABLES

Foreword: Canadian Studies Perspectives

In a psychological sense the border between Canada and the United States is one of the most consciously defended boundaries on the face of the earth. Enormous amounts of Canadian money are spent to reinforce the economic and cultural aspects. Free-trade negotiations are plagued by protectionism and the reemergence of a strong Canadian nationalism. It is often said that while United States ignorance of Canada is benevolent, Canadian knowledge of the United States is malevolent. There is enormous discrepancy in the knowledge of each country concerning the other.

A partial solution to this problem is the rapid development in the United States, in the last fifteen years, of courses on Canada and of formal Canadian Studies Programs. The Canadian government has recognized the value of encouraging the development of courses and research on Canada by making available monetary grants for such activities. Professor Rathbone-McCuan, one of the editors of this volume, received such an award. However, these active efforts alone will not produce the burgeoning of courses and research on Canada needed to redress the knowledge imbalance.

An alternative may be to increase application of the "comparative approach" such as that applied in this work. This approach has been successfully used for a long time, especially in geography, history, sociology, and anthropology. Only in the increasingly popular study of Canadian literature—English and Quebecois—has the comparative approach lagged, perhaps for valid reasons. This popular short-term approach may lead to a demand for greater Canadian-specific content.

Unfortunately, little academic work has been devoted to U.S.–Canadian social policy analyses. This volume, therefore, represents a pioneering effort in the aging social policy area. It presents a continental viewpoint on demography, and then deals with seven specific topics by means of a nation-to-nation analysis. Most of the comparative social science texts have tended to be single-authored or to have originated in one of the two countries. This volume is unique in that it is the work of scholars from both countries, each contributing their expertise. The editors represent gerontological experts from Canada and the United States and must be applauded for undertaking this comprehensive work and bringing it to a successful conclusion. It is hoped that this will be the first of many similar studies that enhance mutual understanding of each country in the other. Greater knowledge of these two great neighbors and their social problems will reinforce the existence of each through greater understanding of the other.

Edward J. Miles

Foreword: Cross-National Gerontology

Cross-national gerontological studies in the United States and, to a somewhat lesser extent, in Canada have largely focused on comparisons of each of the two countries with countries of other continents. Equivalent, collaborative, cross-national data collection by the two North American neighbors has been largely neglected. In this seminal volume the editors (Eloise Rathbone-McCuan and Betty Havens) have presented material representing parallel information from each of the two countries. In so doing, they have made abundantly clear the need for rectifying the dearth of conjoint cross-national research effort.

Despite their ethnocultural similarities and the commonality of their shared landmass, there are differences between the American and the Canadian populations. Major disparities exist in the size and distribution of their respective populations. Differing social, educational, political, economic, and health policy factors have a significant impact upon the ways and means by which each deals with its elderly population. Under these circumstances the demographic techniques of cohort tracking and of examining previous cohort trails have considerable predictive potential for policy formulation.

This volume serves as a timely stimulus for researchers in both countries to rethink their research directions in this field along these lines of enquiry. The implications are clear that such conjoint, comparative investigation is long overdue and could lead to rational policy and viable practice development.

J. A. MacDonnell
Jean M. Maxwell

Acknowledgments

This book is the result of significant cooperation and collaboration on the part of gerontologists within our two countries and across the border. All the chapter contributions reflect the scholarly efforts of the authors, who present their own opinions and not the official positions of the organizations with which they are affiliated.

Appreciation is extended to the Canadian Embassy in Washington, D.C., for granting Eloise Rathbone-McCuan a 1985–86 Faculty and Institutional Research Program award in order to complete this project. The conceptual framework of cross-national gerontological research is supported by the Canadian Association on Gerontology and the Gerontological Society of America. We are gratified by the leadership extended by both professional organizations to promote the advancement of gerontological research and its application for the improved quality of life of elderly persons in Canada and the United States.

A special thank you is extended to all our authors, their institutions, and our colleagues Dorothy Brown, Jane White Hennessey, Solange Lagasse, and Barbara Wescott for their administrative, clerical, and personal support.

Eloise Rathbone-McCuan
Betty Havens

NORTH AMERICAN ELDERS

CHAPTER 1

Introduction

Eloise Rathbone-McCuan and Betty Havens

The rationale for producing this cross-national study of aging in Canada and the United States was to offer scholars, practitioners, and students a comprehensive text about aging in the two countries. Cross-national research and policy analyses in the field of gerontology have become more commonplace as the aging population has come to dominate the social welfare and economic maintenance agenda of many nations. Those multinational concerns have failed to stimulate the production of a text that considers a nation-to-nation analysis between Canada and the United States. The timely production of this text was possible because of a convergence of certain factors and conditions:

1. The editors were aware of the lack of such work available to a variety of audiences. There is a broad spectrum of professionals who have diverse reasons to be concerned with the similarities and differences in the aging process and its impact on citizens in both nations.

2. Until very recently there was an acute shortage of Canadian research, policy, and practice materials that could be used by scholars and students of gerontology. Until the publication of this text there was no single source that included original research on Canadian issues with a comparative data base from the United States. The study of aging in each country and both countries will be further advanced by a text with this dualistic standpoint.

3. Canada and the United States have an interdisciplinary core of gerontologists examining health and social service provision to the aged. Their efforts will be enhanced by the indepth consideration of special groups of high-risk elderly and specialized service delivery issues requiring targeted policies that are addressed in this book.

4. The editorial leadership and institutional support was available from both countries to produce a comparative text. It was a unique opportunity

to involve numerous scholars from the two nations as contributors, providing a broad perspective on aging in North America.

5. The availability of this text is matched by the growing interest in both countries to exchange information beyond national boundaries. Aging is an area with significant social and economic repercussions for many nations which are now seeking applicable social technologies through international exchange.

Cross-national efforts require a commitment to extensive analyses of many similar issues, philosophies, historical trends, and contemporary policies of the countries under comparison. These dimensions with all their variations in and between Canada and the United States afford valuable gerontological data. At the beginning of the project, the editors explored their respective conceptualizations about the cross-national framework to be applied. There are some obvious commonalities, such as: (a) historical development of colonial settlements and the east to west flow of populations during migration cycles; (b) similar geographical patterns and landmass equivalencies with many common regional features distributed from east to west; (c) ethnocultural and legal orientations based upon a Judaic-Christian tradition and later evolved from a British common law tradition supportive of personal and civil liberties; (d) language that evolved from common primary linguistic roots and was complemented by overlapping secondary languages; (e) demographic trends of common age structures with the greatest similarity among the aging and aged cohorts; and (f) educational commitments to the populace to assure availability of higher education and incentives to advance empirically based professional knowledge.

Equally important are the contrasts between Canada and the United States encompassing: (a) the variation in the values of multiculturalism reflected in the mosaic structure of Canada and the multicultural "melting pot" of the United States; (b) different national commitments to the importance of bilingual competencies among Canadians and a determination of a single-language standard in the United States; (c) alternative governmental structures that offer Canadians an extension of majority party rule as distinct from the candidate-party configuration in the United States; (d) different patterns of population density and of mobility within regional areas; and (e) varied histories of political ideologies with social democratic thought dominating in Canada and individual conservatism prevailing in the United States.

In combination these patterns give rise to important but unexplored fields for comparative gerontology. As the critical knowledge base within each country emerges, so does the foundation for serious comparative analyses. It is the goal of this book to present independently produced knowledge integrated into a framework of cross-national conceptualization that takes into account variables which demonstrate both the similarities and differences between Canada and the United States.

RATIONALE FOR CONTENT AND STRUCTURE

To meet the scholarly and applied criteria of comparative data analyses, the editors selected topics that provided vital points of comparison between the two countries. Wherever possible, topical areas were selected to reflect conditions facing the aging population which were of mutual national concern. It was especially important to identify topics that have both immediate and longer-range social policy implications, whether or not the direction of each country's policy was distinct or similar.

In the selection of a northern American focus, the editors applied the United Nations definition of North America that excludes Mexico from the region shared by the United States and Canada. Application of this cross-national definition in no way minimizes the very special importance of the Mexico-America relationship and the unique status of Hispanic elderly in the United States aging population. On the contrary, the special aging issues and unique problems of isolation Hispanic elderly experience within the dominant American culture are separate and distinct cross-national concerns requiring more research.

Topics addressed result from having identified Canadian and United States specialists willing to work independently to capture their particular national perspectives in areas of their own research interests. Seven comparative units are included. The first section on demography and aging was prepared for North America by a single authorship team. Their analysis involved a special challenge. They constructed a profile of aging populations in both countries and thereby give an overview of North American demographic trends. Leroy O. Stone and Susan Fletcher give readers an introduction to the special demographic characteristics of the aging cohorts cross-nationally and indicate important methodological issues present in current analysis and those required to determine future demographic profiles.

The remaining seven comparative units include chapters containing independent data from Canada and the United States relevant to the particular topic. John Myles and Robert B. Hudson contributed chapters describing the current structure and content of federal and provincial/state policies that direct distribution of economic benefits and health and social service coverage for the elderly. Each author analyzes the points at which policies fall short in meeting the current needs of the elderly cohorts eligible for pensions and other economic benefits. Major and minor social policy reforms are suggested to correspond to the particular needs of the aging populations in the two countries.

Neena L. Chappell as well as Laurence G. Branch and Allan R. Meyers document the historical evolution of long-term care and its current status in each country. Long-term care policy in the United States is in massive disarray. Chappell evaluates the importance of redirecting Canadian social policies from institutional priorities to community-based care that also includes allocations of major respite care resources to support informal net-works. Each country relies on a combined set of federal, provincial/state, and local initiatives to provide long-term care to its elderly citizens. Some of the most appropriate care options reflecting the desire and potential of elderly persons to remain in the community are those not supported by current directives and priorities in long-term care policy.

Neither country has achieved satisfactory community-based care options for the older chronic mentally ill population. Dehospitalization has occurred in both countries under the rubric of deinstitutionalization, but the failures of posthospital alternatives are blatant. Colin M. Smith and Nancy J. Her-man trace the historical developments of mental health treatment in Canada. They contribute a unique account of how older chronic mentally ill persons are attempting to survive in the midst of nonsupportive situations. Hashimi follows the historical flux of the American mental health movement's re-sponse to chronically impaired groups. She presents comparative data from New York and Wisconsin that illustrate the state-by-state variations in serving this population. Smith and Herman consider how the provinces of Saskatchewan and Ontario have progressed in their efforts to provide for this population without arriving at effective alternatives.

Anne Martin Matthews and Raymond T. Coward write multidimensional overviews of rural aging concerns that have an impact on significant pro-portions of the elderly population in each country. The current and emerging data on the rural Canadian population are limited in comparison to that available to describe conditions faced by the variety of aged rural dwellers in the United States. The larger body of knowledge about aging in rural America has not stimulated either consistent or comprehensive social policies to address these special needs. Numerous methodological issues, including a universal definition of rurality, are barriers to advancing national and cross-national rural gerontology.

Systems of care for the veteran population are in place in Canada and the United States. Each system is faced with the special care demands of aged veterans and with larger numbers of near-old or young-old veterans from the Second World War and Korean conflict. A. Margery Boyce and Ellen M. Gee describe policies and benefits available to the Canadian veteran population, concentrating attention on the oldest group from the First World War. They discuss the pattern of provincial relationships with the Depart-ment of Veterans Affairs arising from the plan to serve older veterans in the community care systems available to nonveteran elderly persons. Philip G. Weiler discusses the complex bureaucratic structure of the Veterans Administration system from the standpoint of geriatric programs. Demo-graphic trends show that long-term care demands will be placed on the United States system. This will require diverse noninstitutional long-term care options, with implications for the methods and levels of financial com-mitment from the federal government to care for eligible veterans.

Native Americans and Canadians are neglected subgroups in the spectrum of gerontological research and policy analysis. Rosamond Vanderburgh offers an anthropological analysis of the Canadian native cultural revitalization process being undertaken within the Ancinabe band of Southern Ontario. She details the special importance of this cultural reestablishment in giving special status and significance to the role of "elder" among the oldest band members. Paul Stuart and Eloise Rathbone-McCuan approach the concerns of the Native American elderly population from a historical perspective. They account for the evolution of major federal policies dominating all native groups, with long-term care needs being of special significance to the elders and their families.

The final unit addresses cross-national families that have historical and/or current connections between the United States and Canada. Mary Murphy Robertson offers an in-depth analysis of the contemporary experiences that American women have encountered in their roles as wives and mothers married into extended French-Canadian families. She documents how these women have managed to maintain ties to their own parental kin systems in the United States while also adapting to the cultural and family variations in Quebec. Peter Woolfson recounts the past stages of movement of French-Canadian families into the United States and how these family units adapted in the United States. He details how they maintained their Franco-American subculture through their multigenerational groupings. He considers the shifting bonds among the generations with the weakening linkages to traditional Quebec culture.

MAJOR THEMES OF THE BOOK

This research collection is designed for multiple audiences that wish to understand the cross-national content and context of aging in Canada and the United States. This knowledge will be useful for students, researchers, practitioners, and policymakers. The chapters address dimensions of cross-national gerontology. Also, the text provides new scholarly streams that may be introduced into Canadian Studies programs in American universities. In spite of extensive comparative research in the field of Canadian Studies, experts have ignored the economic, social, political, and cultural impact of aging in North America. The structure of the text provides for various user approaches, for example, as a single work used in traditional textbook format or as a unit-by-unit reference source on separate issues as these meet an individual reader's need or interest on a given topic.

The book clusters three theses—education, practice, and policy—each thesis having equal importance to Canadian and United States gerontologists. Research is the necessary link among themes as well as the vehicle through which the authors contributed their information and the editors attempted to build the bridging perspectives. Each of the themes may be of greater or less interest to the individual reader. It is their interconnectedness that gives value to the common concerns of the two countries.

The first goal is to broaden educational perspectives. The contents of the book give evidence of the importance of bringing Canadian—United States comparisons into the forefront of cross-national gerontology. Its availability will encourage Canadian Studies programs to expand course work into social welfare, specifically gerontology and related human services. Canadian students will have a text to study the research of their country's scholars creating the emergent core of a Canadian Gerontology. That is a knowledge base separate from the gerontological knowledge of the United States. Their United States counterparts taking gerontology courses will have an opportunity to study gerontology through a comparative perspective on issues relevant to their northern neighbor nation about which they have little understanding.

Direct practice and service delivery information is a second goal that cuts across all chapters and units. It is critical to reinforce the concept that core gerontological practice principles have a universal quality. Practice methods can be improved through the study of their application in alternative cultural contexts controlled by different policy perspectives and varying delivery structures. Equally important, practitioners need encouragement to develop interest in cross-national applications of helping approaches and intervention systems. The included studies evidence the immediate importance of and potential for the transfer of micro- and macro-gerontological practice technologies between the United States and Canada. Opportunities exist to expose leading practitioners of both countries to the data so as to influence and to advance the quality of practice standards.

The final goal—perhaps the one most heavily emphasized by a majority of the contributors—is cross-national social policy based on internal analyses for each country. Numerous possibilities exist for collaboration among scholars. There are relatively few barriers for the pursuit of every facet of gerontological policy comparison between the United States and Canada once comparable data can be identified. Our overall objective is to foster an understanding of how the elderly populations in Canada and the United States might benefit, now and in the future, were a comprehensive sense of a "North American gerontology" guiding policy formulation and implementation.

I

DEMOGRAPHY

This chapter attempts to make comparisons between Canada and the United States with regard to a few of the basic features of population aging. Scarcity of space precludes any effort to dwell upon unique features of one country for which there is no meaningful analogue in the other country. For example, as is well known, ethnic origin and language are important variables in both countries; but several relevant aspects of these variables differ in noncomparable ways between Canada and the United States. In spite of the fact that the chapter gives emphasis to comparable aspects of population aging between Canada and the United States, we acknowledge the need to keep in mind significant unique features of each country.

The main body of the text starts with a conventional review of selected aspects of population aging in North America (north of the Rio Grande). This review focuses on the past and projected time patterns of population aging, noting the accompanying growth rates and absolute sizes of the older population, as well as the imbalance between the numbers of men and women. Some attention is paid to the subpopulation aged 85 and over.

A special feature of this chapter is the presentation of new cohort-specific data and observations, most of which deal with Canada because of resource constraints. By integrating data from a sequence of censuses, a set of abridged life-tables recently published by Dhruva Nagnur of Statistics Canada Analytical Studies Branch (Nagnur, 1986b), and a long-time series on annual deaths by single years of age, this chapter spotlights aspects of the "demographic trails" left by major cohorts in the course of the aging of population during this century.

The cohort perspective is adopted by first considering rates of entry of new cohorts into the older population. The chapter then turns to an assessment of intercohort and gender differences (within a cohort) in the speed and age pattern of attrition in size as cohorts move toward extinction. Both the United States and Canada are covered in this phase of the work.

Improvement in survival rates is then explored by the study of cohort-specific series of these rates. This exploration is based upon simple transformations of series in Nagnur's life-tables (Nagnur, 1986b) and reconstructions of extinct populations using annual deaths by single year of age. This study is preceded by a substantial comparative view of mortality declines at the older ages in the United States and Canada.

The chapter closes with a brief consideration of some ramifications of the observed intra- and inter-cohort survivorship patterns. The subjects covered in this review are widowhood, living arrangements, and support network help capacity.

CHAPTER 2

Demographic Variations in North America

Leroy O. Stone and
Susan Fletcher

DEMOGRAPHY

When the authors decided to respond positively to the request to include Canada—United States comparative materials in this work, an initial thought was to estimate certain key values for North America as a whole by merging data from both countries. However, it soon became apparent that the results would be swamped by the United States data. To appreciate this point, try to put into your mind the picture of a large elephant standing beside a deer. Keep that picture in mind when you think about the relative sizes of Canada and the United States. (See Figure 2.1.)

We need some arbitrary cutting points to make international comparisons. In both Canada and the United States age 65 is meaningful in terms of the flow of benefits from public resources to groups in society. Using this cutting point for comparison, Figure 2.1 reminds us that in 1985 there were more Americans at least 65 years old than there were people of all ages in Canada. At 28 million, those older Americans were more than ten times as numerous as the 2.6 million Canadians aged 65 and over.

For the purposes of this discussion, let us define *population aging* as a series of increases in the percentage of older persons in the total population, and use age 65 as an arbitrary cutting point to facilitate the international comparison.

In the course of population aging, the age structure of a population may be said to attain higher and higher levels of maturity. Age structure maturation and population aging are equivalent. The opposite of age structure maturation is rejuvenation, as happened during the Baby Boom period from roughly 1946 to 1966.

The term *cohort aging* means a series of increases in the average age of a cohort. When the word *cohort* is used below, it will usually refer to a

Figure 2.1
Total Population and Population Aged 65 and Over, Canada and the United States, 1985

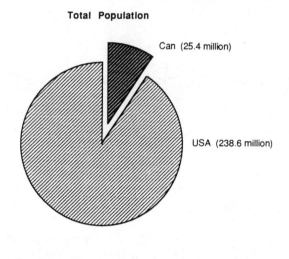

Total Population

Can (25.4 million)

USA (238.6 million)

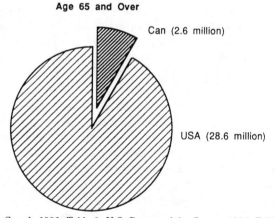

Age 65 and Over

Can (2.6 million)

USA (28.6 million)

Source: Statistics Canada 1986: Table 2; U.S. Bureau of the Census 1984: Table 6.

birth cohort, though the time period (for the set of births that will be deemed to form a cohort) could be large enough to cover what is sometimes considered to be a generation (a period containing a sequence of several annual birth cohorts). The authors support V. W. Marshall's view that it is useful, at least in social gerontology, to think of a generation as being comprised of those whose lives were shaped during a period of history that we now consider to be distinctive because of the special events of that period (Marshall, 1983). This is a different concept of generation than that normally used in demography.

TIME PATTERN OF POPULATION AGING IN NORTH AMERICA

At the mid–1980s the United States has a more mature age structure than does Canada. More than one in nine (i.e., nearly one-eighth) Americans are aged 65 and over, while just over one in ten Canadians are similarly aged. Both populations have begun to show mature age structures, in sharp contrast to the immature ones they had in 1900 when neither country had much more than 5 percent of its population above the age of 65. (Compare L. Bouvier et al., 1975; L. O. Stone and S. Fletcher, 1980; S. A. McDaniel, 1986.)

Population aging since the turn of the century has been gradual, except during the Baby Boom era of about twenty years after World War II, when population aging practically stalled in the United States and was reversed in Canada. That era was a period of age structure rejuvenation for Canada. Contributing to this Canada-America divergence was a strong wave of immigration that was particularly consequential for Canada; for example, immigrants resulting from the Hungarian revolution of 1956.

Another period of marked slowdown in the speed of population aging is drawing near for both Canada and the United States. This period will last from the late 1980s to the end of the first decade of the twenty-first century, based on setting the lower bound of the older population at age 65.

Although this period may look like a "breathing spell" before the real explosion in the number of seniors that will come with the advance of Baby Boomers into retirement age, this view does not take into account the fact that North America is in the midst of a long period of high rates of growth of the population that some call the *oldest-old*. While this growth does not mean accelerated population aging, established research findings about age patterns of intensive usage of social and other supports suggest that it is important for resource utilization.

The latest Statistics Canada and United States Bureau of the Census projections [henceforth the unqualified phrase "the projections" will refer to the 1985 Statistics Canada projections (Statistics Canada 1985a), and the 1984 Census Bureau projections (Bureau of the Census 1984)] suggest a pattern in which Canada will draw somewhat closer to the American level of maturity of population age structure during the remaining years of this century. By the year 2000, roughly 13 percent of Canada's population is expected to be at least 65 years old (Statistics Canada 1985a, Projection 5). Over the same time period the percentage of population aged 65 and over is projected to rise from the current 12 percent to just above 13 percent in the United States (Bureau of the Census 1984, Middle Series Projection

14). During the next century, however, age structure maturation could again proceed more rapidly in the United States than in Canada.

Population aging could accelerate sharply in both countries when the Baby Boomers (those born between 1946 and 1966) begin to penetrate the current main ages for retirement after 2010. The extent of the acceleration is presently uncertain. The chief source of uncertainty is our inability to be confident about what the children and grandchildren of the Baby Boomers will do with regard to family building, since it is these grandchildren who will be the main producers of babies in the opening decades of the twenty-first century.

It seems reasonably certain, however, that there will be substantial population aging over the second and third decades of the next century. As B. J. Soldo states, "The birth cohort of the 1950s is so large that the proportion of elderly between 2001 and 2020 will increase regardless of whether fertility remains at its current low level of about 1.8 children per woman or takes an unexpected turn upward toward an average of 3 children" (Soldo, 1980:10).

The American projections for the percentage of population aged 65 and over in 2020 indicate a figure in the neighborhood of 18 percent (Bureau of the Census 1984: Table 6). The corresponding projections for Canada suggest a figure somewhat about 16 percent. In other words, for North America we can expect that by 2020 the measured level of age structure maturity will rise to at least six percentage points above the current values (Statistics Canada 1985a: 338–42).

Both sets of national population projections envisage further maturation of the country age structures between 2020 and 2030. In 2030 more than one out of five Americans (21 percent) could be 65 or older. The corresponding Statistics Canada projections point to a somewhat lower level of age structure maturity for Canada in 2030 (just below 19 percent aged 65 or more).

GROWTH PATTERNS IN THE SENIOR POPULATION

The aging of the North American population is equivalent to higher than average growth rates for the older population. As is true of population aging itself, the rate of expansion in the total number of older persons has varied from one period to another. The following remarks will focus upon the projected growth rates and changes in the absolute numbers of seniors of different ages.

In contrast with the slow growth of the total population, which is projected to rise at an average annual rate close to 1 percent in both countries during the last two decades of this century, the population aged 65 and over will (barring a major catastrophe) grow more than twice as fast (Table 2.1). The projections for Canada suggest an average annual rate of growth

Table 2.1
Population Growth and Sex Ratio at Selected Ages, Canada and United States, 1920–2030

Average Annual Population Growth Rate					Population In Thousands					Men per 100 Women	
Time Period(1)	Total	65+	75+	85+	Year	Total	65+	75+	85+	65+	85+
Canada											
1920 - 30	1.79	3.72	3.18	1.76	1920	8659.6	406.4	126.8	20.5	104.1	84.7
1930 - 40	1.15	3.36	4.24	4.32	1930	10208.0	557.6	167.1	24.1	104.9	81.2
1940 - 50	2.05	4.12	3.99	5.33	1940	11381.0	744.8	237.9	34.5	108.9	81.6
1950 - 60	3.03	2.92	4.44	4.25	1950	13712.0	1051.3	332.8	52.9	104.1	77.5
1960 - 70	1.95	2.49	3.54	6.96	1960	17870.0	1357.8	480.7	75.4	95.2	77.0
1970 - 80	1.26	3.49	3.08	4.57	1970	21350.9	1695.7	650.7	127.9	82.0	67.2
1980 - 90	1.13	3.49	4.58	3.94	1980	24042.5	2286.9	851.4	186.3	75.0	50.5
1990 - 00	1.20	2.36	3.84	5.76	1990	26749.4	3084.0	1241.4	259.7	73.2	39.9
2000 - 10	0.90	1.56	1.81	3.51	2000	29966.0	3811.1	1718.0	409.2	75.2	40.0
2010 - 20	0.82	2.94	1.34	1.03	2010	32689.9	4405.6	2028.9	552.8	76.3	40.8
2020 - 30	0.70	2.51	3.57	1.70	2020	35368.9	5699.1	2300.0	609.9	77.7	43.0
					2030	37846.5	7127.2	3120.7	713.5	78.3	43.9
United States											
1920 - 30	1.63	3.41	2.88	4.48	1920	105883.4	4950.7	1482.2	212.1	101.4	104.1
1930 - 40	0.74	3.61	3.85	0.75	1930	123101.9	6637.7	1908.9	307.2	102.0	68.4
1940 - 50	1.52	3.73	4.78	7.87	1940	132161.0	9032.5	2642.9	330.2	96.6	67.2
1950 - 60	1.78	3.07	3.72	4.64	1950	152274.0	12398.0	3905.0	590.0	89.5	70.0
1960 - 70	1.33	2.40	4.31	7.54	1960	179325.6	16207.2	5359.3	863.8	82.1	62.9
1970 - 80	1.15	2.71	3.00	4.79	1970	203209.5	20101.1	7669.1	1515.1	72.3	56.1
1980 - 90	1.02	2.41	3.71	4.79	1980	226545.7	25549.4	9968.8	2240.0	67.6	43.7
1990 - 00	0.74	1.02	2.62	4.87	1990	249557.0	31697.0	13662.0	3312.0	66.3	38.4
2000 - 10	0.57	1.22	0.95	3.30	2000	267936.0	34922.0	17244.0	4926.0	65.1	37.8
2010 - 20	0.52	3.81	1.42	0.81	2010	283241.0	39197.0	18879.0	6552.0	66.2	37.6
2020 - 30	0.23	1.93	3.93	2.16	2020	297988.0	54128.0	21568.0	7081.0	79.2	37.8
					2030	304806.0	64579.0	30045.0	8611.0	71.6	40.2

1. Data after 1980 are projections.

Source: U.S. Bureau of the Census 1964: T. 47, T. 189; 1973: T. 189; 1983: T. 43; 1984: T. 6. Statistics Canada 1973: 10,19,29,39,49,59; 1982: T. 5; 1985a: 302–322; and unpublished data from Demography Division.

of just below 3 percent per year (Statistics Canada 1985a: 56) for the population aged 65 and over, while those for the United States point to a level near 2 percent (Bureau of the Census 1984: Table 6).

The twenty-year average annual growth rate at the levels just shown imply substantial increases in the absolute numbers of older North Americans. There were roughly 2.6 million Canadians aged 65 and over in 1985. If the projections prove to be reasonably correct, roughly 4.4 million Canadians will fall within that age range when the leading edge of the Baby Boom generation crosses the age–65 threshold in the year 2010 (Statistics Canada 1985a: 56). At the middle of the 1980s about 29 million persons in the United States were aged 65 and over, and the U.S. Bureau of Census projections suggest that there will be 39 million similarly aged persons around 2010 (Bureau of the Census 1984: Table 6).

Soldo states that "after 2010 the aging of the post–World War II 'baby boom' generation will set off a 'senior boom.' . . . After 2030 the growth of the older population will probably fall sharply again as the small cohorts born during the later 1960s and the 1970s cross the threshold into old age" (Soldo, 1980:7). The projected number of American seniors for the year 2030 stands at about 65 million (Bureau of the Census 1984: Table 6).

A similar picture, though with a very much smaller absolute number, can be painted for Canada, using the latest Statistics Canada projections. They suggest that between 2010 and 2030 the number of Canadians aged 65 and over will jump from 4.4 million to 7.1 million (Statistics Canada 1985a: 56).

Explanation of the Time Patterns of Population Aging and Senior Population Growth

These variations in the growth rates of the total population and of different age groups result mainly from historical cycles in the birth rate. Cycles in international migration are also relevant, but they are of less importance. In recent years the sharp falls in mortality rates at the older ages have also become significant in explaining the time pattern of senior population growth.

Since the purpose of this chapter is to exposit features of population and cohort aging in a comparative North America context, extensive explanations are being omitted.

MATURATION WITHIN THE OLDER POPULATION AGE STRUCTURE

Within the older population itself, the next forty-five years will see rapid growth in the group with more advanced age. The Canadian population aged 75 and over is expected to triple in size to reach about 3 million by

2030. This pattern of very fast growth for the older segments of the senior population is projected for the United States as well. The number of Americans aged 75 and over is projected to rise from roughly 12 million in the mid–1980s to 30 million by 2030. However, both sets of national projections anticipate a moderate tapering off of the growth rate for the 75-and-over age group in the opening two decades of the next century.

In spite of their tiny percentage of the total population (roughly 1 percent in Canada and in the United States at the mid–1980s), the subpopulation aged 85 and over merits careful attention. The number of Americans aged 85 and over could jump from about 2.8 million at the mid–1980s to 4.9 million by the year 2000; and by the year 2030 this subpopulation could comprise nearly 3 percent of the American nation and number 8.6 million. (See C. M. Taeuber, 1983: 3 and U.S. Senate 1986: 11.)

The Canadian projections anticipate a huge growth rate of 4 percent or more per annum for those aged 85 and over in the remaining years of this century, and continuing strong growth (above 3 percent per year) into the first decade of the next. In consequence, the numbers of Canadians in this age range will jump from about 200,000 in the mid–1980s to more than 400,000 by the year 2000. In other words, a veritable population explosion among seniors of more advanced age is underway and will not end soon. (See Stone and Fletcher, 1986.)

A particularly sharp rise will occur among those aged 85 and over, relative to those 65 and more, over the period from 1990 to 2010 (Figure 2.2). After 2010 the percentage of seniors aged 85 years or more will begin to decline as the Baby Boom generation will move strongly into the youngest ranks of the older population. In both countries the percentage of population aged 85 and over will remain at much less than 5 percent up to the year 2030, after which it will commence another strong rise.

The importance of these numbers has been well stated by Soldo:

In 1950, 32 percent of elderly persons were 75 years of age or over; in 2000, some 45 percent will probably be in that category, of which well over half will be 80 years or older. This change has important policy implications which are often overlooked. It is the "old old" (those 75 years of age and over) who generate the most intensive demand for health care services, particularly costly long-term care services (Soldo, 1980:10–11).

A more recent report by the U.S. Senate Special Committee on Aging adds the following observations:

[The 85 +] population is also expected to triple in size between 1980 and 2020 and increase seven times between 1980 and 2050.... [This] has far-reaching implications for public policy because of the high probability of health problems and need for health and social services for this age group.... Because of the increase in the very old population, it is increasingly likely that older persons will themselves have a

Figure 2.2
Percentage Aged 85 or More in the Population above 64 Years Old,
Canada and the United States, 1920 to 2030

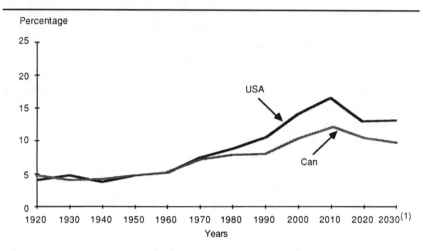

1. Data for 1990 to 2030 are projections.
Source: U.S. Bureau of the Census 1964: T.47, T.189; 1973: T.189; 1983: T.43; 1984: T.6.
    Statistics Canada 1973: 10,19,29,39,49,59; 1982: T.5; 1985a: 302–322; and unpublished
    data from Demography Division.

surviving parent. Four- and five-generation families are becoming more common
(U.S. Senate 1986: 15)

THE IMBALANCE BETWEEN THE SEXES

Also of very great social and economic significance is the rising numerical
predominance of women over men in the older population, which both
Canada and United States have been showing. This predominance will increase slightly over most of the remaining years of this century (Table 2.1).
In the 1980 census of the United States, there were 68 men for every 100
women aged 65 and older. A gradual fall in this ratio is projected for the
year 2000—65 men for every 100 women aged 65 and over. An even greater
imbalance is evident among persons aged 85 years and older.

For both Canada and the United States, the projections envisage a gently
rising ratio of men to women in the older population during the early decades
of the next century. This is partly due to the expected fall in the proportion
of those aged 80 and over during those years, as the Baby Boomers invade
the ranks of seniors. In addition, there is an assumption of gradual decline
in the size of the male-female longevity gap in the years ahead.

The predominance of women in the older population is more pronounced
in the United States than in Canada (Table 2.1). The pattern of sharply

declining ratios of men to women took hold in Canada only within the last 25 years, while it has been evident in the United States since before World War II (Soldo, 1980; U.S. Senate 1986: 19). However, the projections suggest that again a kind of catch-up is going on between the two countries, as they are expected to be very close in sex ratios at the older ages by the turn of the century.

THE 40-YEAR CULTURAL DOMINANCE OF THE BABY BOOM GENERATION AND INCREASED HETEROGENEITY IN FUTURE SENIOR POPULATIONS

The subjects raised in the foregoing discussion comprise much of the standard fare of a demographic overview of population aging in North America. Almost exclusive focus on such subjects has led many to think that if population aging is an increase in the proportion of elderly and this increase is mostly due to fertility, then a profound study of population aging boils down to a phase of fertility analysis. However, there are other worthwhile ways to define aging from a group perspective. One example involves a focus upon the aging of cohorts.

Cohort Demographic Trails

New cohorts with culturally innovative sets of values and traditions are continually entering the senior ages, while others are leaving it. Those leaving it are unlike the cohorts that leave other age groups because they are in the process of leaving the society forever. As they do so, the very character of the society may change fundamentally. Thus the rate at which major cohorts enter and leave the older population may have an impact on the pace of social change, as well as on the complexity of the requirements and options with which the planners and deliverers of social services (in the broadest sense of this phrase) may be confronted. (For related information see McDaniel, 1986: 3–6 and Soldo, 1980: 6.)

So important are the implications of the ideas just set forth that we need a concept to help us focus thoughts upon them, and help orient the study of population aging toward a greater emphasis upon those implications. The authors propose the concept of *cohort trail*, which is the idea that a cohort blazes a path through the society up to the time of its extinction; and upon that extinction leaves behind it a legacy whose breadth and influence depend upon the extent to which that trail managed to be influential and distinctive while the cohort was alive. The character of the population of elders depends upon the distinctive features and the relative dominance of the trails that its constituent cohorts have blazed, and upon the speed with which those cohorts undergo attrition in size toward the moment of extinction. Of particular interest in this discussion is a cohort's demographic trail. This is composed of the time tracks of key demographic variables for that cohort over its life course.

Renewal of the Older Population

For the remainder of this chapter, focus will be placed upon the older population and, to the extent feasible, upon the comparative experiences of different aging cohorts. This focus orients us toward looking at the size and structure of the older population as outcomes of processes of cohort emergence (entry of new cohorts into the ranks of the senior population), and attrition toward eventual extinction. The net result of cohort emergence and extinction is renewal of the older population.

If we set an arbitrary statistical lower boundary for the older population at age 65, we can indicate crudely the trends and fluctuations in the rate of entry of new cohorts into the population of the elderly by measuring the quinquennial changes in the ratio of population aged 65–69 to the aggregate aged 65 and over. This measure is a kind of five-year senior population rate of entry, emergence, or becoming. It should be noted that when the older population gets larger and larger through declining mortality rates at the upper ages, the ratio of population aged 65–69 to those aged 65 and over will tend to decline; thus we should pay particular attention to its pattern of cyclical fluctuation over a series of time periods.

There was a positive momentum (cyclical updrift) of the rate of entry into the older population in Canada from the 1950s to the 1970s, and in the United States from the 1960s to the 1970s (Figure 2.3). The projected index then shows a downdrift over the 1980s and the 1990s in both countries, after which it fluctuates upward with unprecedented strength in the first two decades of the next century.

Baby Boom Generation

This pattern indicates that there is a potential for the Baby Boom generation to become the dominant cultural and economic force (from the viewpoint of cohort determinants of such force) in the older population for a period of over forty years, even though the Baby Boom was only 20 years (1946–66 roughly) in length. The loss of positive momentum in the rate of entry into the older population over the third decade of the next century will merely serve to reinforce the massive presence of Baby Boomers in the older population.

Further support for the notion of extended dominance of the Baby Boom can be found by looking at patterns of retirement and related issues about postretirement incomes. Pension and other retirement income issues, as well as older-worker opportunity issues linked strongly to that generation, will

Figure 2.3
Five-Year Cohort Entry Rate[1] and Momentum of the Entry Rate[2] into the Older Population, Canada and the United States, 1920 to 2030

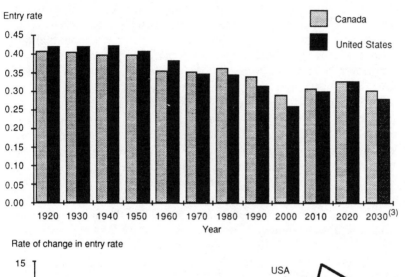

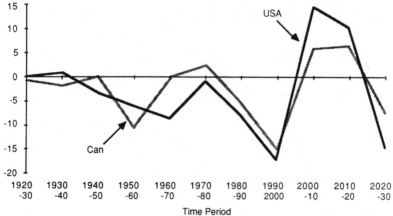

1. Five-year Cohort Entry Rate is the proportion aged 65–69 among all those aged 65 and over.
2. Momentum of the Entry Rate is the rate of change, expressed as a percentage change, from one time point to another (e.g. from 1920 to 1930) in the entry rate.
3. Data after 1980 are projections.

Source: U.S. Bureau of the Census 1964: T.47, T.189; 1973: T.189; 1983: T.43; 1984: T.6. Statistics Canada 1973: 10,19,29,39,49,59; 1982: T.5; 1985a: 302–322; and unpublished data from Demography Division.

be in ascendancy as early as the 1990s. (For supporting comments see Stone and Fletcher, 1980: 89–96.)

New high levels of senior population heterogeneity will likely occur in North America during the first third of the next century. This forecast can be supported by a consideration of the joint operations of cohort entry into the older population and cohort attrition. Offsetting the process of cohort entry into the older population is the perpetual loss of members from any cohort (cohort attrition) in that population. When the attrition rate is slowing down, from cohort to cohort, while the entry rate is strong, high levels of cultural heterogeneity in the older population can be expected. The slowing attrition rate sets up a force that tends toward retardation of the rate of turnover in population composition among elders.

Figure 2.4 points clearly to the slowing down of the rate of cohort attrition among women as we go from earlier to later cohorts in Canada and the United States. Continuation of this pattern points to enhanced levels of heterogeneity in the older population. For example, the cohort aged 45–49 in 1980 will be entering the 80-and-over age group in the same period when there will be very high older population entry rates produced by the Baby Boom generation. A projected 43 percent (as measured from the 1980 base year) of North American women and 20 percent of the men in this cohort will likely be alive and aged 85–89 in 2020. The decade 2010–20 will be the period in which the Baby Boom generation will begin flooding into the currently prime ages of retirement. Thus we have the makings of enormously high levels of heterogeneity in the older population over certain years in the future.

THE RECENT SHARP FALL IN MORTALITY RATES WITHIN THE SENIOR POPULATION

Lying behind the slowing rate of attrition, as we go from earlier to later cohorts of seniors, is the well-known factor of mortality rate changes. This section will briefly review mortality rate changes from a cohort perspective. To set a background for the review, the section commences with a comparison of the recent United States and Canadian patterns of mortality decline at the older ages.

Several analysts of American and Canadian data have called attention to the recent marked declines in mortality rates among elders, particularly women, since the 1960s. (See Nagnur, 1986a; Taeuber, 1983; J. S. Siegel and Davidson, 1984; I. Rosenwaike, N. Yaffe and P. C. Sagi, 1980.) According to Siegel and Davidson:

Age-specific death rates at the older ages for the period 1940 to 1980 reflect a sharp deceleration of the reduction in mortality among the older population during the late 1950s and the early 1960s, as compared with earlier and later years.... The

Figure 2.4
Census Survival Rate for Women in the Cohorts aged 45–49 in 1920,
1950, and 1990, Canada and the United States[1]

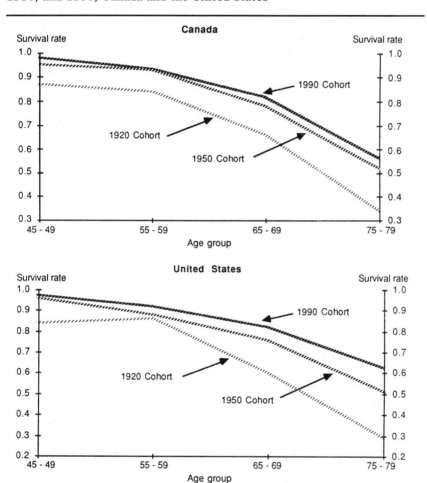

1. Each curve pertains to one cohort. A point plotted on that curve represents the estimated probability of surviving to the next age group. For example, the point above 45–49 is the ratio of the cohort's size at age 55–59 to its size at age 45–49, based on census data and population projections.

Source: U.S. Bureau of the Census 1964: T.47, T.189; 1973: T.189; 1983: T.43; 1984: T.6. Statistics Canada 1973: 10,19,29,39,49,59; 1982: T.5: 1985a: 302–322; and unpublished data from Demography Division.

annual data for the sixties and seventies show that a turning point in the trend of mortality at the older ages was reached about 1968, and that after that year, mortality at these ages resumed a strong downward trend (Siegel and Davidson, 1984:44).

Especially striking has been the decline in the mortality rate for the 85-and-over age group in the United States. This rate did not fall significantly over the period from 1955 to 1967. However, in the 1968–78 period it declined at an average annual rate slightly faster than 2 percent (Fingerhut, 1984; and see also National Center for Health Statistics, 1986).

A 1986 report of U.S. Senate Special Committee on Aging suggests that most of the increasing life expectancy since 1970 has been due to decreased mortality among the middle-aged and elderly population (U.S. Senate 1986: 22). For Canada, Nagnur has done a relevant analysis covering the period from 1921 to 1981. He found that since 1951 mortality rate declines in the older population have contributed significantly to the rising life expectancy at birth. Among women, 37 percent of the 1951–81 increase in life expectancy at birth is attributable to mortality rate declines among women aged 65 and over (Nagnur, 1986b).

In an earlier work, Nagnur indicated:

From 1921 to 1981, there have been significant increases in the expectation of life and survivors at successive ages.... Significant and in some cases remarkable improvements have been registered in the probabilities of survival to older ages—say 65, 75 and 85.... With respect to women, the improvements have been still more spectacular than those for men (Nagnur, 1986a:84).

For some thirty years or so older women in Canada have shown a remarkable series of substantial falls in mortality rates. For example, among women aged 70 years of age or more, the death rate declined by 6 percent or more over each of the six five-year periods between 1951 and 1981 (Stone and Fletcher, 1986, Chart 3.1). Much more recently, in the late 1970s, older men had a similar fall in mortality rates. Prior to that time, older men have had mainly weak and sporadic death rate declines.

One result of the mortality declines just reviewed is a notable advance in life expectancy among seniors. Figure 2.5 shows comparative data for the United States and Canada.

These dramatic falls in mortality have been focused among specific classes of cause of death. Notable are the causes associated with the heart and the cerebrovascular system (Rosenwaike, Yaffe and Sagi, 1980). For further discussion see Nagnur, 1986b; Siegel and Davidson, 1984; Taeuber, 1983.

The mortality declines have been much sharper for women than for men. In the process male-female differences in life expectation at birth approached a peak in the late 1970s in both Canada and the United States. (Compare Siegel and Davidson, 1984: 55–56.) There is now a suggestion that the

Figure 2.5
Life Expectancy at Selected Ages, by Sex, Canada and the United States,
1920 to 1980

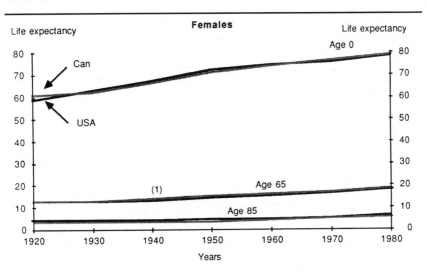

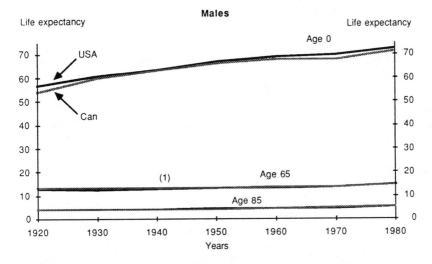

1. USA and Canada are not separately identified when the curves are very close to each other.
Source: Nagnur 1986b: T.C.1; U.S. Department of Health and Human Services 1986: T.6–4.

male-female gap in life expectancy may be decreasing slightly in America. "Between 1981 and 1982, life expectancy for males at birth increased by four-tenths of a year, slightly more than the three-tenths of a year gain for females" (U.S. Senate 1986: 22). In Canada the male-female gap in life expectancy at birth fell slightly (0.26 of a year) from 1976 to 1981 (Nagnur, 1986b).

COHORT PERSPECTIVE ON MORTALITY DECLINES AMONG THE OLDER POPULATION

The following discussion looks at mortality declines in the senior population from a cohort perspective. The data are limited to Canada in this example. One primary data source is a very recent publication of abridged life-tables by Dhruva Nagnur (Nagnur, 1986b). Further observations from the cohort viewpoint may be made through the use of a long series of annual deaths by single years of age to reconstruct extinct cohorts, using the Method of Extinct Generations (F. Depoid, 1973; F. Bayo, 1972; I. Rosenwaike, 1968).

Each curve in Figure 2.6 plots an aspect of the demographic trail of a birth cohort. Each one of these curves refers to a group that was in the 45–49 age range on June 1st of a specific year. For example, the top curve of the graph for females refers to the group of women who were aged 45–49 years on June 1, 1946, and who would then potentially be 85–89 years of age in 1986. The decline in this curve reflects the decreasing likelihood, as age rises, that all those women aged 45–59 years in 1946 would attain ages of 85–89 years in 1986.

Generally, as we move from the earliest cohort (aged 45–49 in 1921) to the latest (aged 45–49 in 1946), we see rising curves of life-table survival rates above age 60, and the rise grows sharper as age increases up to the age group 85–89. A comparison of the cohort-specific curves for women indicates that survival changes have improved most notably in the 80 and over age range. For instance, the earliest cohort (45–49 years in 1921) had a 50 percent chance of surviving from the age group 80–84 to that of 85–89; but the later cohort of women aged 45–49 years in 1946 had a 70 percent chance of survival between these two age groups.

Both the cohort-to-cohort mortality rate improvements and the sex differences within a single cohort can be summarized by a cohort-specific index of life expectancy at age 65. This index is a weighted average length of life beyond age 65 (it is not an equivalent measure to the usual life expectancy variable). The weight for any length is rough approximation of the probability of living that long, given that the person has reached age 65. This joint probability was estimated by the senior author from the survival rates embedded in Nagnur's abridged life-tables (Nagnur, 1986b), with the data series being reorganized to track the experiences of individual birth cohorts over time.

Among women, the cohort aged 45–59 in 1946 had an approximate life expectancy (when they became 65) some 5 years greater than that of the cohort aged 45–49 in 1921. This overall rise of the life expectancy index,

Figure 2.6
Life-table Survival Rates¹ for Selected Cohorts at Nine Time Points, by Sex, Canada

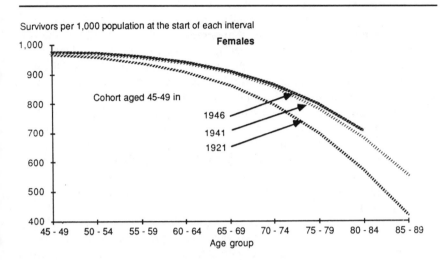

Survivors per 1,000 population at the start of each interval

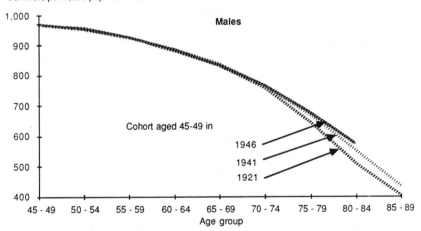

Survivors per 1,000 population at the start of each interval

1. The estimated probability of surviving to the next age group is multiplied by 1,000.
Source: Nagnur 1986b, Appendix Tables.

from a value of 15.2 for the oldest to 20.2 for the youngest of the selected cohorts of women, far outstripped the corresponding one among the male cohorts of similar vintages. The males aged 45–59 in 1921 had (when they reached age 65) an approximate life expectancy index value of 12.6, not much below that of 13.3 for those aged 45–49 in 1946. The gap between men and women of the same cohort, with regard to the life expectancy index, widened gradually from the oldest to the youngest cohorts.

Because of potential problems with the quality, at ages 80 and over, of the estimates for the denominators of the death rates upon which life-tables are based, and because of the actuary's tendency to close off the life-table by using mathematical functions that represent hypotheses about the real age pattern of mortality at the upper ages, it is desirable to supplement the life-table data when dealing with survival rates at advanced ages. One way of doing this is through the method of extinct generations. Based on a number of assumptions, this method involves using death data to reconstruct most of the population aged 80 and over at a given time (say, January 1, 1986) from deaths at age 80 and above over a series of subsequent years. The reconstruction relies upon the fact that the population at age 80, at the start of a year, is a major (though not the only) contributor to the number of deaths at age 80 in that year, the deaths at age 81 the next year, the deaths at age 82 two years hence, etc. (See Rosenwaike, 1981; Bayo, 1972; Depoid, 1973; A. J. Coale, 1984.)

A notable by-product of the use of deaths to reconstruct the population aged 80 and over by single years of age in each year from 1926 to 1971 is a set of survival rates for approximate cohorts. These rates show a pattern in which the more recent cohorts of women are surviving beyond age 80 at significantly higher rates than did earlier cohorts. Figure 2.7 shows these data for two selected approximate cohorts of men and women: those estimated to have crossed the age–80 threshold in 1931 and 1971. Each of these two groups is followed over time, and Figure 2.7 shows the proportions surviving to approximate ages 81, 82, 83, etc., up to 100 or more.

For women the survival curve for the 1971 cohort (those who arrived at age 80 in 1971) lies well above that of the 1931 cohort, except near the initial and terminal ages in Figure 2.7. The curves for men suggest some improvement but only to a slight degree. For example, among women the percentage surviving to age 90 (given their arrival at age 80) increased from 20 percent for the 1931 cohort to 34 percent for that of 1971. In other words, the survival rate from age 80 to age 90 among the stated female cohorts improved from one in five to one in three. The corresponding improvement for men was only from 17 percent to 23 percent.

Women aged 80 years in 1941 had less than a 10 percent chance of attaining the age of 92 and a 6 percent chance of turning 94. Only 30 years later in 1971, as many as 20 percent of 80-year-old women could expect to celebrate their 92nd birthdays and 12 percent their 94th. After age 94, however, survival chances diminish rapidly.

BRIEF REVIEW OF SOME RAMIFICATIONS

These systematic intercohort improvements in survivorship have implications that are deep and widespread both for scientific study and for public

Figure 2.7
Percentage Surviving to Each Age Above 80, Given Arrival at Age 80,
Canada, Cohorts Aged 80 in 1931 and 1971[1]

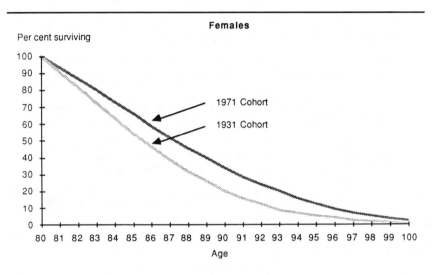

Females

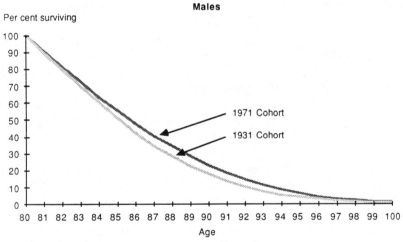

Males

1. In this chart a cohort is a group of persons who were aged 80 at a start of a particular year.
Source: Dominion Bureau of Statistics 1954: T.20; 1957: T.23; 1963: T.D6; 1968: T.D5.
       Statistics Canada 1974: T.14.

policy concern. The available space remaining requires us to be brief and introductory in covering the subject of ramifications. This section considers three specific topics: widowhood rates, living arrangements, and support network resiliency. (For more in-depth discussions of these subjects, see

Siegel and Davidson, 1984; Soldo, 1980; Stone, 1986; Stone and Fletcher, 1987.)

Cohort Age Patterns of Widowhood Rates

The foregoing discussion would lead one to expect that men are being especially well favored with declining widowhood rates, while women may have to wait quite a while longer to see the kinds of male mortality declines that would greatly change their exposure to widowhood. Of course, the encounter with widowhood often triggers a whole range of life-style adjustments, not the least of which are those that involve the microsociety that is alive within a person's home.

The age pattern of the triggering of these adjustments is especially important for the design of social services related to compensation for the effects of the declining help capacity of informal support networks. The extent of stability or change in these age patterns is relevant to the effort of keeping the design of social services up to date in the face of shifting patterns or volumes of demand.

Stone (1986) has portrayed the course of widowhood rates for selected birth cohorts. For women, there has been a basically stable age pattern for the course of widowhood rates over a series of at least five birth cohorts, from that born in 1887–91 to that born in 1907–11. For each of these cohorts, the curve of widowhood rates makes its marked upturn (acceleration) at about age 55. However, the widowhood rate at each age decreases slightly as we go from the earliest to the latest cohorts.

The data for the two latest cohorts considered in Stone (1986) suggest significant recent declines for women in widowhood rates. For example, in the 1887–1901 cohort of women the widowhood rate reached 20 percent at about age 54. In contrast, the cohort of women born between 1917 and 1921 reached the average age of 58 before they were 20 percent widowed.

Among men, the situation is quite different. First, the drop in the age-specific widowhood rates over cohorts is much more distinct than it is for women. Secondly, the shape of the curve is not nearly as stable as that for women. The curve for men has been flattening markedly; that is, the inflection point (the point of sharp acceleration in rates) has been pushed back quite noticeably to higher and higher ages over the set of five cohorts from that born in 1887–91 to that born in 1907–11.

These observations would suggest that as we go from the earlier to more recent cohorts we should expect to see a gradual decline in the speed of changes in living arrangements related to the experience of widowhood at the upper ages. Working against this decline would be significant increases in divorce rates at those ages. (For related discussion, see P. C. Glick, 1979: 303–305.) However, keep in mind that peak divorce rates for a cohort would have been reached long before the cohort has entered the prime retirement years.

Cohort Age Patterns of Living Arrangements

Given the systematic and relatively stable age patterns of widowhood rates within cohorts, we would expect to see similar patterns of living arrangement. This is to say, as a cohort ages, its distribution over alternative living arrangements should change in a characteristic way.

By using a crude living arrangement classification, Stone and Fletcher were able to find empirical support for the idea that a single real cohort can be expected to exhibit systematic age-associated variation in living arrangement distribution (Stone and Fletcher, 1987). To achieve this result they reorganized data for a series of censuses into cohort series and prepared special estimates when a census failed to provide data for one of the living arrangement classes or did so for an age group wider than the one for which data were needed.

The initial results of this work include the finding that there was a steady increase in the percentage living alone from the age group 65–69 to that of 80–84, within the cohort of men and women born between 1896 and 1901. This percentage peaked for these women in the 80–84 age group (contrary to what one sees in cross-sectional census data), and climbed much more sharply among women than men. It continued to climb among the men into the 85-and-over age group. After the percentage living alone passed its peak for this cohort, there began a sharp rise in the proportion that resided in institutions. In the 85-and-over group 40 percent of the women and 30 percent of the men in the cohort were living in institutions.

Broader Issues Regarding Social Support

These patterns and developments with regard to living arrangements are but symptoms of larger issues touching the whole field of formal and informal social supports. Age patterns of cohort attrition, such as those indicated earlier in this chapter, help to produce a progressive loss of informal support-network members as the average age of a cohort climbs beyond 60. This loss tends to reduce the average ability of the support networks to respond effectively to members' declining functional capacity. If the tendency is actualized, the declining network help capacity may be more important than the mere existence of declining functional capacities in causing a resort to formal-organization supports (G. G. Fillenbaum and L. M. Wallman, 1984). For a related discussion that indirectly refers to impacts of cohort attrition, see G. C. Myers and K. G. Manton (1983: 13–17).

What changes can we expect in the age pattern of average helping capacity of informal support networks for elders if life expectancy at the upper ages continues to rise? Let us assume that mortality declines will lower the rate of family break-up due to death at a given age (e.g., age 80). By keeping families together for longer periods of time, other factors being constant, the life expectancy increase causes the phase of steep decline (with rising average cohort age) in the mean helping capacity of the informal networks to be pushed upwards toward higher and higher chronological ages.

If we can assume that the helping capacity of affected informal networks is inversely related to the demand for certain formal organization services, the mortality decline would tend to push the steep incline in demand for such services to higher and higher ages. For example, we should expect to see a rise in the mean age at entry to nursing homes. Referring to the situation in the United States, J. Treas and V. L. Bengtson say that:

... goodly numbers of couples today can look forward to marriages of startling duration. Even though higher divorce rates offset declines in early widowhood, today one in five couples in their first marriages can expect to celebrate a golden wedding anniversary. Even among those who have remarried, one in 20 will someday be able to look back on a union lasting 50 years (Treas and Bengtson, 1982:15–6).

There is at least one offsetting factor, however. If the difference between men and women in mortality improvements remains at current levels or fails to narrow quickly, we might still see the emergence of unusually large numbers of very old women (aged 85 and over) with support networks weakened severely by loss of spouse and comprised substantially of persons who themselves would be of or entering advanced age. Thus, when their husbands are finally lost, widows of advanced age may still face about the same number of years of widowhood as they formerly did. Further, because of the process of functional aging in their peer generation, the average helping capacity of their husbandless informal support networks (at the date of entry to widowhood) would be significantly below the level it would have been if widowhood had struck earlier.

A significant proportion of the women who might in the future be facing a substantial length of widowed life after losing their husbands at advanced age could find that the hazard of an onset of financial indigence begins to rise to disturbing levels. In fact, unless they have been spared the high levels of personal expenditure often associated with long-term care services from formal organizations, a substantial percentage of the intact families that would have been surviving for twenty years or more after giving up or losing their right to earned income will already have been faced with this hazard before the death of one spouse.

CONCLUSION

In closing, let it be noted that we have set out to help chart a new course for the demographic analysis of aspects of population aging. We are calling for a reduction in the attention given to the overall proportion of seniors in society, and to consequent overemphasis on analysis of fertility rates as the driving force behind that proportion. We advocate that a focus on aspects and ramifications of cohort entry into the senior ranks and subsequent extinction would lead to new advances in the useful study of population aging. It would be particularly helpful in highlighting the ways in which service demands and effective service design can be sensitive to the shifting pattern of cohort dominance within the older population.

The authors of this chapter are solely responsible for errors and judgments herein. We are grateful for the enthusiastic support of several persons in the preparation of the paper: Jean Coward, Suzanne DesBiens, and Heidi Walton for bibliography assembly and editing; Hubert Frenken, Lena Jarvlepp, Susan Kee, Gislaine Lafortune, and Diane Traynor for text and graphics editing; and Vasile Nedulcu for graphic design. Abundant and valuable critical commentaries on drafts were received from M. V. George, Betty Havens, Karol J. Krotki, Dhruva Nagnur, Paul Reed, Ira Rosenwaike, and Paul Shaw.

REFERENCES

Bayo, F. (1972). Mortality of the Aged. *Transactions of the Society of Actuaries,* 24, 1–24.

Bouvier, L., Atlee, E., and McVeigh, F. (1975). The Elderly in America. *Population Bulletin,* 30(3).

Canada. Dominion Bureau of Statistics (1954). *Vital Statistics 1951.* Ottawa: Minister of Trade and Commerce.

Canada. Dominion Bureau of Statistics (1957). *Vital Statistics 1956.* Ottawa: Minister of Trade and Commerce.

Canada. Dominion Bureau of Statistics (1963). *Vital Statistics 1961.* Catalogue, 84–202. Ottawa: Minister of Trade and Commerce.

Canada. Dominion Bureau of Statistics (1968). *Vital Statistics 1966.* Catalogue 84–202. Ottawa: Minister of Trade and Commerce.

Canada. Statistics Canada (1973). *Population: 1921–1971.* Catalogue, 91–512. Ottawa: Minister of Industry Trade and Commerce.

Canada. Statistics Canada (1974). *Vital Statistics: Deaths 1971, Volume 3.* Catalogue 84–206. Ottawa: Minister of Industry, Trade and Commerce.

Canada. Statistics Canada (1982). *1981 Census of Canada: Population.* Catalogue 92–901. Ottawa: Minister of Supply and Services.

Canada. Statistics Canada (1983). *Intercensal Annual Estimates of Population by Sex and Age for Canada and the Provinces.* Catalogue 91–518. Ottawa: Minister of Supply and Services.

Canada. Statistics Canada (1985a). *Population Projections for Canada, Provinces and Territories 1984–2006.* Prepared by M. V. George and J. Perreault, Demography Division. Catalogue 91–520. Ottawa: Minister of Supply and Services.

Canada. Statistics Canada (1985b). *Vital Statistics, Births and Deaths: 1983, Volume 1*. Catalogue 84–204. Ottawa: Minister of Supply and Services.

Canada. Statistics Canada (1986). *Postcensal Annual Estimates of Population by Marital Status, Age, Sex and Components of Growth for Canada, Provinces and Territories, June 1, 1985, Volume 3*. Catalogue 91–210. Ottawa: Minister of Supply and Services Canada.

Coale, A. J. (1984). Estimation of Expectation of Life at Advanced Ages. *Genus, 40* (3–4), 185–90.

Depoid, F. (1973). La mortalité des grands vieillards. *Population,* Juillet-Octobre (4–5), 755–92.

Fillenbaum, G. G., and Wallman, L. M. (1984). Change in Household Composition of the Elderly: A Preliminary Investigation. *Journal of Gerontology, 39*(3), 342–49.

Fingerhut, L. A. (1984). Changing in Mortality among the Elderly: United States 1940–78. Supplement to 1980. *Vital & Health Statistics.* Series 3, No. 22a. DHHS Pub. No. (PHS), 84–1406a. Public Health Service. Washington: U.S. Government Printing Office, April.

Glick, P. C. (1979). The Future Marital Status and Living Arrangements of the Elderly. *The Gerontologist, 19*(3), 301–9.

Marshall, V. W. (1983). Generations, Age Groups and Cohorts: Conceptual Distinctions. *Canadian Journal of Aging, 2*(2), 51–62.

McDaniel, S. A. (1986). *Canada's Aging Population.* Toronto: Butterworths.

Myers, G. C., and Manton, K. G. (1983). Some Socio-demographic Observations Relating to Unpaid Productive Role in an Aging Society. Unpublished paper.

Nagnur, D. (1986a). Rectangularization of the Survival Curve and Entropy: The Canadian Experience 1921–1981. *Canadian Studies in Population, 13*(1), 83–102.

Nagnur, D. (1986b). *Longevity and Historical Life Tables (Abridged), Canada and Provinces 1921–1981*. Ottawa: Statistics Canada, Social and Economic Studies Division.

Rosenwaike, I. (1968). On Measuring the Extreme Aged in the Population. *Journal of the American Statistical Association, 63,* 99–112.

Rosenwaike, I. (1981). A Note on New Estimates of the Mortality of the Extreme Aged. *Demography, 18*(2), 257–66.

Rosenwaike, I., Yaffe, N., and Sagi, P. C. (1980). The Recent Decline in Mortality of the Extreme Aged: An Analysis of Statistical Data. *American Journal of Public Health, 70*(10), 1074–1080.

Siegel, J. S., and Davidson, M. (1984). Demographic and Socioeconomic Aspects of Aging in the United States. *Current Population Reports: Special Studies.* Series P–23, No. 138. U.S. Department of Commerce, Bureau of the Census.

Soldo, B. J. (1980). America's Elderly in the 1980s. *Population Bulletin, 35*(4).

Stone, L. O. (1986). Cohort Aging and Support Networks. In George Maddox and E. W. Busse (eds.), *Aging: The Universal Human Experience.* New York: Springer Publishing Company. (In press.)

Stone, L. O., and Fletcher, S. (1980). *A Profile of Canada's Older Population.* Montreal: Institute for Research on Public Policy.

Stone, L. O., and Fletcher, S. (1987). The Hypothesis of Age Patterns in Living

Arrangement Passages. In Victor W. Marshall (ed.), *Aging in Canada: Social Perspectives*. Toronto: Fitzhenry and Whiteside.

Stone, L. O., and Fletcher, S. (1986). *The Seniors Boom: Dramatic Increases in Longevity and Prospects for Better Health*. Catalogue 89–515. Ottawa: Minister of Supply and Services Canada.

Taeuber, C. M. (1983). American in Transition: An Aging Society. *Current Population Reports: Special Studies*. Series P–23, No. 128. U.S. Department of Commerce. Bureau of the Census.

Treas, J., & Bengtson, V. L. (1982). The Demography of Mid- and Late-Life Transitions. *The Annals of the American Academy of Political and Social Science*, 464, 11–21.

United States of America. Department of Commerce. Bureau of the Census (1964). *Census of Population: 1960. Characteristics of the Population. United States Summary. Volume 1. Part 1.* Washington: U.S. Government Printing Office.

United States of America. Department of Commerce. Bureau of the Census (1973). *Census of Population: 1970. Characteristics of the Population. United States Summary. Volume 1. Part 1.* Washington: U.S. Government Printing Office.

United States of America. Department of Commerce. Bureau of the Census (1983). *Census of Population: 1980. General Population Characteristics. United States Summary. Volume 1. Part 1.* Washington: U.S. Government Printing Office.

United States of America. Department of Commerce. Bureau of the Census (1984). Projections of the Population of the United States, by Age, Sex, and Race: 1983 to 2080. *Current Population Reports*. Series P–25, No. 952.

United States of America. Department of Health and Human Services. National Center for Health Statistics (1986). *Vital Statistics of the United States: 1981. Volume 2—Mortality, Part A.* Washington: U.S. Government Printing Office.

United States of America. Senate Special Committee on Aging (1986). *Aging America—Trends and Projections.* 1985–86 Edition. Washington: U.S. Government Printing Office.

II

SOCIAL POLICY

World War II operated as a watershed in the social policy formulation of both countries. The period prior to World War II was essentially one of social insurance while the postwar era marked a transition to social security. A major difference between the United States and Canada is the universal publicly insured health care system in Canada, which has been assessed as adding the equivalent of one-third, on average, to the incomes of older Canadians. The Medicare/Medicaid provisions in the United States are neither universal nor as comprehensive, and hence, do not have a similar effect of supplementing the incomes of older Americans.

Another problem encountered in comparing Canadian and United States pension systems and related social policy is a lack of agreement on what constitutes *poverty*. The Canadian *low income cutoffs* are set so that 58.5 percent of income is expended on necessities. This may be contrasted with the United States poverty line, which is $5,763 (adjusted for family size) and the comparable Canadian dollar value of the United States poverty line, using the Organization of Economic and Community Development purchasing power conversion, which is $7,903. This issue is especially important when trying to sort out the goals of income policies that may have either antipoverty objectives or income security goals.

As Myles notes, the Canadian system has three tiers, i.e., public, public contributory, and private. By contrast, the United States system as described by Hudson relies on only the latter two tiers. When this difference is further related to the differences in the health care systems, the two North American income policy approaches have created very different systems, structures, and benefits levels.

Both countries have recently experienced threats to existent policies and benefits from a progressively conservative electorate. Hudson and Myles point out that benefits to older persons have suffered but the public outcry against these reductions was so substantial that benefit losses were not as great as they were for the nonelderly population. As a result of the positive orientation to old age income security, the relative impoverishment of the elderly population versus children in the two countries has decreased. This fact must not be interpreted to mean that benefits to the older age group should be redirected as benefits to children and youth. Rather it should alert policymakers in both countries to the importance and necessity of addressing and solving the problems of poverty among children and youth in their own right.

Both authors describe the special problems encountered by older women in maintaining an adequate income. Myles places special emphasis on this issue by highlighting the relatively high levels of poverty among older women on the basis of their greater likelihood to be widowed, to live longer following age 65, to require supportive services as well as on the basis of their lower income and pension generation compared to their male counterparts. In part, this is reflected in his discussion of the homemakers' pension proposals that arose from what was known in the late seventies and early eighties as the *Great Canadian Pension Debate*. The unfortunate consequence of concentrating the current debate on homemakers' pensions has been to ignore reform of the overall income security system as public sentiment and political pressure have been defused.

The increased public perception that *means testing* is an appropriate basis for benefit determination in at least health care, and possibly also in income security programs, threatens to undermine universality in all related programs in the United States and to a lesser extent in Canada.

CHAPTER 3

Social Policy in Canada

John Myles

INTRODUCTION

Canadians who have followed debates on social policies for the elderly during the past decade might well be excused if they are now somewhat confused. In the late seventies and early eighties there was a broad consensus that Canada's old age security system was inadequate. The *Great Pension Debate*, as it was called at the time, was not a debate about the facts of the matter but about the choice between public and private solutions to the problem. As the recession deepened in the early eighties, however, talk of reform was replaced by talk of restraint and cutbacks. By 1984, the Great Pension Debate, a debate over how to enhance the system, had been replaced by the debate over universality—whether to restrict Canada's universal Old Age Security benefits to those in need.

Making sense of these debates is no easy task. The first reason is because the policies are complex. Michael Prince (1985) lists over twenty public revenue and expenditure programs for the elderly. (See Table 3.1.) Even more confusing are the competing claims about the relative merits of these programs. For some, universal social benefits are the foundation of the "good society"; to others, these benefits provide unneeded and unwarranted subsidies to the rich.

An understanding of these matters is important for several reasons. In Canada, as elsewhere, public programs for the elderly represent the single largest component in the budget of the modern welfare state. As a result, old age policies are a major public issue. As the population continues to age, Canadian political life will be increasingly affected by what Hudson (1978) has called the *graying* of the state budget. Equally important, these programs are the main source of income for the elderly. In 1981 government programs provided 45.5 percent of the income going to aged couples and

Table 3.1
Components of Canadian Retirement Income Policy

1. Cash Programs:
   - Old Age Security
   - Canada Pension Plan/Quebec Pension Plan
   - Guaranteed Income Supplement
   - Provincial and Territorial Government Income Supplements for the Elderly
   - Veterans Disability and Surviving Dependent Pensions
   - Retirement Benefits'under the Unemployment Insurance Program
   - Provincial Social Assistance
   - Rental and Homeowner Assistance for the Elderly

2. Tax Deductions:
   - Registered Pension Plan Contributions
   - Registered Retirement Savings Plans Contributions
   - CPP/QPP Contributions
   - Income up to $1000 from any pension or savings plan other than CPP/QPP

3. Tax Exemptions
   - Tax exemptions for those over age 65
   - Exemptions are available to families supporting older members

4. Tax Waivers
   Persons aged 65 or more for health insurance premiums in the three provinces (Alberta, British Columbia and Ontario) with such premiums

Source: M. Prince, "Startling Facts, Sobering Truths and Sacred Trust," in A. Maslove, ed., *How Ottawa Spends 1985: Sharing the Pie* (Toronto: Methuen, 1985), 118–19.

51.3 percent of income to elderly unattached individuals (National Council of Welfare, 1984a).

HISTORICAL OVERVIEW

Building the System: From Social Assistance to Social Security

In an essay written to commemorate the 50th anniversary of the International Labor Organization, Guy Perrin (1969) suggested that the history of modern social security could be divided into two major periods: the social assistance era prior to the Second World War and the period of social security proper following the war. Prior to World War II, social programs in Europe and elsewhere were largely designed as a form of social assistance to the poor. Benefits were low and usually targeted toward those of limited means. Nowhere were they intended to provide elderly workers with a level of income sufficient to permit withdrawal from economic activity, i.e., to retire, in advance of physiological decline.

The transition to social security involved two novel principles of distribution. The first was the principle of universality. Coverage and benefits were extended to all citizens or, alternatively, to all members of the labor force. The second was the principle of *substitutive benefits* or income security. This required benefits related to the worker's earnings at a level sufficient to provide continuity in living standards in the event of unemployment, illness, or retirement. This is what distinguishes the "modern" welfare state. No longer are old age pensions merely to provide subsistence for those who fall out of the labor market. Instead, old age pensions became a "retirement wage" sufficient to permit (or induce) the older worker to withdraw from the labor market.

The result of this development was to break the historic link between public provision and the "poor." Modern old age security systems were designed to provide income security to the expanding middle strata of the postwar period—workers with average incomes and stable employment and the professionals and managers of the new middle class. The poor were not excluded. Rather, the boundaries of public provision were expanded. This gradual process of middle class incorporation was subsequently to prove of enormous political importance. As a result of their incorporation, the growing middle strata became allies rather than enemies of the welfare state.

Social Assistance for the Elderly: The Old Age Pensions Act

Perrin's description fits the Canadian case rather well. Canada entered the era of "social assistance" with the passage of the Old Age Pensions Act in 1927. The act was neither universal nor generous. It provided for a pension of $20 per month to those over 70 and yearly incomes less than $365. In the last year of operation (1951), less than half of those over age 70 were receiving benefits and benefit levels had risen to a maximum of $480 per year at a time when the average production worker was earning $2,460 per year (F. H. Leacy, 1983). What is remarkable, however, is that the act was passed at all. Whereas many other industrialized countries had already implemented a broad infrastructure of social measures for unemployment, sickness and old age (P. Flora and J. Alber, 1981), this was the only major social policy introduced in Canada prior to World War II.

Universality: The Old Age Security Act

The first step into the social security era came with the Old Age Security Act (OAS) of 1951. Benefit levels remained fixed at $40 per month, but the means test for those over age 70 was removed, making benefits universal. This created the first tier in Canada's emergent income security system for the elderly. In the same year, the Old Age Assistance Act (OAA) extended means-tested benefits to those aged 65–69. It remained in place until 1970 by which time eligibility for the universal pension (OAS) had been reduced to age 65.

Income Security: The Canada Pension Plan

Universal flat benefits were insufficient to allow most elderly workers to leave the labor force without a significant drop in living standards. In Canada and other countries where the flat-benefit principle was adopted (for example, Britain and Sweden) income security required a second tier of contributory pensions. This was achieved in 1965 through the Canada Pension Plan and the Quebec Pension Plan (C/QPP). The effect of the legislation was to create a national, contributory pension scheme in which benefits are linked to past contributions. The scheme would pay benefits of up to 25 percent of average adjusted earnings to a ceiling equivalent to half the average wage. Initially there was a retirement test (continued earnings resulted in reduced benefits) until age 70, a practice eliminated in 1974.

The C/QPP and OAS are now the core of Canada's old age security system. The traditional one-earner couple, for example, receives two OAS check (one for each partner) each month plus whatever C/QPP benefits have been earned through contributions.

More Social Assistance: The Guaranteed Income Supplement

Since it would take some years before workers would accumulate benefits under C/QPP, the Guaranteed Income Supplement (GIS) was adopted as an interim measure in 1967. It subsequently became a permanent program and provides a monthly income-tested supplement to those over 65. In 1975 the Spouse's Allowance was introduced to supplement the income of low-income couples in which one member is old enough to qualify for GIS and the other is between ages 60 and 64. In 1972 the Government of British Columbia added a provincial supplement as a "top-up" to GIS, and five other provinces subsequently followed suit. The elderly also benefit from a variety of federal and provincial tax rebates, credits, and exemptions.

Public Policy and Private Pensions

The programs described above represent what is conventionally considered to be Canada's *public income security system* for the elderly. The public-private distinction, however, conceals the true extent of government activity in the field of pensions. Pensions, like insurance, are a major industry. Governments affect this industry in three ways: (1) by establishing how much of the industry will be "nationalized"; (2) by regulations; and (3) by subsidies.

Governments do not nationalize pensions in the way they nationalize other industries, i.e., by expropriating and becoming the legal owner of existing productive resources. Instead, pensions and other forms of insurance are nationalized by "expropriating" the market for these services. This is done by creating public systems that reduce or eliminate the demand for private coverage. This is why the insurance industry (and the Government of Ontario where the industry is concentrated) opposed the Canada Pension Plan (K. Banting, 1985; B. Murphy, 1982). Though unsuccessful in blocking the legislation, they succeeded in setting the maximum benefit at 25 percent of the average wage. The *intended* effect was to ensure that a substantial portion of the pension market would be left intact for the private pension industry to exploit. Since combined benefits from OAS and the C/QPP were well below conventionally understood poverty levels, even the average worker could be expected to seek additional private coverage.

Government policies also regulate the conditions under which private pension plans can be established. Who is to be covered, the nature of the benefits provided, and the entitlements of workers when they change jobs are all subject to public regulation. This has been an active area of policy debate in recent years about which we shall say more later. The point, however, is that the quality of private plans is also an "effect" of government policy.

Third, private occupational pensions (Registered Pension Plans or RPPs) and personal savings for retirement (Registered Retirement Savings Plans or RRSPs) receive enormous subsidies from the government in the form of tax concessions on contributions and earnings. Thus a sizeable portion of private benefits originate in public expenditures and these expenditures are far from insignificant. In 1981 total public and private expenditures for retirement income security were just over $28 billion, of which tax expenditures accounted for $7.6 billion (Prince, 1985).

CURRENT POLICY AND PROGRAMS

Evaluating the System

By 1975 the Canadian federal government, along with the provinces, had developed the elaborate and complex income security system described above. How well does the system perform?

Income policies for the elderly can be evaluated against two broad objectives: an antipoverty objective and an income security objective. To measure poverty, we shall follow the practice of the National Council of Welfare and use Statistics Canada's *low-income cut-offs*. This is a more conservative measure than used by other agencies, but serves the useful purpose of refuting criticism that the poverty lines are too high. (American readers should not equate these low-income cut-offs with conventional poverty lines used in the United States. Such comparisons would suggest the poverty rate among the elderly is higher in Canada than in the United States when, in fact, the reverse is true (P. Hedstrom and S. Ringen, 1985). Income Security means more than avoiding poverty. It implies that the elderly can maintain preretirement living standards during their retirement years. Income security is measured by means of a replacement ratio: the annual value of all public pensions divided by annual earnings just prior to retirement.

Table 3.2 shows the extent to which current programs meet the antipoverty and income security objectives of low and moderate income earners in Canada. The *poverty gap* measures the difference between the poverty line and maximum benefits; the replacement rate measures benefits as a percentage of preretirement earnings. The main conclusion from Table 3.2 is that the system is unable to meet either target but is more successful in satisfying the antipoverty than the income security objective.

Income Security

The first panel shows that the income security system (OAS and C/QPP) provides little real security to the elderly. Those who were poor before retirement are considerably poorer after retirement and only the two-earner couple with moderate earnings manages to escape poverty. In the absence of other sources of income all remain eligible for social assistance. Among Western countries Canada is unique in maintaining an income security system with maximum benefits below social assistance rates. This is by design. When the C/QPP was established, it was assumed that private pensions would expand to meet the retirement income objectives of Canada's

Table 3.2
Public Pension Income, Canada, 1984

Earnings Before Retirement	Public Pension Income After Retirement			
	Without GIS		With GIS	
	Poverty Gap	Replacement	Poverty Gap	Replacement
1. Low Income[1]				
Single Earner	-4,131	.51	-1,991	.81
One Earner Couple	-4,074	.79	-354	1.18
Two Earner Couple	-2,800	.60	+283	.70
2. Moderate Income[2]				
Single Earner	-2,030	.35	-941	.51
One Earner Couple	-1,974	.49	+696	.73
Two Earner Couple	+576	.40	+1,971	.55

1. Low income for single earners and one-earner couples is 1/2 the average wage and for two-earner couples joint income is 3/4 of the average wage.
2. Moderate income for single earners and one-earner couples is equal to the average wage and for two-earner couples joint income is 1 1/2 times the average wage.
Source: Derived from National Council of Welfare, *Pension Reform* (Ottawa: Ministry of Supply and Services, 1984).

aged. This expectation was never realized. In 1965 when the legislation was passed, 38 percent of the paid labor force was covered by private pensions. By 1980 this figure had risen to only 44 percent (National Council of Welfare, 1984c).

Preventing Poverty

The second panel of Table 3.2 shows the extent to which the system meets the antipoverty objective. The Guaranteed Income Supplement is intended to ensure that the elderly will not fall below the minimum required for subsistence. As indicated, GIS brings the incomes of couples to a point just above or just below the poverty line, but leaves a significant poverty gap for single retirees. Trends in poverty in old age confirm this pattern. The poverty rate among elderly couples declined from 41.4 percent in 1969 to 11.1 percent in 1983. The rate among unattached individuals also declined but was still 57.5 percent in 1983 (National Council of Welfare, 1985b).

Women and Pensions

The high poverty rate observed among the *unattached elderly* is rooted in the gender-specific character of the aging process: most of the unattached are elderly widowed females. Retirement is the first major event of the aging process; the second is widowhood. Because of gender differences in longevity, most widowed persons are women and most women become widows. Accordingly, we must also assess the system's capacity to prevent poverty and to provide income security in the face of this second major event in the aging process. Table 3.3 shows the economic impact of widowhood for the survivors of the couples identified in Table 3.2. Here the replacement ratios are not based on preretirement earnings but on public pension benefits prior to the death of the spouse.

The results are startling. All widows can expect a sharp drop in income to levels well below the low income cut-off. The failure of OAS and C/QPP to provide adequate income security has a cumulative effect on elderly women. The GIS improves the situation somewhat but still leaves a substantial poverty gap.

These are the major failings of the retirement income system in Canada. A system that provided real income security would make the Guaranteed Income Supplement and other social assistance measures redundant. Instead, over 50 percent of Canada's elderly are eligible for such assistance. The Canadian system does better in meeting the antipoverty objective for couples, but fails miserably when the spouse (usually male) dies. In a ten-nation comparison of the support provided to elderly survivors in the mid-seventies (Union Bank of Switzerland, 1977), Canada ranked last. It is from this context that the policy debates of the seventies and eighties emerged.

THE POLITICS OF INCOME SECURITY

The Great Pension Debate: The Failure of Reform

The Great Pension Debate was launched in 1975 when the Canadian Labour Congress proposed that C/QPP benefits be doubled. The debate was not over the antipoverty objectives of the system. There was general concensus that targeted benefits to the low-income elderly, especially elderly women, should be improved. The main point of confrontation was over the use of the public system to improve income security. A review of the debate

Table 3.3
Public Pension Income for Surviving Spouse, Canada, 1984

Earnings Before Retirement[1]	Public Pension Income After the Death of a Spouse			
	Without GIS		With GIS	
	Poverty Gap	% Pre-Death Income	Poverty Gap	% Pre-Death Income
Surviving Spouse				
a. Low Income	$		$	
One Earner Couple	-5,151	.37	-2,501	.58
Two Earner Couple	-3,877	.45	-1,864	.60
b. Moderate Income				
One Earner Couple	-3,890	.44	-1,871	.58
Two Earner Couple	-1,391	.56	-596	.62

1. For definitions of low and moderate income, see Table 3.2.
Source: Derived from National Council of Welfare, *Pension Reform,* (Ottawa: Ministry of Supply and Services, 1984).

is useful not only for what it tells us about old age policies but also the insight it provides into the forces shaping policy in Canada.

The core of the debate was rather simple: whether to meet the income security needs of Canada's workers through expansion of the C/QPP, or through improving private sector plans. The cleavages in the debate were also clear. The public sector option was promoted by organized labor, women's rights groups, a variety of social reform lobbies, and the antipoverty lobby. It was recognized that the major reason persons required GIS was the inadequacy of private pensions and the C/QPP. The major opposition came from Canadian business.

As Banting (1985) points out, this societal cleavage was overlaid by a second conflict system within the state. The two major antagonists in the area of pension reform have traditionally been Canada's two most populous provinces, Ontario and Quebec. Quebec took a leadership role in the initial C/QPP legislation while Ontario opposed it. Conflict between the two provinces over additional reforms has continued. On balance, the federal government has leaned toward public sector solutions, especially in the early periods of the debate, as evidenced by the Lazar Commission proposals made by senior federal officials (Task Force on Retirement Income Policy, 1980).

On the face of it, the public sector solution would seem to have been irresistible. The C/QPP already had all of the qualities lacking in private sector alternatives: universal coverage of the labor force, immediate vesting of benefits, portability, indexing, and survivors' benefits. Most ironic, in view of the usual business attacks on public sector "inefficiency," it had the advantages of ease of administration and low overhead costs. By almost any standard it was judged superior to private sector alternatives (Task Force on Retirement Income Policy, 1980).

An additional factor favoring a public sector solution was the lack of consensus by business on improvements to private sector plans (Banting, 1985). Large firms were prepared to accept mandatory private pensions to solve the coverage problem, but small business was not. The financial sector urged modest indexing based on *excess interest*, but the large industrial firms were opposed. What then led to the eventual failure of the public sector reform coalition? To answer the question, it is necessary to examine the nature of the opposition.

To find the business community lurking behind the failure to reform Canada's old age security system is far from self-explanatory. In 1951 big business supported legislation to abolish the means test and introduce universal benefits (Murphy, 1982). In the sixties the insurance industry fought the C/QPP reforms, but received only tepid support from the industrial sector. In the late seventies a more cohesive business coalition, with major industrial firms as the dominant partner, emerged to oppose further public sector expansion. The reason for this, Banting observes, was that the "battle over public pensions had become a battle over one of the commanding heights of the Canadian economy" (1985:59). By the mid-seventies the accumulated assets of the private pension funds were the largest source of new investment capital in the Canadian economy (Calvert, 1977). Any expansion of the C/QPP would transfer the economic power of the pension funds from the private sector to the state. It was no longer a matter of protecting the pension market for insurance and trust companies; expansion of the public system was a threat to the entire business community.

Interprovincial conflicts were also rooted in issues of capital formation. In the 1960s Quebec took the lead in promoting the C/QPP not merely to provide better pensions but also to create a capital pool to finance Quebec's economic development and reduce financial dependence on English Canada. And it was the promise of a cheap source of capital that swung the other provinces behind the plan. As one provincial official remarked: "The main reason for us was the creation of a large fund. It would provide money for development here and give us more liberty in the money markets. The fund was certainly the main reason for me; it was the reason" (R. Simeon, 1972:175–76). The funds of the Canada Pension Plan soon became the major source of provincial borrowing. In Quebec the government agency through which the QPP funds are channelled became the largest purchaser of common stocks in Canada.

But despite the importance of the funds, the government of Ontario continued to oppose expansion of the C/QPP and had the veto power to do so. Governed from 1943 to 1985 by the Conservatives, Ontario is the headquarters of Canada's major financial and industrial corporations. Its power of veto made the Ontario government the private sector's most important and reliable ally.

Thus the reform coalition favoring a public sector solution faced formidable obstacles: a broad alliance of business interests that became increasingly cohesive as the debate evolved; and a federal structure that allowed the government of Ontario to veto reform. Whether the reform alliance would have been able to overcome these obstacles is a question now lost to history. As the recession deepened, the forces for reform began to dissipate. Labor did not give up its objectives; but as unemployment began to rise, attention turned to other matters and resources were deployed to defend past achievements. At the same time a profound cleavage emerged within the federal government. Monique Begin, minister of health and welfare, continued to press for public sector reform, but faced growing opposition from the powerful Finance Department where the concern was to restore "business confidence" and to encourage investment. Neither objective would be enhanced by expansion of the C/QPP.

The erosion of the reform movement was also hastened by the emergence of a break between organized labor and the women's movement over the appropriate method of dealing with the problems of elderly women. This was clearly the most critical issue facing the pension system and the one most likely to arouse broad public sympathy for the reform movement. The focus of the cleavage was on the issue of *pensions for homemakers*.

Pensions for Homemakers

The poverty of elderly women is associated with several factors. First, limited participation in the labor market means that they acquire few pension credits during their working lives and those acquired are worth less because of the low wages earned by women. Second, survivor benefits depend entirely on the value of pensions earned by men. If these benefits are low, survivor benefits will be even lower. The major thrust of the reforms advanced by labor and antipoverty organizations was to improve the value of benefits that both men and women earn from their time in the labor market. This would improve the situation of women in the paid labor force and also result in higher survivor benefits.

Women's organizations supported this thrust, but sought to go further to recognize the economic and social value of domestic labor by including a pension for homemakers (L. Dulude, 1981) in the C/QPP. Currently, the only recognition of domestic labor is the *child dropout provision* under which women are not penalized for years out of the labor force raising small children when C/QPP benefits are calculated. The proposal also sought to end survivor benefits—on the grounds that they entrench the dependency of wives—and mandatory splitting of accumulated pension credits between husbands and wives. A form of credit splitting has been enacted. As of January 1, 1987 either spouse in a continuing marriage can apply to divide C/QPP retirement pensions earned during their life together. After a one-year separation divorced spouses may apply for a division of all pension credits acquired during their life together. But it was the homemakers' pension proposal that became most controversial and resulted in the split in the reform movement.

Though opposed by some women's organizations, the proposal won increasing support in the women's movement, particularly from the National Action Committee on Women representing 250 member organizations, and was included in the recommendations of the Parliamentary Task Force on Pension Reform (1983). The proposal would allow families whose main wage earner earns above the average wage to make contributions to provide C/QPP benefits for a spouse who is not in the labor force or who earns less than half the maximum annual pensionable earnings. Single parents, adults caring for the aged or the infirm, and low-income families would be included but exempt from making contributions. Contributions and benefits would be based on the assumption that the domestic labor of an unpaid homemaker is equal to half the average wage.

Critics in the labor movement and other reform lobbies pointed out that the proposal did not provide a pension for homemaking but a subsidy to homemakers not in the paid labor force. The majority of women in the paid labor force are also homemakers, doing their domestic labor evenings and weekends. If these women earn less than half the average wage, their final benefits would be lower than those received by women not in the labor force. Nor was the presence of children or other dependents a condition of the proposal. Nonlabor force spouses who perform no domestic labor (e.g., those with paid housekeepers) would also be eligible. In effect, the scheme would not be a payment for domestic labor but a benefit for families where one spouse is not in the paid labor force. As the National Council of Welfare (1984b) demonstrated, the majority of elderly women would do better financially with a 50 percent increase in the earnings replacement rate of the current plan. The proposal was significant because it received support of both major parties and thus has some prospect of being enacted into law.

By appearing to address the most important problem among Canada's elderly—poor elderly women—it defused much of the political pressure for a broader reform of the system.

The Attack on Universality

With the deepening recession of the early eighties, debates over social policy took on a new complexion. Rising unemployment and a general decline in economic activity meant more social expenditures and a rising federal deficit. As a result, discussions turned from expansionary reforms to reducing expenditures. Canada's universal social programs, including Old Age Security, became an immediate target. Soon-to-be Prime Minister Brian Mulroney gave the attack its classic formulation. In the 1984 election campaign he questioned the practice of providing universal social benefits to bank presidents and other well-to-do individuals when the funds could be used to relieve the poverty of the needy.

To Mulroney's surprise, the right of bank presidents to Old Age Security benefits was defended by virtually everyone except bank presidents. This included not only labor, women's, and old age organizations but also the antipoverty lobbies. Their defense of universality was based on the *middle class incorporation thesis*, i.e., it is necessary to include the middle class in social programs or it will not defend them when they come under attack. In the end the prognosis proved to be accurate. Faced with mounting criticism, Mulroney backed away and announced that universal social benefits were a "sacred trust" to be defended at all costs.

The attack on universality went through two more phases. Once in power, Mulroney allowed his finance minister and leading conservative ideologue, Michael Wilson, to reopen the debate. Wilson announced his personal opposition to universality, implying that some income test would be included in his first budget. Public outcry forced Mulroney to repudiate Wilson, his most important cabinet minister.

Unable to dismantle universal benefits, Wilson turned to the more traditional conservative strategy of slow erosion. In his May 1985 budget, he announced partial deindexation of both family allowances and old age security to save the federal treasury some 4 billion dollars over the next five years. Public outrage was worse than before. After two months during which the threat to deindex old age benefits monopolized parliamentary and public debate, Mulroney forced his finance minister to retract.

The core of the Conservative critique was that universal social benefits were subsidizing the well-to-do. There is considerable irony in this since, historically, universal flat benefits were seen as providing income security that would enhance equality (K. Bryden, 1974). In the discussions that led to the reforms of 1951, there was a clear preference in government for an earnings-based system in which benefits would reflect contributions. In contrast, a flat pension paid from a progressive tax system would result in considerable redistribution. OAS proved to be inadequate to the task, but it became the first element and most redistributive component of an emergent income security system. The attack on universality was intended to remove OAS from the income security system and restore it to the status of poor relief it had prior to 1951. The result would be to erode an income security system that the studies of almost a decade had shown to be inadequate.

On the face of it, the more conservative forces in the new government had suffered an enormous defeat, and this was the way its first year in power was interpreted by the popular press. What went unnoticed was that by 1985 the Great Pension Debate of the preceding decade had entirely dissipated. Proposals to expand the C/QPP disappeared from the political agenda and a modest set of reforms for those already covered by private plans was introduced in December 1985. After almost a decade of debate, the result was to reinforce the economic divisions that had generated the debate in the first place: better pensions for those covered by private plans and nothing for the majority who are not. Even more remarkable was the success of the new government in expanding Canada's welfare state for the rich.

Income Security for the Rich

The proposal to deindex OAS was only one of two proposals to "reform" Canada's old age security system in the Wilson budget. The second was to expand the old age security program for upper-income Canadians, the Registered Retirement Savings Plans (or RRSPs). RRSPs have become a major component of Canada's retirement income system. Though not usually considered part of the public system, the public costs of the program are great. Individuals are encouraged to save for retirement by allowing them to make tax-deductible contributions into a registered retirement savings plan. Returns on these investments are then allowed to accumulate free of tax.

Before the 1985 budget, individuals who belonged to a private pension plan (RPP) to which they contributed less than $3,500 were able to contribute the difference to an RRSP up to a combined ceiling of 20 percent of earned income. Those not in a private plan could contribute 20 percent of earned income to a ceiling of $5,500. High-income earners are able to contribute more (sheltering more income from taxes) and, given the tax structure, they receive a larger tax subsidy for each dollar contributed. A high-income earner in the 50 percent marginal tax bracket receives a benefit of $500 for a $1,000 contribution, whereas a modest-income person with a marginal tax rate of 20 percent receives a $200 benefit. As a result, low-income earners have less opportunity to contribute and receive a lower subsidy when they do.

This initial advantage is subject to the magic of compound interest. The

Table 3.4
Tax-Saving for Single RPP/RRSP Contributors Before and After 1985 Budget, 1990

Earnings	Before Budget	After Budget	Increase
$20,000	$ 414	$ 414	$ 0
$30,000	1,205	1,409	204
$40,000	1,295	1,776	481
$50,000	1,554	2,442	888
$60,000	1,554	2,753	1,199
$70,000	1,628	3,138	1,510
$80,000	1,761	4,328	2,567

Source: National Council of Welfare, *Giving and Taking: The May 1985 Budget and the Poor* (Ottawa: Minister of Supply and Services, 1985), p. 7.

Canadian Council on Social Development (1985) points out that a $5,000 investment at 10 percent interest accumulating tax-free will grow to $150,000 in 30 years or about $110,000 when taxes are paid on withdrawal. If tax were paid on the interest by an upper-income earner as it was being earned, the same investment would grow to $20,000. "Thus," the Council concludes, "the majority of money in RRSPs is the tax assistance, not the original contribution" (1985:11).

The major change in the May 1985 budget expanded this income security system for Canada's well-to-do. The ceiling on contributions was raised from $5,500 to $15,500. Table 3.4 shows the distribution of benefits from this change. It was clearly a windfall for the rich. The estimated cost of the change for the year 1990–91 will be an additional $235,000,000 in lost revenues (National Council of Welfare, 1985a). Ironically, a decade of debate that began to ensure adequate income security for Canadian workers ended by enhancing income security for the well-to-do.

CONCLUSION

The major thrust of postwar social legislation in all capitalist democracies was away from the *poor law conceptions* of the welfare state toward income security programs that incorporate the stable working class and middle-income earners. The consequences were both political and economic. Programs built on the twin pillars of universality and income security provided a political foundation for a broadly based coalition of lower- and middle-income earners supportive of welfare state expansion and resistant to cuts.

This process of *middle-class incorporation* did not go as far in Canada as in some countries, but its consequences were significant, the failure of the new Conservative government to change Old Age Security being a case in point.

The neoconservative attack on the welfare state has sought to reverse this trend and has proceeded on two fronts. The first is an attempt to return to the *social assistance tradition* of the prewar period. The attack has not been on the welfare state for the poor but rather on the incorporation of the stable working class and middle-income earners into the welfare state. The key word in the neoconservative lexicon is *rationalization*: transfer dollars should be spent "efficiently" for those most in need. The object is to return the field of income security to the marketplace. The state would prevent starvation but not provide the means for workers to maintain continuity in their standard of living when they leave the market as a result of illness, unemployment, and old age.

This does not mean the middle strata are being abandoned. Rather they are being weaned away from the postwar welfare state and incorporated into a new "welfare state" that subsidizes wealth accumulation. Workers with average and above average incomes are being encouraged to rely on private pensions (RPPs) and personal savings (RRSPs) for income security. The political and economic consequences of such programs are the obverse of the public programs. The public system redistributes income in favor of low-income earners and creates solidarity between middle- and low-income earners. Private plans and RRSPs redistribute income to high-income earners and build alliances around the ownership of wealth. The more the middle classes become dependent on these programs the more ready they will be to support the expansion of the welfare state for the rich and to abandon traditional alliances with the less fortunate.

REFERENCES

Banting, K. (1985). Institutional Conservatism: Federalism and Pension Reform. In J. Ismael, ed., *Canadian Social Welfare Policy: Federal and Provincial Dimensions*. Kingston and Montreal: McGill Queen's University Press.

Bryden, K. (1974). *Old Age Pensions and Policy-Making in Canada*. Montreal: McGill Queen's University Press.

Calvert, G. (1977). *Pensions and Survival: The Coming Crisis of Money and Retirement*. Toronto: Financial Post.

Canadian Council on Social Development. Analysis of the May 1985 Budget. *Social Development Overview Supplement*, 3, 1985.

Dulude, L. (1981). *Pension Reform with Women in Mind*. Ottawa: Canadian Advisory Council on the Status of Women.

Flora, P., and Alber, J. (1981). Modernization, Democratization and the Development of Welfare States in Western Europe. In P. Flora and J. Alber, eds., *The*

Development of Welfare States in Europe and America. New Brunswick, N.J.: Transaction Books.

Hedstrom, P., and Ringen, S. (1985). *Age and Income in Contemporary Society: A Comparative Study*. Stockholm: Institute for Social Research.

House of Commons, Canada (1983). *Report of the Parliamentary Task Force on Pension Reform*. Ottawa: Ministry of Supply and Services.

Hudson, R. (1978). The 'Graying' of the Federal Budget and Its Consequences for Old Age Policy. *The Gerontologist, 18*(5), 428–40.

Leacy, F. H. (1983). *Historical Statistics of Canada*. Ottawa: Ministry of Supply and Services.

Murphy, B. (1982). *Corporate Capital and the Welfare State: Canadian Business and Public Pension Policy in Canada Since World War II*. Master's thesis, Carleton University, Ottawa.

National Council of Welfare (1984a). *Sixty-five and Older: A Report by the National Council of Welfare on the Incomes of the Aged*. Ottawa: Ministry of Supply and Services.

National Council of Welfare (1984b). *Better Pensions for Homemakers*. Ottawa: Ministry of Supply and Services.

National Council of Welfare (1984c). *A Pension Primer*. Ottawa: Ministry of Supply and Services.

National Council of Welfare (1985a). *Giving and Taking: The May 1985 Budget and the Poor*. Ottawa: Ministry of Supply and Services.

National Council of Welfare (1985b). *Poverty on the Increase*. Ottawa: Ministry of Supply and Services.

Perrin, G. (1969). Reflections on Fifty Years of Social Security. *International Labour Review, 99*(3), 249–90.

Prince, M. (1985). Startling Facts, Sobering Truths, and Sacred Trust: Pension Policy and the Tories. In A. Maslove, ed., *How Ottawa Spends: Sharing the Pie*. Toronto: Methuen.

Simeon, R. (1972). *Federal-Provincial Diplomacy: The Making of Recent Policy in Canada*. Toronto: University of Toronto Press.

Task Force on Retirement Income Policy (1980). *The Retirement Income System in Canada: Problems and Alternative Policies for Reform*. Ottawa: Ministry of Supply and Services.

Union Bank of Switzerland (1977). *Social Security in Ten Industrial Nations*. Zurich: Union Bank of Switzerland.

CHAPTER 4

Social Policy in the United States

Robert B. Hudson

INTRODUCTION

Older persons have featured prominently in the development of social policies in the United States. Their place in American social welfare policy stems from a number of factors, including popular attitudes toward government and governmental intervention, historical circumstances that helped launch welfare policies, and the ways age-related programs have grown and developed over time.

Resulting from this development is an array of age-related policies notable for its program rationale and overall expenditure levels. Much of American social policy owes its development to factors common to all industrial nations, but the aging have played a special role in the American case. For many years their social standing and economic situation rendered the aging relatively noncontroversial beneficiaries of governmental social policy initiatives. These initiatives enabled them to play an important role in the development and expansion of social welfare programs.

This supportive environment, built on the legitimacy of the aged as a policy constituency and their usefulness to other actors in the policy process, has been subjected to new pressures during the past decade. Along with rising program costs and demonstrable program successes have come new questions about the nature and extent of need within the older population. Short-term economic conditions and long-term population trends have led to widespread concern about the future viability of the Social Security system. Recognition of poverty and attendant problems among younger populations has introduced the issue of intergenerational equity to social policy debate. Added to these pressures have been the initiatives of the Reagan Administration to reduce the federal government's domestic social policy presence. Lastly, enormous federal budget deficits and the inability of the administration or Congress to deal with them effectively make remote the possibility of major program enhancements and place added constraints on existing programs.

This chapter recounts this policy growth, reviews patterns of developments, and addresses present and future policy issues.

HISTORICAL OVERVIEW

Before the New Deal programs of the 1930s, American social policy toward the aged remained in the Poor Law and colonial traditions: benefits were meager, eligibility was based on ad hoc determinations of abject need, administration was purely local, and efforts to assure family responsibility for frail elders were widespread. Exceptions were found only in the case of veteran benefits developed after the Civil War, benefit plans for federal and some state government workers and means-tested old age benefits for the destitute elderly in a dozen states (E. Kutza, 1981; J. Axinn and H. Levin, 1982).

The New Deal and After

The major breakthrough in social policy came with the Social Security Act of 1935. Through this legislation, the federal government took on— albeit incompletely and unevenly—responsibilities associated with the modern welfare state. The act established federal responsibility to intervene in the name of promoting the general welfare, introduced the notion of entitlement to benefits by selected groups, and institutionalized the idea of outdoor or cash relief.

The elderly were prominently featured in the politics and provisions of the original Social Security Act. Old Age Assistance, a means-tested, state-administered program served as Title I of the legislation, and Title II was Old Age Insurance, the initial social insurance program in the U.S. The destitution of most of the aged during the Depression, the need to stimulate economic activity, and great concern with finding jobs for younger workers have each been cited as contributing to the central positioning of age-related programs during the period (A. Schlesinger, Jr., 1958; W. Graebner, 1981).

The period from the late 1930s to the early 1960s is often considered to be one of little social welfare activity in the U.S. This is only partially true. Major amendments to the Social Security Act in 1939 added survivors to the Old Age Insurance program. The inclusion of survivors under the act represented an important break with the original OAI rationale that benefits would only be made available on the basis of one's own previous work history (M. Derthick, 1979). This provision and that made a quarter of a century later to weight the benefit formula toward low-income workers are the principal ways in which the strict earnings-related insurance rationale of the original legislation has been modified. Disability insurance was added to the act in 1956, creating the current Social Security cash program, Old Age, Survivors, and Disability Insurance (OASDI).

Other developments and changes also helped expand and institutionalize Social Security. First was the total and immediate popular acceptance of the program. Surveys showed that whatever opposition had existed about the program on ideological or other grounds had essentially disappeared by the 1940s (M. E. Schiltz, 1970). Second was the gradual inclusion of new occupational groups in the system. Political considerations initially prevented making the compulsory coverage as inclusive as program architects would have preferred. Since then, however, virtually all occupations have been brought in: the self-employed, employees of nonprofit organizations, farmers, domestic workers, and most recently, those federal workers hired after January 1984. In 1950, 64 percent of all workers participated in the system; by 1983, that figure had risen to 95 percent (U.S. Senate, 1984).

Benefit levels have also risen dramatically. The first major increases took place in the early 1950s. Since then benefits have risen substantially, first through ad hoc increases enacted in what appear to be election year cycles (E. R. Tufte, 1978) and, since 1973, through cost-of-living adjustments whenever inflation exceeds 3 percent annually. However, in 1986 Congress voted a benefit increase for recipients even though the 3 percent inflation threshold level had not been reached.

The Great Society and After

A second major wave of social policy initiatives took place during the Great Society years of the 1960s. While many of the programs and much of the rhetoric focused on younger persons and different problems—the unemployed, the poor, the sick, the young, and minority groups (J. L. Sundquist, 1968)—the elderly would prove to be major beneficiaries of activities during these years. Indeed, the program with the longest incubation period and which quickly became the most expensive was Medicare, the health insurance program for the elderly.

Federally financed health insurance was kept out of the original Social Security package of the 1930s for fear of its being sufficiently controversial to derail the entire legislative package. The Truman Administration tried to advance the idea, first with proposals covering much of the population and later targeted only on the elderly. These efforts were soundly defeated by Republicans and conservative Democrats, and little further progress was made during the 1950s.

Toward the end of that decade and especially in the wake of John F. Kennedy's victory in 1960, Medicare proposals again came to life. Public hearings were held around the country that brought forth well-publicized accounts of financial devastation to older persons and their families because of catastrophic health care costs. Lyndon Johnson's landslide victory in the 1964 election made enactment a foregone conclusion. So certain was passage that the Republican leadership added what was to become Part B (physicians' and other supplemental medical coverage) in order that the Democrats might not claim exclusive credit for what had by then become a very popular cause (T. Marmor, 1970).

Two lesser-known pieces of age-related legislation were also enacted in the high-water legislative year of 1965. The Medicaid program emerged as something of a "sleeper" from the heated Medicare debate. Medicaid (Title XIX of the Social Security Act) transformed a five-year-old program of grants to the states for the medically indigent elderly (the so-called Kerr-Mills program) into an entitlement program for the categorically and medically indigent of all ages. An important and unanticipated development in the Medicaid program has been the enormous growth in expenditures for long-term care services and facilities. These costs now constitute nearly half of Medicaid expenditures. The principal federal social services program for the aged, the Older Americans Act, was also enacted in 1965. This is an age-based, expressly nonmeans-tested, grant-in-aid program that finances nutrition, employment, transportation, in-home, and other social services through a network of state, substate, and vendor agencies. Expenditures under the social services titles of the legislation now total nearly $700 million and have helped to develop an aging-based agency and service infrastructure throughout the country.

Employment problems confronting middle-aged and older workers were addressed by the Age Discrimination in Employment Act of 1967. That legislation was designed to prohibit arbitrary discrimination based on age and to foster ability rather than age criteria in employer decisions about hiring and promotion. Major amendments in 1978 expanded coverage under the act to individuals up to age 70; and in 1986 all age restrictions were removed, effectively eliminating the purely legal grounds for mandatory retirement. Despite these provisions, there has been a gradual but long-term growth in the proportions of older men opting for early retirement. Workers may take early retirement under Social Security beginning at age 62 (with an actuarially based reduction in benefits), and 65 percent of men and 76 percent of women opt for such benefits before age 65 (J. H. Schulz, 1985).

The early 1970s saw the last legislatively sustained period of aging program liberalization. Major Social Security amendments in 1972 brought about an immediate 20 percent increase in OASDI benefits and introduced the cost-of-living adjustment to the Social Security benefit structure. These amendments also contained the new Supplemental Security Income program for the impoverished aged, the blind, and disabled. SSI replaced the three separate federal grant-in-aid programs covering these populations with a program administered nationally through the Social Security Administration and which guaranteed a minimum benefit nationwide to the eligible populations.

Age-related legislation enacted during the last ten years has differed from the programs reviewed to this point in that it has been largely regulatory and restrictive in purpose and impact. Major legislation regarding private pensions, the Employee Retirement Income Security Act (ERISA), enacted in 1974 established guidelines for funding and insuring pension plans. It required that vesting requirements be standardized and eased in order for plans to receive preferential federal tax treatment (R. L. Clark and D. L. Baumer, 1985). ERISA also created a major new retirement instrument, the Individual Retirement Account. The tax treatment of IRA's contributions was greatly liberalized in 1981, but these tax benefits were significantly reduced by the tax reform legislation of 1986. Considerable controversy has been generated around continuing inadequacies of private pension coverage and benefits, especially as they affect women, and around ways to improve the equity and efficiency of targeting tax preferences in retirement legislation. However, little additional headway has been made in the current antiregulation, deficit-reduction atmosphere in Washington.

The New Era of Constraints

Concerns with rising costs and future obligations associated with age-related programs has emerged as the principal policy issue affecting the elderly in the 1980s. This shift represents a major break with much of the preceding fifty-year period, marked as it was by gradual and occasionally dramatic expansion of programs and benefits.

Most significant in this regard were the changes made to the OASDI program by the Social Security Amendments of 1983. Included in the package of the tax increases and benefit reductions were an increase in the tax rate on covered wages and salaries, a phasing in early in the next century of an increase in the age of eligibility for full Social Security benefits, taxation on up to one-half of Social Security benefits for those beneficiaries whose income exceeds $25,000 for single persons or $32,000 for couples, and inclusion of all new federal government workers in the Social Security system. The tortuous process leading to this mix of tax increases and benefit reductions, and presumably to long-term solvency for the system, is recounted in Paul Light's *Artful Work* (1985).

Health care policy is the other principal area where major cost containment efforts affecting the elderly have been instituted. In 1984 a new prospective payment system for hospitals under the Medicare program was introduced in response to Medicare expenditures having increased from $3 billion in 1967 to over $70 billion in 1985. This new system reimburses hospitals a fixed amount based on a series of diagnostically related groupings (DRGs) rather than retrospectively on the basis of costs incurred in the care of individual patients. It was expected that savings would result from hospitals choosing to discharge patients sooner than formerly in order either to avoid absorbing the care costs of "overstayers" or to retain the savings resulting from early discharges. The effects of this new system on quality of care, especially premature hospital discharges, is the subject of current debate and research.

Patterns of Development

Over the last half-century programs for the elderly have enjoyed an unrivaled expansion in eligibility criteria, benefit levels, and federal funding participation. There continue to be, nonetheless, great disparities in income within the aged population and between the older and younger populations.

In accounting for these differences, it must be understood that the United States inaugurated welfare state programs for the elderly and other groups later than other industrial nations, has historically devoted fewer resources than comparable nations to its welfare state programs, and has placed relatively greater emphasis on the needs of the aged than have other countries. In short, the United States has been "late, low, and slow" when it comes to social welfare policy development.

The relative tardiness of the United States in embarking on national welfare programs is well known. The Social Security Act came a generation or more after initial efforts had been made elsewhere, and expenditures under that act (which has contained all of the major welfare state programs in the United States) remained very low for a full twenty-five years after its passage. Disability coverage was not added until 1956 (1950 under the public assistance titles), and the two major health care programs enacted in 1965 covered only the elderly and poor. The timing of universal American social program development can be seen in Table 4.1.

As to expenditures, Table 4.2 shows that despite significant increases over the twenty-five-year-period 1953 to 1978, the United States still trails selected other industrial nations in the proportion of gross national product devoted to social security programs. The relative weighting toward old-age benefits can be seen from the cross-national expenditure data in Table 4.3. The United States allocates a greater portion of its income maintenance to the elderly than does any other country, except Austria, despite having a younger age profile than any of the advanced European nations. Were public health care financing data included, the U.S. position would be more distinctive yet, given the near-exclusive concentration of the Medicare program on the elderly.

It is important that this pattern of American spending be easily and appropriately interpreted to stress how little is allocated toward families

Table 4.1
Dates of Introduction of Selected Social Programs

	Industrial Accident	Sickness Ins.	Pension Ins.	Unemployment Ins.	Family Allowance	Health Ins.
Germany	1884	1883	1889	1927	1954	1880
U.Kingdom	1906	1911	1908	1911	1945	1948
Sweden	1091	1910	1913	1934	1947	1962
Canada	1930	1971	1927	1940	1944	1972
U.S.	1930	- - - -	1935	1935	- - - -	- - - -
France	1898* 1946**	1930	1910	1914# 1959## 1967	1932	1945

*Employer Liability   #Unemployment Assistance
**Compulsory   ##Collective Labor Agreements
Source: R. T. Kudrle and T. R. Marmor (1981). The development of welfare states in North
America, in P. Flora and A. J. Heidenheimer, eds., *The Development of Welfare States in
Europe and America* (p. 83). New Brunswick, N.J.: Transaction Books. Derived from
Table 3.1 and sources cited therein.

Table 4.2
Social Insurance Expenditure as a Percentage of GNP/GDP

	1953-1955	1965-1967	1975-1977
Great Britain	9.6	12.9	17.2
France	13.3	15.4	24.8
Sweden	10.1	15.1	28.0
United States	4.6	7.8	13.6
West Germany	14.7	17.4	23.8

Source: A. J. Heidenheimer, H. Heclo, and C. T. Adams, *Comparative Public Policy: The
Politics of Social Choice in Europe and America,* 2nd ed. (New York: St. Martin's Press,
1983). Table 7.1 and sources cited therein, especially International Labor Organization,
The Cost of Social Security, various years.

Table 4.3
Expenditures on Main Items of Income Maintenance, 1972–1973

	Old Age & Invalidity Pension	Child Allow-ance	Sickness Cash Benefits	Unemploy-ment Related	Means Tested Public Assistance	Other
G.Britain	63	7	12	9	9	0
France	56	20	11	2	4	7
Sweden	62	14	18	4	3	0
U.States	73	0	4	7	12	4
W.Germany	72	3	8	3	4	10

Source: Organization for Economic Cooperation and Development, *Public Expenditure on Income Maintenance Programmes* (Paris: OECD, 1976), p. 20, Table 2. Cited in A. J. Heidenheimer, H. Heclo, and C. T. Adams, *Comparative Public Policy, p. 214.*

and children rather than how much is allocated toward the old. The relatively low American spending levels overall, the higher percentage devoted toward means-tested public assistance programs, and the total absence of any kind of a family allowance program speak directly to historical American attitudes toward government intervention, the welfare state, and the basis on which public benefits should be made available to different population groups.

These high levels of public expenditures directed toward the aged are very much the result of economic, demographic, and political developments throughout the West. Economic expansion and aged population growth are the most obvious. The catalyst transforming these fundamental trends into proximate program reality has been the constituencies and expectations which grew up once the programs were underway. Social insurance programs, such as OASDI in the United States, are formal entitlements that take on a political life of their own. The program and the concerns of both those running it and benefitting from it create a political reality in which policy creates its own politics. This is a reversal of how the policy process is usually thought to exist and, as such, represents a development of enormous importance.

The political presence and popularity of the aged has been a major contributing factor to program growth. The number and size of age-based interest groups in the United States has no equal elsewhere. Membership in the American Association of Retired Persons alone now numbers more than 25 million. How these numbers are translated into political influence has been subject to extensive debate (F. Cottrell, 1971; R. H. Binstock, 1972; H. Pratt, 1976; P. Light, 1985), and pressures emanating from the organized aging have not been seen as central to some major age-related enactments (M. Derthick, 1979; P. Schuck, 1980; V. Burke and V. Burke, 1974). But there is no question that the presumably special needs of the aged have been both cited and used by other groups and officials in pursuit of various electoral and programmatic agendas. This has been most especially the case in the cases of Medicare (T. Marmor, 1970) and welfare reform during the Nixon Administration (D. P. Moynihan, 1973). The aged have enjoyed a particular legitimacy and utility in the social welfare state as it has developed "out of the liberal mold" (G. V. Rimlinger, 1971) in America.

It is again important to note that the policy standing of the aged in the United States must be seen alongside that of other actual or potential constituency populations. The relative absence of class-based politics in the United States combined with the ingrained tenets of nineteenth-century liberalism have precluded the development of broad-based public programs for workers and their families. These realities alone would place the elderly in a relatively advanced position; that they are also consonant with offering assistance to a group with the social and economic characteristics long considered unique to the old makes the distinctions sharper yet.

CURRENT POLICY AND PROGRAMS

Program and Expenditure Growth

There has been a remarkable growth in the number of age-related programs and in expenditures under those programs over the last twenty-five years. Depending on who is counting, the number ranges from forty-seven (U.S. House, 1977), to eighty (C. L. Estes, 1979), to 147 (R. Stanfield, 1978). Roughly three-quarters of these programs were enacted between 1960 and 1980.

The listing compiled by the House Select Committee on Aging, for example, finds multiple age-related programs in the following areas: income maintenance programs (6); employment and volunteer programs (9); health care programs (7); housing programs (6); social service programs (10); transportation programs (4); and training and research programs (6). While a number of these programs served aged and nonaged alike, just over one-half of them have age as an eligibility criterion.

Expenditure growth under U.S. aging programs has been equally dramatic. From an estimated $18 billion in 1960, expenditures on behalf of older persons (in current dollars) jumped to $104 billion in 1978, and to $216 billion in 1983 (U.S. Senate, 1982; J. R. Storey, 1983). Expenditures on behalf of the elderly now constitute just over one-quarter of all federal spending.

The initiatives of the Reagan Administration have fundamentally altered long-standing assumptions about federal program and expenditure growth. More important than the actual reductions the administration has achieved has been its bringing into question the notion that these expenditures are essentially uncontrollable. As documented in a number of Urban Institute studies (J. L. Palmer and I. V. Sawhill, 1984; Storey, 1983; M. R. Burt and K. J. Pittman, 1985), the record of success is mixed, but is remarkable nonetheless given the background of the 1970s.

The Reagan Administration has had greater success in forestalling new program initiatives than in curtailing expenditure growth. On the first point, as Storey observes: "There have been no initiatives by the administration to increase the incomes of the needy aged through transfer payments, improve directly medical or institutional care, protect the elderly against crime, improve employment opportunities for older workers, or construct more housing for the elderly" (1983:22). Nonetheless, the Administration has not attempted to transform the scope and structure of the major aging-related programs to the same extent that it has a number of programs targeted largely on younger individuals (D. L. Bawden and J. L. Palmer, 1984).

Demography and the structure of the major entitlement programs (OASDI, Medicare, SSI, Medicaid) have generated increasing program expenditures through this period, but the Congressional Budget Office (cited in Storey, 1986) has estimated that administration efforts have reduced what the amount would have been by $26 billion. The largest dollar reductions came in Social Security ($8.7 billion) and Medicare ($12.3 billion), but the largest proportional cuts were made in smaller health programs (22 percent) and community service programs (39 percent). Had not Congress resisted some of the administration proposals, the cuts would have been twice (Social Security) and five times (Medicaid) as great (Storey, 1986).

Eligibility: Social Insurance and Public Assistance Programs

The size, acceptance, and place of the social insurance system under Social Security has been unquestionably the hallmark of social welfare policy development in the United States. The ascendancy of social insurance is important in at least three contexts.

First, its central position is a relatively new development. As recently as 1950, expenditures under the former Old Age Assistance program exceeded those under OASI (Derthick, 1979). Today, there are over 36 million recipients of social insurance benefits, 24 million of whom are retired workers and their spouses and 5 million of whom are widows and widowers. By contrast, 2 million older persons are SSI recipients (one-quarter of these older persons eligible by reason of disability or blindness), a figure that has remained nearly constant for a decade. Largely because of the growth and acceptance of OASDI, Old Age Assistance/SSI has largely "withered away," much as the program founders had envisaged (G. Y. Steiner, 1966).

That this withering away has not occurred in the case of the other means-tested income program under Social Security—Aid to Families with Dependent Children—raises the second point. Aged program beneficiaries receive a much higher proportion of their program benefits through social insurance programs than do nonaged beneficiaries. OASDI and Unemployment Insurance offer important assistance to nonaged dependents, survivors, the disabled, and the unemployed, but there are major policy gaps for low-income and single-headed families, the long-term unemployed, childless couples, widows under age 60, and impoverished single persons.

Third, on a more positive note, the cash social insurance programs are fundamental to the well-being of today's aged. The OASI program provides 40 percent of the aggregate aged income in the United States, and much of that assists persons who are poor and many more who would be poor without it. Social Security constitutes over half of the income for 94 percent of aged households with less than $5,000 in total income, and for 78 percent of such units with incomes between $5,000 and $10,000 (Y. P. Chen, 1985). More than any other source, Social Security is responsible for the poverty rate among older Americans having declined from 35 percent in 1959 to 14.2 percent in 1985.

The Reagan Administration attempted to make cuts in both social insurance and public assistance programs affecting the aged but, as indicated, met with only limited success. After experiencing "a Social Security Dunkirk" (Light, 1985) in 1981 by proposing a 25 percent cut in early retirement benefits, the Reagan Administration (and the Congressional leadership) delegated alterations in Social Security to the bipartisan commission that fashioned important changes in its 1983 report. The administration proposed a 2.8 percent cut in SSI, but Congress ended up by increasing benefits by 8.6 percent (Storey, 1986). The relative sanctity of SSI in the administration's eye resulted from the realization that the stringent ability-to-work criteria it used in slashing assistance programs for younger individuals could not be readily applied to SSI recipients.

Program Locus: Washington and the States

A major objective of the Reagan Administration has been to decentralize public program responsibilities, thereby reducing the presence of Washington in citizens' lives and also making program administration "closer to the people."

Specific attention was focused on grant-in-aid programs, which involve transfers of varying levels of federal responsibility and funds to state and substate governments and to individuals. Since 1960 the number of such grants expanded to over 500, and expenditures under them had reached

$93 billion or 11.7 percent of the total federal budget by 1983 (G. B. Mills and J.L. Palmer, 1984). There was also widespread criticism that many of these Great Society programs had failed to live up to their advance billing (J. L. Pressman and A. Wildavsky, 1979; D. Stockman, 1975). Similar concerns were expressed in the case of grants-in-aid focusing on older persons (Estes, 1979; Binstock et al., 1985; R. B. Hudson, 1986).

The Reagan Administration has had a mixed record in seeking to restructure and cut spending for grant programs. Its major successes came in 1981 when it brought about recessions of 13 percent and was able to consolidate fifty-five categorical grants into nine block grants (G. E. Peterson, 1984). However, various administration attempts to turn AFDC and Food Stamps over to the states while federalizing portions of the Medicaid program were not successful.

The elderly have been less affected by these changes than other groups. This is, in part, because a disproportionate share of old-age benefits are outside of the grant-in-aid system (OASDI, Medicare, and SSI). The grant-in-aid programs focused heavily on the aged have not fared so poorly as have other programs. Medicaid cuts were limited and waivers to the states were granted to facilitate development of community-based services for the elderly. There were heavy cuts in housing programs, but these must be phased in over time because of long-term contractual commitments made earlier.

The grant legislation targeted exclusively on the elderly and responsible for creating a network of state and substate agencies serving older people was left almost untouched. The Older Americans Act was excluded from grant consolidation attempts, and its funding has continued at a level just under 1 billion dollars. Once widely criticized for its lack of focus and measurable accomplishment, this legislation has come to serve as an important political bulwark in the 1980s, whatever its programmatic shortcomings may be (R. B. Hudson, 1986).

FUTURE ISSUES

The aged have fared relatively well in the context of the truncated American welfare state. They were prominently featured in the New Deal legislation, shared fully in the program expansion spawned by mid-century economic growth, and have been less adversely affected by recent program cuts than other populations.

This generalization is clouded by long-standing and continuing areas of unmet need and by shifting demographic and political trends. Well-known subpopulations of the old continue to suffer from ill health, low income, and social isolation. This might seem anomalous given the overall social welfare standing of older Americans, but therein lies a major source of the problem. As long as there continue to be gaps in coverage for younger populations, many Americans will continue to arrive at old age with histories of low wages, poor health, limited education, and marginal family and social supports.

The liberalization of age-related policy over the last twenty-five years has markedly enhanced the prospects of both economic security and life-style continuity in old age. However, in the absence of expanded policies for working-age populations and/or enhanced benefits for the low-income aged, poverty in old age and that which accompanies it are not about to disappear in the United States.

REFERENCES

Axinn, J., and Levin, H. (1982). *Social Welfare: A History of the American Response to Need*. New York: Longman.

Bawden, D. L., and J. L. Palmer (1984). Social Policy Challenging the Welfare State. In J. L. Palmer and I. V. Sawhill, eds., *The Reagan Record*. Cambridge, Mass.: Ballinger.

Binstock, R. H. (1972). Interest-Group Liberalism and the Politics of Aging. *Gerontologist, 12*, pp. 265–80.

Binstock, R. H., Levin, M., and Weatherley, R. Political Dilemmas of Social Intervention. In R. H. Binstock and E. Shanas, eds., *Handbook of Aging and the Social Sciences* (pp. 589–615). New York: Van Nostrand Reinhold.

Burke, V., and Burke, V. (1974). *Nixon's Good Deed*. New York: Columbia University Press.

Burt, M. R., and Pittman, K. J. (1985). *Testing the Social Safety Net*. Washington: Urban Institute.

Chen, Y-P. (1985). Economic status of the aging. In R. H. Binstock and E. Shanas, eds., *Handbook of Aging and the social sciences* (pp. 641–65). New York: Van Nostrand Reinhold.

Clark, R. L., and Baumer, D. L. (1985). Income Maintenance Policies. In R. H. Binstock and E. Shanas, eds., *Handbook of aging and the social sciences* (pp. 666–96). New York: Van Nostrand Reinhold.

Cottrell, F. (1971). *Government and Non-Governmental Organizations*. Washington: White House Conference on Aging.

Derthick, M. (1979). *Policymaking for Social Security*. Washington: Brookings Institution.

Estes, C. L. (1979). *The Aging Enterprise*. San Francisco: Jossey-Bass.

Graebner, W. (1981). *A History of Retirement*. New Haven, Conn.: Yale University Press.

Hudson, R. B. (1986). Capacity-Building in an Intergovernmental Context: The Case of the Aging Network. In B. W. Honadle and A. Howitt, eds., *Perspectives on management Capacity-Building* (pp. 312–33). Albany: State University Press of New York.

Hudson, R. B., and Strate, J. (1985). Aging and Political Systems. In R. H. Binstock and E. Shanas, eds., *Handbook of aging and the social sciences* (pp. 554–85). New York: Van Nostrand Reinhold.

Kutza, E. (1981). *The Benefits of Old Age*. Chicago: University of Chicago Press.

Light, P. (1985). *Artful Work: The Politics of Social Security Reform*. Washington: New York: Random House.

Marmor, T. (1970). *The Politics of Medicare*. London: Routledge Kegan Paul.

Mills, G. B., and Palmer, J. L., eds. (1984). *Federal Budget Policy in the 1980's*. Washington: Urban Institute Press.

Moynihan, D. P. (1973). *The Politics of a Guaranteed Income*. New York: Vintage.

Palmer, J. L., and Sawhill, I. V., eds. (1984). *The Reagan Record*. Cambridge, Mass.: Ballinger.

Peterson, G. E. (1984). Federalism and the States: An Experiment in Decentralization. In J. L. Palmer and I. V. Sawhill, eds., *The Reagan Record*. Cambridge, Mass.: Ballinger.

Pratt, H. (1976). *The Gray Lobby*. Chicago: University of Chicago Press.

Pressman, J. L., and Wildavsky, A. (1979). *Implementation*. Berkeley: University of California Press.

Rimlinger, G. V. (1971). *Welfare Policy and Industrialization in Europe, America, and Russia*. New York: John Wiley.

Schiltz, M. E. (1970). *Public Attitudes toward Social Security, 1935–1965*. Washington: Social Security Administration, U.S. Government Printing Office.

Schlesinger, Jr., A. (1958). *The Politics of Upheaval*. Boston: Houghton Mifflin.

Schuck, P. (1980). The Graying of Civil Rights Law. *The Public Interest*, 60, 69–93.

Schulz, J. H. (1985). *The economics of aging*. Belmont, Calif.: Wadsworth.

Stanfield, R. (1978). Services for the Elderly: A Catch–22. *National Journal*, 10, 1718–21.

Steiner, G. Y. (1966). *Social Insecurity: The Politics of Welfare*. Chicago: Rand McNally.

Stockman, D. (1975). The Social Pork Barrel. *The Public Interest*, 35, 3–30.

Storey, J. R. (1983). *Older Americans in the Reagan Era*. Washington: Urban Institute.

Storey, J. R. (1986). Policy Changes Affecting Older Americans during the First Reagan Administration. *Gerontologist*, 26, 27–31.

Sundquist, J. L. (1968). *Politics and Policy: The Eisenhower, Kennedy, and Johnson years*. Washington: Brookings Institution.

Tufte, E. R. (1978). *Political Control of the Economy*. Princeton: Princeton University Press.

U.S. House of Representatives, Select Committee on Aging (1977). *Fragmentation of services for the elderly*. Washington: U.S. Government Printing Office.

U.S. Senate, Special Committee on Aging (1982). *Developments in Aging: 1981*. Washington: U.S. Government Printing Office.

U.S. Senate, Special Committee on Aging (1984). *Developments in Aging: 1983*. Washington: U.S. Government Printing Office.

SUMMARY

A major drawback to comparative cross-national research on income security and related health and social policies is our lack of comparable data based on uniform standard definitions. The very recent efforts of the Luxembourgh Income Study to arrive at standard definitions and to produce comparable data for Canada, Germany, Israel, Norway, Sweden, the United Kingdom and the United States has begun this process. It is based on the concept of the median disposable (post-tax and transfer) income. This effort should be encouraged and augmented for comparative United States and Canadian studies. In particular Canadian and United States gerontologists must arrive at comparable definitions and data relative to the health care benefits and systems as components of income security policy and social security systems of both countries.

A cross-national assessment of the impact of the erosion of universality on the aging population and the various subpopulations is of critical importance to inform practitioners and policy makers in both countries. An advantage to constructing this area as one for cross-national study is that it enables these questions to be removed from the narrow political arena of either country and placed in the border, more neutral and more appropriate arena of policy analysis and development. The progress toward income security systems reform could be anticipated and should be sought from this cross-national approach.

III
LONG-TERM CARE

The most important portion of the health care spectrum in both countries for the aging population, and especially for the "old-old" is long-term care. The roots of long-term care are in the family, which has traditionally cared for frail older members. The health care systems and medical industrial complex in the United States and Canada have been dominated by physicians, acute care hospitals, and proprietary, usually for-profit, institutions. These components are the most expensive, least flexible, overutilized, and inappropriate to an aging population.

Long-term care, both that delivered in institutions, generally referred to as *nursing homes*, and in the community, as *formal care* and *informal support*, is described by the authors within the policy context of each nation. Chappell briefly documents the historic development of health care in Canada as the background to her analysis of long-term care. Branch and Meyers note the legislative bases for long-term care developments in the United States as the background to their descriptive critique.

The two chapters highlight the remarkable lack of data available on noninstitutional long-term care in the two countries. Chappell explicitly identifies some of these shortcomings, especially the difficulty in assuring data comparability across the ten provinces and territories and in arriving at anything which approximates Canadian national data. Consequently she often relies on Manitoba data because of availability and accessibility. Branch and Meyers, faced with some similar problems, were able to draw on the National Health Interview Survey for some information; however, they too disproportionately use Massachusetts data because of availability. These shortcomings in data do not adversely affect the chapters, but they do draw attention to intranational comparative problems in each country that serve to impede progress toward cross-national comparisons and research strategies.

In this major area of policy concern largely stimulated by perceived budgetary constraints, the authors are extremely sensitive to the various policy issues and debates. As a result, each chapter raises policy concerns and addresses them with research that may serve to clarify the key issues. The authors also pose further questions that ought to be of concern to practitioners and policymakers in the United States and Canada. For example, both Chappell and Branch and Meyers provide evidence that informal support from family and friends to frail elderly persons does not disappear with the involvement of formal community care. They further document the lack of appropriateness of institutional long-term care for much of the population and the ability of the community-based services and informal care givers to provide appropriate long-term care at home.

Once again in these chapters the reader will be struck by the fact that aging issues, including the provision of long-term care, are women's issues. The major consumers of long-term care are frail elderly women; the major providers of both formal and informal long-term care are middle-aged and older women. Having made these points, the gerontological community continues to know virtually nothing about the sustained impact of care giving on these women. Perhaps we are creating the situation for the next cohorts to become long-term care service users because of the stress both societies are placing on women care givers.

The authors call to our attention that not all consumers of long-term care are elderly. Branch and Meyers note the use of these programs by mentally retarded adults, and both chapters identify long-term care service consumption by the younger physically disabled adult population. These consumers are noted only to alert the reader to the necessary scope of long-term care programs and to caution against making the assumption that all long-term care consumers are necessarily the aged. This point is frequently overlooked by gerontologists.

Major attention is drawn to the issues surrounding service delivery, assessment criteria, access to care, and the dynamics of financing long-term care in both the institutional and community programs. In the examples provided the importance of the systemic provision of case coordination and care management is explicitly mentioned as a program imperative. This leads to descriptive discussions of the need to coordinate and integrate long-term care within and between the community and the institutional facilities and with all the other components of health services. Failing appropriate policy decisions on these issues of long-term care, our countries will remain host to the fragmentation of services, the inappropriate and largely unproductive competition between programs for scarce resources, the incomplete documentation of needs and service consumption, and the lack of adequate care for the frail elderly.

CHAPTER 5

Long-Term Care in Canada

Neena L. Chappell

INTRODUCTION

This chapter examines formal long-term care in Canada today, including both institutional and community components. Throughout, both federal and provincial levels are discussed, although it is frequently hazardous to make provincial comparisons, as the provinces differ in regard to their health services. However, it is important to understand both the federal and provincial roles in long-term care. The federal government has had an impact on the evolution of the system through its command of monetary resources and its ability to set national standards and priorities. The provinces however, have responsibility for health. The division of authority between the federal and provincial levels reflects the decentralized Canadian governmental system.

At the time of Confederation, in 1867, the British North America Act made no mention of welfare measures, either income security or social services. Responsibility for quarantine centers, marine hospitals and "special" groups, such as the armed forces and veterans, was assigned to the federal government while responsibility for other hospitals, asylums, charities, and charitable institutions was assigned to the provinces. Any jurisdiction not assigned federal responsibility was to be within the provincial domain if it arose later (J. Sirois, 1940). Provincial responsibility for health has been confirmed in the patriated Canadian Constitution. Nevertheless, the federal government has played an important role in the focus of long-term care (N. L. Chappell, 1980; 1987).

BACKGROUND TO LONG-TERM CARE

People have always helped one another in times of illness, both individually and collectively. This was usually done in the home. Organized agencies were delivering services in the home in the eighteenth century. For example, in 1838 when the Grey Nuns, a religious nursing order, were formed, they visited the sick in their own homes. In 1898 the Victorian Order of Nurses (similar to the Visiting Nurses Association) was established to provide nursing services in the home (L. Wilson, 1982). By the turn of the century, local governments and industries provided some health care services and some insurance options. During the Depression of the 1930s, thousands could not afford care. The lack of central coordination and standardization of services from one local area to another became obvious. Local social services simply could not meet the demand (K. Bryden, 1974).

After the Depression federal participation developed. A research and training program in medicine and assistance in hospital construction were implemented in 1945 (L. Marsh, 1975). These two measures encouraged more personnel into medicine and ensured hospital construction throughout the country. The 1957 Hospital Insurance and Diagnostic Services Act insured hospital care for the entire population. This act established cost sharing between the federal and provincial governments for hospitals. Care institutions such as nursing homes and homes for the aged were excluded. With hospitals insured, they became a major arena for practicing medicine. In 1968 the Medical Care Act was implemented, providing national insurance for physician services. By 1972 all ten provinces and the two territories belonged to the cost-shared medical insurance program. To be eligible for federal cost sharing, a provincial plan had to include universal coverage, reasonable access to services, portability of benefits, comprehensive services, and nonprofit administration by a public agency. The hospitals and medical care delivery systems contract with the public insurance plans to provide care at specified rates of reimbursement. Payment from the government sector is analogous to that of group insurers such as Blue Cross and Blue Shield. Provincial governments and medical associations negotiate fee schedules. Most physicians are paid on a fee-for-services basis. Cost sharing started with the federal government matching every dollar the provinces spent on approved services. The provinces controlled overall health expenditures, but the federal government controlled service eligibility.

In 1977 cash grants (a type of block funding) from the federal to the provincial governments were instituted. This limited the rate of growth in federal costs by divorcing funding from specific expenditures. It gave the provinces more control over health expenditures because transfers were no longer tied to specified services, but a very expensive complex of medical services was already in place.

The national insurance schemes established a medical and an institutional focus within the health care system. As C. W. Schwenger and J. M. Gross (1980) point out, these are the two most expensive forms of care. Community-based programs are not covered by any comprehensive national insurance and have tended to develop as add-ons to the cost of existing institutional and medical care. This is in contrast to the community services in Great Britain that were insured simultaneously with hospital and institutional care under the National Health Services Act.

In 1966 the Canada Assistance Plan Act provided payment for some health care services not covered by hospital insurance and medicare. However, unlike the insurance act, the Canada Assistance Plan was designed for those meeting a means test. Each province administers its social assistance program with no uniformity among the various provinces (S. S. Lee, 1974; M. LeClair, 1975). In some provinces homes for the aged come under this provision, but other provinces do not have similar institutions and those that might be considered similar are not uniformly covered. The Canada Assistance Plan does not provide national or comprehensive coverage for nonhospital, nonphysician-related services.

National involvement has assured a health care delivery system with a medical emphasis. This is demonstrated by the role played by physicians within the system. R. G. Evans (1976) has noted that physicians control approximately 80 percent of insured health care costs. Although only about 19 percent of total health care expenditures go directly to physicians, the physicians control or influence hospital admission, prescribing of drugs, ordering of tests, and recommending return visits. By and large it is physicians who make the decision to use expensive health services, not the client or patient (J. E. Bennett and J. Krasny, 1981; A. S. Detsky, 1978).

Hospital costs represent about a half of total insured expenditures. Disentangling physician practice from hospital utilization appears impossible, but clearly physicians play a major role in the use of these institutions. Patients usually have access to hospitals only if admitted by a physician. The very name of our health care system, Medicare, reflects the central role of physicians. This supports acceptance of a medical model of health and illness (E. G. Mishler et al., 1981). This biomedical perspective focuses on cure and acute care rather than on chronic illness and long-term care.

Both dollar and utilization figures confirm the physician and institutional focus within our system. For the period 1970–79, 50 percent of insured health care costs went to hospitals and nursing homes, i.e., institutional care, 25 percent went to salaries for professional services (including but not exclusive to physician services), 10 percent went to drugs and appliances, and only 15 percent to all other costs (Statistics Canada, 1983). In terms of use, the Canada Health Survey (Health and Welfare Canada and Statistics Canada, 1981) revealed one or more visits to a physician by 85 percent of elderly persons in the previous year. Although figures for community care are difficult to obtain, it is estimated that in 1981, .8 percent of elderly persons received meals on wheels, 3.5 percent transportation services, 4.3 percent homemaker or home help services, 4.3 percent assistance with shopping and banking, and 2.7 percent nursing or other medical calls at home (Statistics Canada, 1983).

The focus on hospitals reinforces short-term acute care, although the major illnesses among elderly persons are chronic. Long-term care institutions (referred to as *homes for the aged, nursing homes,* and *personal care homes*) have been the major long-term care service. Only a minority of elderly individuals reside in long-term care institutions and a medical focus is not the major emphasis required by an aging society.

CURRENT POLICY AND PROGRAMS

Institutional Care

At any one time most elderly individuals are not in long-term institutional care; most live in the community. In 1981, 6.7 percent of elderly individuals lived in long-term care institutions (i.e., nursing homes and institutions for the elderly and chronically ill). However, fully 33 percent of those aged 85 and over lived in long-term care institutions in that year (N. L. Chappell et al., 1986). While the proportion in facilities at one time is small, one-quarter to one-third of elderly persons can expect to spend some time in a long-term care facility before they die.

With the assistance of Statistics Canada and Stone and Fletcher, we were able to examine provincial trends by identifying those classed as inmates of institutions in the 1981 census. (See Table 5.1.) While this category is broader than long-term care institutions, the majority of elderly individuals in this category are in these residences.

Looking at the provincial comparisons, the two northern territories have the lowest percentage of their population in institutions, partly as a result of their small percentages of elderly and their geographically scattered populations—factors that make institutions less feasible. Among the provinces, Nova Scotia shows the lowest percent at 5.1 percent, while Alberta is the leader with 10.1 percent of the elderly population in long-term care institutions. The reasons for provincial variations include policy variations, differing histories, and diverse population characteristics. For all provinces and territories significantly more of the old elderly are in long-term care institutions.

In all provinces there are roughly 3 percent more women than men residing in these institutions. The two territories are different. In the Yukon a greater proportion of elderly men are in these institutions while percentages are roughly comparable in the Northwest Territories.

Utilization of nursing homes has been studied quite extensively in Manitoba. N. P. Roos et al. (1987) examined nursing home use as related to nearness to death. They report large and regular increases in nursing home use in each of the four years prior to death, both for number of days stayed and percent living in nursing homes. However, even for very elderly females, 73 percent were not in these institutions.

Table 5.1
Percentage of Elderly in Institutions* by Age and Gender for the
Provinces, 1981

Province	Age			Gender	
	% of Pop'n 65+	% of Pop'n 65–74	% of Pop'n 75+	% of Women 65+	% of Men 65+
Canada	7.3	2.3	15.7	8.7	5.4
Newfoundland	5.8	2.2	12.7	7.0	4.5
P.E.I.	6.4	1.5	13.2	7.7	4.8
Nova Scotia	5.1	1.8	10.6	6.1	3.8
New Brunswick	6.5	2.2	13.3	7.9	4.7
Quebec	7.4	2.8	16.1	8.7	5.6
Ontario	7.2	2.2	15.5	8.8	5.1
Manitoba	7.0	2.1	14.7	8.5	5.2
Saskatchewan	7.2	1.9	15.3	8.8	5.3
Alberta	10.1	3.2	21.0	11.4	8.4
British Columbia	7.2	2.0	15.9	8.8	5.3
Yukon	4.1	0.0	13.3	1.6	5.8
N.W.T.	2.7	2.2	3.6	2.5	2.8

Sources: Unpublished tabulation from the 1981 Census of Canada designed by Leroy Stone and
  Susan Fletcher for the forthcoming *Fact Book on Aging in Canada* (1986); and Statistics
  Canada, *Population, Age, Sex and Marital Status,* 1981 Census of Canada. (Ottawa:
  Minister of Supply and Services, 1982), CS92–901, Table 1.
*Inmates of institutions as defined by the 1981 Census of Canada.

These findings are of particular interest when compared with the use of
physician services and hospitals. Elderly persons make few ambulatory visits
to physicians. There is a general, but not linear, increase in hospitalization
with age. Further, major increases in hospital use occurred during the last
month prior to death, irrespective of age. Finally Roos et al. (1987) note
that fully 40 percent of those aged 75–84, and 45.7 percent of those aged

85 and over, spent fourteen days or less in any institution in the year prior to death.

Given the increased pressure on long-term institutional beds with an aging population and the suggestion that concomitant pressure on acute hospital beds is not evident, what about the much discussed bed blocker issue? Geriatric patients in acute hospitals who have recovered from the acute stage of illness but for whom transfer to rehabilitation or chronic care facilities or home care programs is delayed, have been a concern. Analyses by E. Shapiro and N. P. Roos (1981) suggest that while there are geriatric patients in Manitoba acute hospitals awaiting transfer, the solution to this problem does not necessarily lie in the provision of more beds. They argue a central community-based agency for assessing need, coordinating home care services, and admitting persons on a priority of need basis to long-term treatment or care facilities is more appropriate than building more beds.

Long-term institutional care, of course, has been heavily criticized. Aside from the cost, many (D. J. Baum, 1977; E. Goffman, 1961) have charged that these institutions have a custodial focus and are oriented toward institutional management rather than the individual's needs. Another concern is inadequate treatment for psychiatric disorders. D. Robertson (1982) estimates that 30 percent to 50 percent of those in institutions have some psychiatric conditions.

There are neither simple nor obvious answers for improving institutional services to the elderly and providing alternative types of care. Of note, the majority of elderly individuals are not in institutions, either acute or long-term. Many individuals are relatively healthy during old age. Overwhelmingly, the elderly themselves prefer to remain in familiar surroundings in their own homes in the community. They do not prefer long-term institutional care. One of the difficulties is that long-term institutional care tends to be a no exit system rather than one designed for rehabilitation and return to the community. The national health care insurance system promotes not only institutional care but also medical care. However, many of the needs of people as they age more appropriately call for community support, much of which is nonmedical.

Community Care

A major shortcoming in the formal health care system is its failure to meet the needs of the chronically ill elderly (Chappell et al., 1986). If it is assumed that the importance of chronic disease should be measured as the extent to which one's ability to function is impaired, a broad definition of health is called for. Such a definition would include economic, social, and psychological as well as medical aspects. Community care, a relatively neglected aspect of the system, is necessary for meeting needs in an aging society.

Not until the 1970s was there substantial growth in home health services. It was recognized that existing residential resources were best able to meet the needs of the very sick (nursing homes) and the very well (housing units), but less able to meet the needs of those in the intermediate range (B. Havens, 1981). Alternatives tended not to fill the gaps in a continuum of care required to meet the diverse needs of a heterogeneous elderly population (L. Heumann, 1978). Early home care programs tended to offer medically oriented services and to be a means of shortening hospital stays. They were not viewed as a means of treating and maintaining people needing chronic or long-term care in the community.

In the late seventies the large percentage of individuals at the lowest levels of care in nursing homes was critically examined. For example, L. Dulude (1978) reported that 45 percent of elderly persons in nursing homes in 1975 were in self-sufficient or level 1 care. Most of these people could remain in the community with the proper supports. Intermediate levels of community support are also considered less expensive than institutional care (M. Lalonde, 1974). The aging of the population raised concerns that an increasing elderly population would place greater and costly demands on an already expensive medical care system, which heightened a search for alternatives.

The Department of National Health and Welfare had established a committee for developing pilot home care programs as early as 1957. By 1967 there were only twenty-six programs operating in six provinces. In 1974 a Federal-Provincial Working Group on Home Care was established. In 1975 it reported that the number and variety of home care programs was growing but with little consistency in objectives, eligibility criteria, services offered, staffing, terminology, or funding. The report (National Health and Welfare, 1975) argued for federal-provincial initiatives to correct this lack of uniformity. At that time Manitoba was the only province providing a universal home care program, one not dependent on medical authorization.

During the mid- to late seventies, home care programs developed to an extent, and a broad definition of services also evolved. Home care was viewed as a service in its own right rather than primarily as a means of shortening hospital stays. Social services were considered necessary in addition to medical services. The need for coordination with other health services was accepted. The report of the Working Group (National Health and Welfare, 1975) stated a broad definition which is regarded as the guideline for home care programs:

Home Care should be regarded as a basic mode of health care that coordinates and/or provides the variety of personal health and supportive services required to maintain or to help function adequately in the home, those persons with health and/or social needs related to physical or mental disability, personal or family crises or to illness of an acute or chronic nature. A pre-requisite is that the home is judged to be a viable place where treatment or care can be provided. Supportive services include social services and other services to assist such persons and their families (1975:13).

The different kinds of needs that can be met through home care have been classified as: basic (necessary for maintenance of the person, e.g., assistance with preparing food or bathing), supportive (helping to cope with the indirect affect of illness, e.g., personal attention, company, or reassurance), and remedial or therapeutic (requiring professional intervention and treatment, e.g., medical, nursing or family counselling (E. Shapiro, 1979). Basic and supportive needs are usually met by the individual or by families and friends while remedial needs are provided by professionals. The Manitoba Home Care Program is an example of a community-based program. It has a coordinated entry point. A range of services is available after an initial assessment by a nurse and a social worker. No unilateral restriction from medical, nursing, social, or financial condition exists. Services are provided at no cost to recipients.

Home care is usually considered a necessary component within a continuum of care, one which has recently received widespread recognition. S. B. Kammerman (1976) reviewed services in eight countries and concluded that needs were fairly uniform. A common theme was for services enabling the elderly to remain in their own homes as long as possible. This includes community support services at one end of a continuum of care.

Despite increasing awareness of the importance of community services, the decentralized Canadian system and the lack of national coordination make the compilation of utilization statistics difficult. The independent jurisdiction of the provinces relative to health matters makes generalization to the entire country problematic. A lack of uniformity remains in program objectives, criteria, funding sources, services available, personnel and terminology (Government of Canada, 1982). Recognizing the need for documenting what exists, the federal-provincial/territorial subcommittee on home care compiled a list of services in the provinces in 1985. From that document, we were able to construct Tables 5.2 and 5.3.

All provinces and the Northwest Territories (no information is available for the Yukon) list some services, but vary in terms of the services offered, the need for physician certification, age restrictions, and user fees. The data confirm the interprovincial diversity existing in home care services, both in types of services provided and in access to services.

ISSUES FOR THE FUTURE

Our formal health care system is organized around physician and institutional services. Care of the elderly calls for long-term community care. If one is unaware of this need, efforts and dollars will continue to be directed toward improving the imperfect medical/institutional system. More energy

Table 5.2
Selected Home Care Characteristics, Interprovincial Comparisons

PROVINCES	DATE PROGRAM BEGAN	ELIGIBILITY			USER FEES	
		Physician Cert., Referral/ Supervision Required	Income Restrictions	Age Restrictions	Medical Services	Support Services
Newfoundland	1975 - home care prog. (acute care). **1982** - home support program for senior citizens **1985** - home care prog. (Continuing Care)	Home Care Prog.	Home Support Program	Age 65+ for home support program	No	No
P. E. I.	1970 - home care prog. 1971 - visiting home-maker services	Home Care Prog.	No	No	Medical Supplies	Visiting Homemaker Services[3]
Nova Scotia	1978 - homemaker services program. **1981** - homecare demon-stration projects[2]	No	No	Age 60+ for home Care	Nursing Services	All Services[3]
New Brunswick	1972 - home care program (acute care) **1980** - home care program (chronic care) **1981** - extra-mural hospital	No	No	Age 65+ home care program (chronic)	No	No
Quebec	1970 - home care program	No	No	No	Medication	Meals
Ontario	1975 - home care prog. **1979** - home support prog. for the elderly **No date** - visiting homemakers & nurse services	Home Care Prog.	No	Age 65+ for home support program	Visiting Nurse Ser.[3]	Home support prog. & visiting home-maker services[3]
Manitoba	1974 - home care program	No	No	No	No	Meals, transport-ation
Saskatchewan	1981 - home care program	No	No	No	No	Portion of initial $60.00 in cost of services, full cost of additional services[3]
Alberta	1978 - coordinated	Yes	If only support ser-vices req'd.	Access to speci-fic services	No	Meals, all other services used after two weeks to a max. of $300/month.
British Columbia	1983 - Continuing care program	Yes	No	No	No	Homemaker services[3] adult day care
N.W.T.	1975 - Home care program (Yellow-knife) **1980** - home-care program (Hay River, Fort Smith) **1984** - home care program (Inuvik)	No	No	No	No	Meals, all other support services[3]

Source: This table was abstracted from data compiled by the Health Insurance Division, Health and Welfare Canada, based on information submitted through the provincial representatives to the federal/provincial/territorial subcommittee on home care.

1. All programs available in St. John's only; similar services may or may not be available elsewhere.
2. Demonstration projects are underway in two counties with one additional program receiving government funding.
3. User fees are levied on a sliding scale based on income and/or subsidies or other financial assistance provided.

Table 5.3
Home Care Services, Interprovincial Comparisons

PROVINCES	MEDICAL							SUPPORT			
	Nursing	Supplies/ Equipment	Physio- Therapy	Occupa- tional Therapy	Speech Therapy	Respiratory Therapy	Homemaker	Meals On Wheels	Transportation	Maintenance	Other
Newfoundland	Yes	Home Care	Yes	Yes	Acute	Acute	Yes	No	No	Home Support	Social Work
P.E.I.	Home Care	Home Care	Home Care	Home Care	Home Care	No	Yes	No	Visiting homemaker	No	Dietetic Services, budgeting.
Nova Scotia	Home Care projects		No	No	No	No	Yes	No	No	Home Support	Child Care, budgeting
New Brunswick	Yes	Yes	Yes	Extra mural hospital	No	Extra mural hospital	Extra mural hospital	Extra mural hospital	No	No	Social work, dietetic services.
Quebec	NO INFORMATION AVAILABLE										
Ontario	Home Care Visiting nurses	Home Care	Home Care	Home Care	Home Care	No	Yes	Yes	Home Support	Home Support	Day care for seniors, Wheels-to-Meals, social work, security checks
Manitoba	Yes	Yes	Yes	Yes	Yes	Yes	Yes	Yes	Yes	Yes	Adult day care, respite care, day hospital
Saskatchewan	Yes	No	No	No	No	No	Yes	Yes	Wheels-to-Meals	Yes	Child care, budgeting
Alberta	Yes	Yes	Yes	Yes	Yes	Yes	Yes	Yes	Yes	Yes	Wheels-to-Meals
British Columbia	Yes	Yes	Yes	No	No	No	Yes	Yes	To adult Day Care	Yes	Adult Day Care
N.W.T.	Yes	Yes	Yes	Yes	Yes	Yes	Yes	Yes	Yes	Yes	Child care, diet, psych. services.

Source: This table was abstracted from data compiled by the Health Insurance Division, Health and Welfare Canada, based on information submitted through the provincial representatives to the federal/provincial/territorial subcommittee on home care.

and more money directed toward redistributing physicians or building more long-term institutional beds will not meet the needs of an aging society.

Recognition of the importance of community and social services for an increasingly older aging population is occurring when a powerful, expensive, and complex medical system is already in place. That basic system has not undergone transformation despite various facts. McKeown (T. McKeown and C. R. Lowe, 1966; McKeown et al., 1975), R. J. Dubos (1963) and J. B. McKinlay and S. M. McKinlay (1977) have demonstrated that medical intervention is not the primary cause of declines in mortality in this century. R. Maxwell (1975) and G. R. Weller and P. Manga (1982) have shown that the major diseases of old age are chronic not acute illnesses, and health care expenditures are not necessarily correlated with health outcomes. S. L. Syme and L. F. Berkman (1981) and K. R. Grant (1984) have shown that social class and poverty are significantly correlated with health.

This is not to deny that physicians successfully mend bones, use drugs to stop the spread of infections, or perform important surgery. However, more doctors, drugs, and hospitals are not necessarily better for an aging society (A. Wildavsky, 1977). There are several reasons why the system is slow to change. The power, influence, and complexity of the existing medical-industrial complex is one. The role of physicians in controlling access to medical care has been discussed earlier.

The power of the medical-industrial complex is reflected in society's acceptance of those services as more important than social services. Community and social services tend to be equated with tasks which one normally does for oneself or on which one receives assistance from family and friends. Some of these tasks, e.g., homemaker, handyman, and meal services, are seldom thought of in terms of formal agencies. When they are provided formally, there is a historical tendency to equate them with welfare, and to make them means-tested, stigmatizing recipients (W. J. Tenhoor, 1982). These programs run the risk of being cut in times of economic constraint. Social services are frequently preventive in nature, and while prevention is generally accepted as less costly than diagnosis and treatment, its efficacy may be obscure.

Amid the focus on physician services and institutional care, and the skepticism surrounding formal community supportive care, concerns have arisen about the feasibility of long-term community care. A major concern is the cost of services, given the current expense of medical services. Community and supportive services are viewed as add-ons to an already expensive system. This argument may be taken further by suggesting that formal community services will substitute for services supplied by family and friends (M. Biaggi, 1980). Supporting this argument, older persons with limited family relationships are prime candidates for institutionalization when they become sick (E. Shanas, 1979). It is feared that community and social services will lead to a "shirking of family responsibility" for its aging members.

This argument assumes that these services can and should be provided by the informal network, and that it will not provide care if it can be obtained elsewhere. Studies designed specifically to assess this proposition are not abundant but those which do, suggest it is false.

A Canadian cross-sectional study of a representative sample of persons aged 65 and over found that over half (55 percent) receive assistance from informal sources, while only 15 percent receive assistance from formal sources (Chappell, 1985; N. L. Chappell and B. Havens, 1985). Of those receiving assistance, either formal or informal, fully 94% receive assistance from informal sources. Among the 15 percent receiving formal care, 80 percent receive care from informal sources at the same time, confirming the provision of informal care even when formal care is provided. Comparing two random samples of elderly individuals living in the community, one receiving formal home care services and the second without services, the home care recipients receive more informal care than the nonrecipients. Recipients also have significantly worse health as measured by several indicators.

The argument that formal community services substitute for assistance received from family and friends appears to be incorrect. Further, current studies are documenting the predominance of informal assistance over formal care to elderly individuals. It has been well documented that even in relation to illness episodes, most individuals do not seek professional help (L. Pratt, 1973). C. G. Helman (1978) and D. Blumhagen (1980) report that between 80 percent and 90 percent of episodes are managed without recourse to expert knowledge. Use of formal services is not proportionately large at any time, even with provision of formal community supportive services.

Other studies suggest formal support is necessary for the informal caregivers to continue their role; i.e., it fulfills a preventive function. Those providing care, especially wives of disabled spouses, have been identified as a group at risk for deteriorating health. A. Fengler and N. Goodrich (1979) have identified these individuals as the *hidden victims*. C. L. Johnson and D. J. Catalano (1983) have studied the importance of social and emotional support for the care giver to prevent depression and deteriorations in health.

Another concern related to cost is the fear that there will be endless demand for community services if they are formally established. While little data are available, R. L. Kane (1985) reports that in British Columbia the demand curve for community services plateaued after two years. He argues that the key to control is a universal program administered from a single entity with a fixed budget. The experiences in British Columbia, Manitoba, and Ontario all suggest that services can be provided within a fixed budget. With about 10 percent of the nursing home budget, these governments offer a desirable package of home care services (R. A. Kane and R. L. Kane, 1985).

Part of the rationale for establishing these services is that they will reduce the use of more expensive forms of care, i.e., physician services, hospital, and long-term institutional care. In their study Kane and Kane (1985; Kane, 1985) did not find evidence of institutional care displacement in the aggregate, but they argue the presence of an alternative system of care makes it more feasible to implement a policy to restrict building more institutional beds. Havens (1985) notes that savings in a mature system occur primarily in less use of acute care hospital beds by long-term care patients. Supporting this argument, preliminary data for Manitoba adult day care users (Chappell and Blandford, 1983) suggest that this relationship may exist.

P. J. Levin (1985) points out that while there has been a continued growth in long-term care beds, it has been less than expected and less than dictated by the increase in the number of elderly. The continued increase of 2 percent per year of individuals aged 65 and over, and the fact that they use the majority of long-term care mean that large decreases in use of other sectors cannot be expected.

There seems to be evidence that providing formal community and social services can decrease use in more expensive sectors. Given the way the system operates, evidence suggesting such a relationship can strongly support providing these services. A major problem with the system, as discussed by R. G. Evans (1984), is that no one part of the system has responsibility for either cost or treatment effectiveness. Physicians, hospital management, and government have had little incentive or pressure until recently to adopt less costly care. A comprehensive, systematic mechanism to measure results or relate costs to outcome does not exist. Canada does not even conduct a periodic national health survey. The assumption that more dollars spent on health care will be reflected in better health outcomes has not been established.

New treatments, new facilities, and increased capacity have been demonstrated to increase utilization. Innovations in the system continue to be added piecemeal without corresponding changes in the system. Evans's (1981) solution for cost control is similar to that discussed by Kane and Kane (1985); i.e., the system must be treated as a whole. This means if a new type of care is introduced specifically to substitute for another, then the corresponding component must be withdrawn. For example, if substitutes for in-patient hospital care are introduced, then the relevant in-patient capacity must be phased out. It is provincial governments that have the authority to decrease this capacity.

Despite the billions of dollars spent on health care in this country, little goes into research. Effectiveness in preventing, postponing, or lessening morbidity, mortality, or suffering is not adequately assessed. Side effects and the relevance of treatment to quality of life have to be considered. The system must respond to effective versus ineffective interventions. Questionable forms of treatment use and care must be discarded. The system must be flexible enough to change to meet the needs of society as it changes and as our knowledge about services evolves.

REFERENCES

Baum, D. J. (1977). *Warehouses for Death: The Nursing Home Industry*. Don Mills, Ont.: Burns and MacEachern.

Bennett, J. E., and Krasny, J. (1981). Health Care in Canada. In D. Coburn, C. D'Arcy, P. New, and G. Torrance, eds., *Health and Canadian Society: Sociological Perspectives*. Don Mills, Ont.: Fitzhenry and Whiteside.

Biaggi, M. (1980). *Testimony before the Select Committee on Aging, House of Representatives*, 96th Congress, Washington, DC.

Blumhagen, D. (1980). Hyper-tension: A Folk Illness with a Medical Name. *Culture, Medicine and Psychiatry, 1*, 197–227.

Bryden, K. (1974). *Old Age Pensions and Policy-Making in Canada*. Montreal: McGill-Queen's University Press, 15–21.

Chappell, N. L. (1980). Social policy and the elderly. In V. W. Marshall, ed., *Aging in Canada: Social Perspectives*. Don Mills, Ont.: Fitzhenry and Whiteside.

Chappell, N. L. (1985). Social Support and the Receipt of Home Care Services. *Gerontologist, 25*, 47–54.

Chappell, N. L. (1987). Canadian Income and Health Care Policy: Implications for the Elderly. In V. W. Marshall, ed., *Aging in Canada: Social Perspectives* (2nd ed.). Markham, Ont.: Fitzhenry and Whiteside.

Chappell, N. L., and Blandford, A. A. (1983). *Adult Day Care: Its Impact on the Utilization of Other Health Care Services and on Quality of Life*. Ottawa: NHRDP, Health and Welfare Canada.

Chappell, N. L., and Havens, B. (1985). Who Helps the Elderly Person: A Discussion of Informal and Formal Care. In W. Peterson and J. Quadagno, eds., *Social Bonds in Later Life*. Beverly Hills, Calif.: Sage Publications.

Chappell, N. L., Strain, L. A., and Blandford, A. A. (1986). *Aging and Health Care: A Social Perspective*. Toronto: Holt, Rinehart and Winston of Canada.

Detsky, A. S. (1978). *The Economic Foundations of National Health Policy*. Cambridge, Mass.: Ballinger Publishing Co.

Dubos, R. J. (1963). Infection into Disease. In D. J. Ingle, ed., *Life and Disease*. New York: Basic Books.

Dulude, L. (1978). *Women and Aging: A Report on the Rest of Our Lives*. Ottawa: Advisory Council on the Status of Women.

Evans, R. G. (1976). Does Canada Have Too Many Doctors? Why Nobody Loves an Immigrant Physician. *Canadian Public Policy II*, 147–60.

Evans, R. G. (1984). *Strained Mercy: The Economics of Canadian Health Care*. Toronto: Butterworth and Company (Canada).

Fengler, A., and Goodrich, N. (1979). Wives of Elderly Disabled Men: The Hidden Patient. *Gerontologist, 19*, 175–84.

Goffman, E. (1961). *Asylums: Essays on the Social Situation of Mental Patients and Other Inmates*. New York: Anchor Books.
Government of Canada (1982). *Canadian Government Report on Aging*. Ottawa: Minister of Supply and Services.
Grant, K. R. (1984). The Inverse Care Law in the Context of Universal Free Health Insurance in Canada: Toward Meeting Health Needs through Social Policy. *Sociological Focus, 17*, 137–55.
Havens, B. (1981). Social Planning Implications of Needs Assessment. In A. A. J. Gilmore, A. Svanborg, M. Marois, W. M. Beattie, and J. Piotrowski, eds., *Aging: A Challenge to Science and Society, Vol. 2, Medicine and Social Science*. Oxford: Oxford University Press.
Havens, B. (1985). A Long-Term Care System: A Canadian Perspective. *The Feasibility of a Long-Term Care System: Lessons from Canada*. Tampa, Fla.: International Exchange Center on Gerontology, 19–27.
Health and Welfare Canada and Statistics Canada (1981). *Canada Health Survey*. Ottawa: Minister of Supply and Services, 169.
Helman, C. G. (1978). Feed a Cold, Starve a Fever—Folk Models of Infection in an English Suburban Community, and Their Relation to Medical Treatment. *Culture, Medicine and Psychiatry, 2*, 107–37.
Heumann, L. (1978). Planning Assisted Independent Living Programs for the Semi-Independent Elderly: Development of a Descriptive Model. *Gerontologist, 18*, 145–52.
Johnson, C. L., and Catalano, D. J. (1983). A Longitudinal Study of Family Supports to the Impaired Elderly. *Gerontologist, 23*, 612–18.
Kammerman, S. B. (1976). Community Services for the Aged: The View from Eight Countries. *Gerontologist, 16*, 529–37.
Kane, R. L. (1985). *The Feasibility of a Long-Term Care System: Lessons from Canada*. Tampa, Fla.: International Exchange Center on Gerontology, 1–19.
Kane, R. A., and Kane, R. L. (1985). The Feasibility of Universal Long-Term Care Benefits. *New England Journal of Medicine, 312*, 1357–64.
Lalonde, M. (1974). *A New Perspective on the Health of Canadians. A Working Document*. Ottawa: National Health and Welfare.
LeClair, M. (1975). The Canadian Health Care System. In S. Andreopoulos, ed. *National Health Insurance: Can We Learn from Canada?* New York: John Wiley, 11–93.
Lee, S. S. (1974). Health Insurance in Canada—an Overview and Commentary. *New England Journal of Medicine, 290*, 713.
Levin, P. J. (1985). A Comparison, from a Hospital Administrator's Viewpoint, between Three Canadian Provinces' Long-Term Care Programs and the U.S. Non-System. *The Feasibility of a Long-Term Care System: Lessons from Canada*. Tampa, Fla.: International Exchange Center on Gerontology, 28–36.
Marsh, L. (1975). *Report on Social Security for Canada*. Toronto: University of Toronto Press, xxii.
Maxwell, R. (1975). *Health Care: The Growing Dilemma*. New York: McKinsey & Co.
McKeown, T., and Lowe, C. R. (1966). *An Introduction to Social Medicine*. Philadelphia: F. A. Davis.

McKeown, T., Record, R. G., and Turner, R. D. (1975). An Interpretation of the Decline of Mortality in England and Wales during the Twentieth Century. *Population Studies, 29,* 391–422.

McKinlay, J. B., and McKinlay, S. M. (1977). The Questionable Contribution of Medical Measures to the Decline of Mortality in the United States in the Twentieth Century. *Milbank Memorial Fund Quarterly* (Summer).

Mishler, E. G., Amarasingham, L. R., Hauser, S. T., Osherson, S. D., Waxler, N. E., and Liem, R., eds. (1981). *Social Contexts of Health, Illness and Patient Care.* Cambridge, Mass.: Harvard University Press.

National Health and Welfare (1975). *Report on the Federal-Provincial Working Group on Home Care Programs.* Ottawa: National Health and Welfare.

Pratt, L. (1973). The Significance of the Family in Medication. *Journal of Comparative Family Studies, 4,* 13–35.

Robertson, D. (1982). Establishing New Services: Canada as a Case Study. In D. Coakley, ed., *Establishing a geriatric service.* London: Croom Helm, 199–216.

Roos, N. P., Montgomery, P., and Roos, L. (1987, forthcoming). Health Care Utilization by the Very Elderly in the Years Prior to Death. *Milbank Memorial Quarterly.*

Schwenger, C. W., and Gross, J. M. (1980). Institutional Care and Institutionalization of the Elderly in Canada. In V. W. Marshall, ed., *Aging in Canada: Social Perspectives.* Don Mills, Ont.: Fitzhenry and Whiteside, 248–56.

Shanas, E. (1979). The Family as a Support System in Old Age. *Gerontologist, 19,* 169–74.

Shapiro, E. (1979). *Home Care: A Comprehensive Overview.* Ottawa: Policy, Planning and Information Branch, Health and Welfare Canada.

Shapiro, E., and Roos, N. P. (1981). The Geriatric Long-Stay Hospital Patient: A Canadian Case Study. *Journal of Health Politics, Policy and Law, 6,* 49–61.

Sirois, J. (1940). *Report of the Royal Commission of Dominion-Provincial Relations, 2.*

Statistics Canada (1983). *Fact Book on Aging in Canada.* Ottawa: Minister of Supply and Services.

Syme, S. L., and Berkman, L. F. (1981). Social Class, Susceptibility and Sickness. In P. Conrad and R. Kern, eds., *The Sociology and Health and Illness: Critical Perspectives.* New York: St. Martin's Press, 35–44.

Tenhoor, W. J. (1982). United States: Health and Personal Social services. In M. C. Hokenstad and R. A. Ritvo, eds., *Linking Health Care and Social Services.* Beverly Hills, Calif.: Sage Publications, 25–59.

Weller, G. R., and Manga, P. (1982). *The Reprivatization of Hospital and Medical Care Services: A Comparative Analysis of Canada, Britain and the United States.* Revision of paper presented at the 10th World Congress of Sociology, Mexico City, Mexico.

Wildavsky, A. (1977). Doing Better and Feeling Worse: The Political Pathology of Health Policy. *Daedalus, 106,* 104–123.

Wilson, L. (1982). Historical Perspectives: Canada. In W. M. Edwards and F. Flynn, eds., *Gerontology: A Cross-National Core List of Significant Works.* Ann Arbor, Mich.: University of Michigan Press, 3–18.

CHAPTER 6

Long-Term Care in the United States

Laurence G. Branch and Allan R. Meyers

INTRODUCTION

Long-term care (LTC) is one of the most ethically and economically por-
tentous problems facing health care systems in industrialized countries. It
is also one of the most complicated and most difficult to understand.

Acute care takes place in specialized identifiable settings, affects a cross-
section of the population, and usually has clearly defined clinical parameters
(i.e., diagnoses, treatment protocols, and outcomes). LTC takes place in a
number of settings (including recipients' homes and a variety of institutions),
disproportionately affects older people, and has both vague parameters and
ambiguous outcomes.

Acute care is capital-intensive, depending mainly upon skilled professional
providers and sophisticated technology. LTC is labor-intensive and uses low
technology. Formal LTC depends heavily upon paraprofessional and nonprofessional paid personnel. Informal LTC relies to a great extent upon
unpaid, and therefore poorly documented, contributions of money and effort
from recipients' family members (mostly female), neighbors, and friends.
Finally, there are reasonably good national data on acute care, but relatively
few LTC data bases. LTC data have questionable validity and refer mainly
to one component of LTC, namely, institutional services (nursing homes,
rest or convalescent homes, and chronic disease/rehabilitation hospitals).

Within the practical and conceptual limits set by these considerations, we
shall try to provide an overview of LTC. We remind the readers at the
outset, however, that LTC is more than nursing homes and LTC clients are
more than the old-old. It includes care in the home provided by families as
well as formal services. LTC clients include people of all ages, not only
older adults.

BACKGROUND TO LONG-TERM CARE

The need for LTC often reflects dependency in one or more activities of daily living (ADL), e.g., bathing, dressing, transferring from a bed to a chair, eating, toileting, grooming, or walking across a small room (J. J. Callahan and S. S. Wallack, 1981). Dependency reflects a combination of physiological, emotional, and environmental factors that may change over time. A physiological factor could be the disabling consequences of a stroke. Environmental factors could be a spouse's inability to continue assisting with ADL or an inability to locate or to afford someone to assist with ADL needs.

Figure 6.1 presents data from the National Health Interview Survey (NHIS) (B. Feller, 1983) relating age to the prevalence of ADL dependency in the civilian (i.e., nonmilitary and noninstitutionalized) population. The prevalence of dependency approximately doubles with each successive age cohort to age 75 and triples thereafter.

Second, Figure 6.1 shows that dependency affects people of all ages. While increasing age is a major correlate, it is neither a necessary nor a sufficient condition for dependency. National nursing home data confirm this, as approximately 10 percent of nursing home residents are less than 65 years old (A. Sirrocco, 1985).

Age-specific percentages of institutionalized people with at least one ADL dependency range from 77 percent of those under age 65 to 96 percent of those aged 85 or over (Sirrocco, 1985). Studies suggest that three subsets of adults have chronically high levels of dependency: (1) older adults, especially the old-old in their eighties or older; (2) younger adults with major disabling conditions (e.g., spinal cord injury, cerebral palsy, or degenerative neurologic conditions); and (3) mentally retarded or chronic mentally ill adults. There are similarities among the three subgroups, but each subgroup differs in terms of resources and appropriate services.

As an example of the resource differences, about 95 percent of older adults have Medicare coverage for acute medical care, while only small proportions (25 to 30 percent) of young people with disabilities qualify for Medicare (A. Meyers et al., 1985). There are also gender differences in the three subgroups. The male to female ratio of older people with at least one dependent condition (Figure 6.1) decreases from 1.2 in the youngest cohort to 0.8 in the oldest. Age-specific sex ratios in nursing homes decrease from 1.0 among residents under age 65 to 0.3 among those aged 85 and older (Sirrocco, 1985). Younger adults disabled by spinal cord injuries, on the other hand, are most likely to be male (D. W. Anderson and R. L. McLaurin, 1980).

The subgroups differ in other ways too. Most dependent older adults have family members from whom they receive financial, instrumental, and affective support (P. Doty et al., 1985). It appears that physically disabled younger adults also have informal support networks. In contrast, mentally

Figure 6.1
Age-Specific Disability Rates in the United States

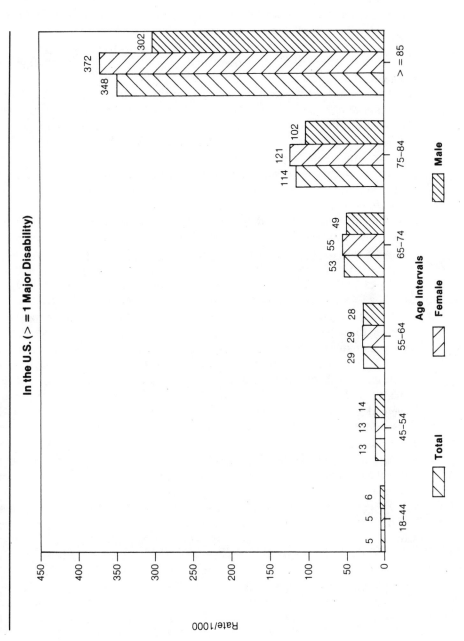

In the U.S. (> =1 Major Disability)

retarded adults and chronic mentally ill adults are less likely to have informal social supports, particularly if they are deinstitutionalized former residents of state hospitals and schools (M. Greenblatt and M. Norman, 1983).

These differences among the three subgroups have important consequences for LTC. They also highlight the importance of flexible LTC policies which have the ability to respond quickly and appropriately to changing dependency needs.

There is no comprehensive estimate of the total need for LTC. An approximation, based on 1977 data by a task force from the U.S. Department of Health and Human Services, estimated that about 6 million people needed LTC (P. D. Fox, 1981). That figure included 3.6 million living in the community, the 1.8 million residents of LTC institutions, and 0.6 million people living in board and care homes. More recent 1982 data (Sirrocco, 1985) indicate a decline from 1.8 million to 1.5 million residents in LTC institutions.

Current trends suggest dramatic growth in the groups at risk of needing LTC, most notably among the old-old who are experiencing the highest growth rate of any age group. Recent estimates projected an increase of more than 100 percent in the number of people aged 85 or older between 1983 and 2000 (from 2.5 million to 5.1 million), with increase to 7.7 million by 2025 (Fox, 1981; I. Rosenwaike, 1985).

Figure 6.2 shows that there has been a marked increase in life expectancy among those who have already reached age 65. This process has been called the rectangularization of the late-life mortality curve because of the greater longevity for more people (J. Fries, 1980). This trend is expected to continue at least until the turn of the twenty-first century. Some have suggested that there may be a corresponding rectangularization of late-life morbidity and dependency which would reduce the future need for LTC (Fries, 1980). Others contend that as life expectancy in old age increases, the level of disability in each age group remains the same or may in fact increase (L. Verbrugge, 1984; E. L. Schneider and J. A. Brody, 1983; K. Manton and B. Soldo, 1985: B. Soldo and K. Manton, 1982). Little evidence exists to support either contention. (Also see Stone and Fletcher, Chapter 2.)

There are limited data on the current patterns of formal LTC service use, and most of these reflect institutional LTC. Quantitative data suggest that there are three patterns of use: (1) people in their last year of life having time-limited but relatively intensive LTC needs; (2) people having active rehabilitation needs, usually following an acute hospital discharge; and (3) people having prolonged care needs.

The best available quantitative data are derived from life-table reconstructions of the 1976–77 national nursing home admission cohort (K. Manton, 1982). These data (Figure 6.3) show that a third of admissions are for a month or less, and more than half are for three months or less.

Figure 6.2
Life Expectancy at Age 65, 1900–1978

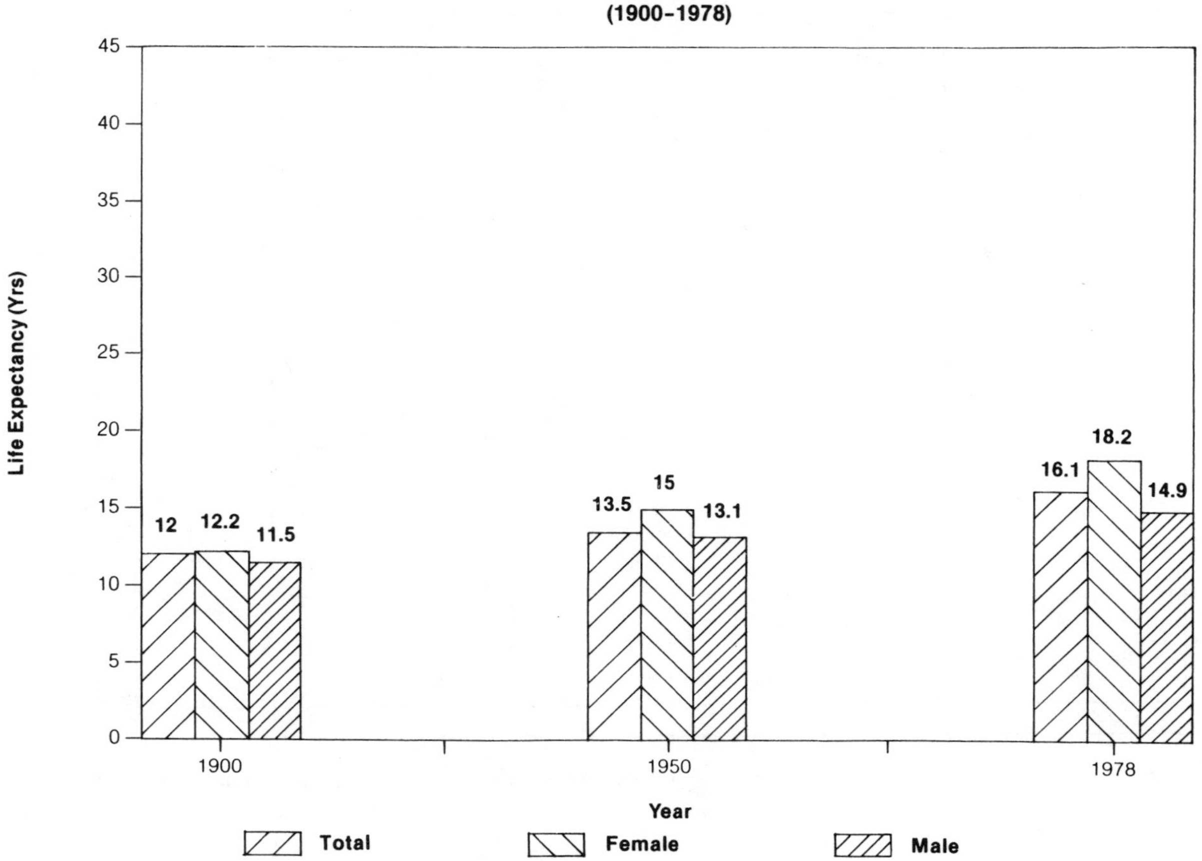

(1900–1978)

Life Expectancy (Yrs)

45 — 40 — 35 — 30 — 25 — 20 — 15 — 10 — 5 — 0

1900: 12 12.2 11.5
1950: 13.5 15 13.1
1978: 16.1 18.2 14.9

Year

Total   Female   Male

Figure 6.3
Nursing Home Lengths-of-Stay (Life-Table Estimates—1976–1977)

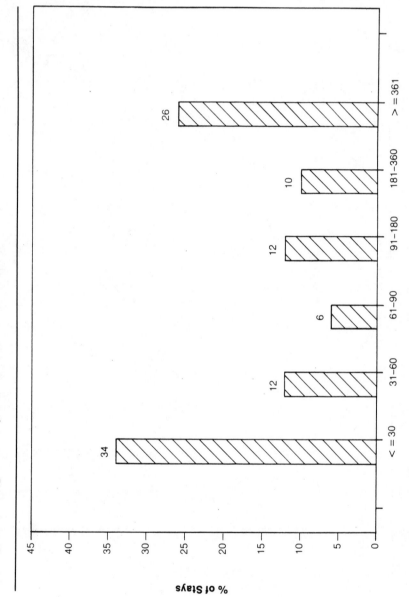

About a quarter of admissions are of relatively long duration, a year or more.

CURRENT POLICIES AND PROGRAMS

Current Supply

Institutional long-term care. Nursing homes are the cornerstones of formal LTC. The most recent data indicate there are about 18,000 nursing homes, with about 1,500,000 beds in the United States (Sirrocco, 1985). By comparison, there are approximately 1,100,000 acute hospital beds.

Most nursing homes are relatively small (a median size of about 85 beds). The vast majority of homes (about 80 percent) and beds (almost three-quarters) are private for-profit. About 14 percent of homes and 20 percent of beds are private nonprofit (sponsored by ethnic, religious, service, or fraternal organizations), and about 4 percent of homes and 7 percent of beds are public. The Veterans Administration also provides LTC as described by Weiler in Chapter 12. Comparisons between the 1979 and 1982 data on LTC show a growth in the proportion of privately owned for-profit nursing homes and beds.

There are three categories of nursing homes: Skilled Nursing Facilities (SNFs); Intermediate Care Facilities (ICFs); and Rest Homes (also known as retirement or convalescent homes). All three are differentiated by the amount and kind of professional services provided. There are also distinctions within types. SNFs include active medically oriented rehabilitation programs (e.g., following strokes, heart attacks, or hip fractures) that are eligible for Medicare reimbursement; maintenance care for the chronically disabled that are typically reimbursed by Medicaid; and those with both kinds of care. A subset of ICFs specialize in the care of mentally retarded people and are called ICF-MRs. Table 6.1 presents the numbers of homes and beds of each type in 1982. Table 6.2 shows the minimum criteria for each type of home in the state of Massachusetts.

LTC institutions are above all places of residence. There are important differences in principal goals: SNFs emphasize intensive medical, nursing, or rehabilitative care; ICFs emphasize custodial care; and rest homes emphasize shelter for people who are reasonably independent. Although states have considerable latitude in criteria, the Massachusetts example identifies distinctions among levels of nursing home care used in most states (Committee on Nursing Home Regulation, 1986).

Figure 6.4 shows the uneven distribution of nursing home beds among states in the United States. Analysis of the distribution indicates no discernable relationship to either the absolute or relative sizes of the aged or dependent populations nor to any other criterion of need. The study suggests

Table 6.1

U.S. Nursing Homes and Nursing Home Beds by Level of Care

Level of Care	Homes	Beds
Skilled Nursing	7,032	855,096
Intermediate Care	5,564	442,277
Other or Unknown	13,253	131,813
Total	25,849	1,429,186

Source: A. Sirrocco, An Overview of the 1982 National Master Facility Inventory Survey of Nursing Land Related Care Homes, *Advanced Data from Vital and Health Statistics, III,* DHHS Pub. (PHS) 85–1250, 1985.

a closer relationship between the density of nursing home beds and state Medicaid program reimbursement (U.S. General Accounting Office, 1983).

There are other types of LTC facilities, some of which are of considerable regional or local importance, but about which there are few national data. These include chronic disease and rehabilitation hospitals, and a limited supply of congregate or sheltered housing. The main purpose of the latter is to provide housing for older people who are largely self-sufficient, but who require some consistent or intermittent assistance with ADLs or Instrumental Activities of Daily Living (IADLs).

Home-based long-term care. There are two types of home-based LTC: medical home care, which addresses active medical or rehabilitation problems; and social home care, which addresses nonmedical ADL and IADL needs (e.g., personal grooming other than bowel and bladder care, housekeeping, household chores, and shopping). The practical distinctions between the two kinds of service are often artificial, contributing to fragmentation and duplication of services, but the organizational and financial distinctions are profound.

Medical home care is provided by certified home health agencies, which may be proprietary, private and nonprofit (e.g., Visiting Nurse Associations), or public. Certified home health agencies can be reimbursed from both the federal Medicare program and the federal-state Medicaid programs.

Each state establishes its own requirements for certification. Certified agencies must provide skilled nursing and home health aide services, and additional services from among physical, speech respiratory, or rehabilitation therapy, and consultation with social workers and nutritionists. Some certified agencies provide specialized medical, dental, mental health services, and podiatry. A few experimental programs employ nurse practitioners as

Table 6.2
Level of Care Criteria for Massachusetts Nursing Homes

Levels of Care: State Requirements

Level	Nursing Care/Supervision	Other Treatment	Minimum Nursing	Other Requirements	Financial Assistance
Skilled Nursing Facilities	Skilled nursing 24 hrs. day, 7 days a week. Full-time Director of Nurses (a Registered Nurse with 2 yrs. experience, 1 yr. in administrative capacity); full-time Supervisor of Nurses during the day shift, 5 days a week for facilities with more than 1 unit.	Organized programs of therapeutic services (occupational, physical, speech, hearing and language) to help patients attain optimum level of functioning.	Total of 2 hrs. of nursing care for each patient each day, at least 15 minutes of this care by a licensed nurse (LPN or RN) and 1 hour and 15 minutes by nurses aide.	Each patient must be seen by a doctor every 30 days. Written care plan for each patient which includes: diagnoses, significant conditions, medication, treatment(s) diet, mental condition, bathing and grooming schedule, and routine daily activities. Each plan must be kept current and be revised every 30 days.	Medicaid and Medicare
II	Same as Level I	Same as Level I	Same as Level I	Same as Level I	Medicaid (A nursing home decides voluntarily whether it will participate in the program.)
III *Intermediate Care Facility*	Routine nursing 24 hrs. a day 7 days a week with periodic skilled nursing available full-time. Supervisor of Nurses, RN with 2 yrs. experience.	Physical, occupational, speech, hearing, and language therapy may be provided for patients whose condition is stabilized so that they need only supportive nursing care and observation. *Additional nursing if required,* in the event of a minor illness, where patient is not transferred to a higher level of care.	Total of 1.4 hrs. of nursing care for each patient each day, at least 25 minutes of this care by a licensed nurse (LPN or RN) and 1 hr. by a nurses aide.	Each patient must be seen by a doctor every 90 days and every 60 days for a patient receiving Medicaid Written care plan revised only every 90 days.	Medicaid (A home participates voluntarily.) Medicare will not pay for this level of care.
IV *Residential Care Facility*	Protective supervision for residents who do not need nursing or doctor-related services.	Minimum care and basic services.	At least a licensed consultant nurse, 4 hrs. per month per unit (floor or ward).	Every resident must be seen by a doctor every 6 months.	Medicaid Medicare will not pay for this level of care.

Source: Commonwealth of Massachusetts, 1979.

Figure 6.4
Licensed Nursing Home Beds per 1,000 Age 65 and Over, 1980

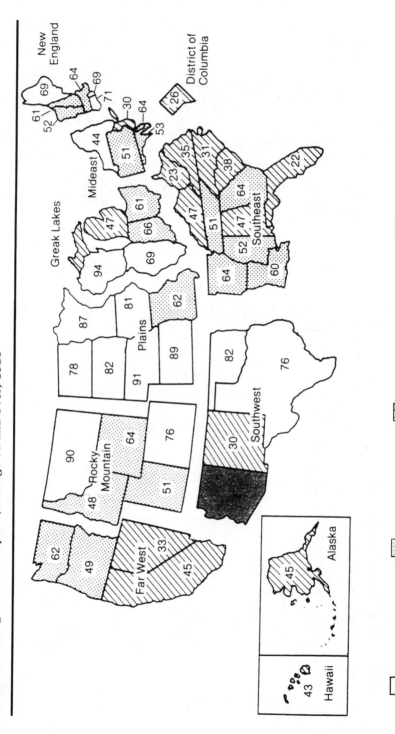

69–94 (15 States)   48–66 (19 States)   22–47 (15 States and D.C.)   No data (1 State)

a/ Data for Colorado and Vermont are for 1979.

Source: U.S.G.A.O., 1983.

primary care providers and case managers. Most programs require consumers to have primary care physicians who are responsible, at least nominally, for care plans.

Social home care is most frequently provided by Area Agencies on Aging (so called Triple-A Agencies), private nonprofit organizations created by the Older Americans Act (OAA, 1965) (National Association of State Units on Aging, 1982). These agencies receive most of their funds from the Administration on Aging, part of the U.S. Department of Health and Human Services. They may receive funds under Title XX (Social Services) of the Social Security Act. In some states, including Massachusetts, they also receive substantial state funds. There are about 670 agencies throughout the United States. There are no data on the total number of clients they serve, but in at least one state (Massachusetts) there are more social home care clients than nursing home patients (L. Branch and N. Stuart, 1984).

To qualify for Administration on Aging funding, Area Agencies on Aging must provide a specified range of services, including information and referral; case management; chore, homemaker, transportation; and meals (both community meal sites and home-delivered Meals-on-Wheels). If their resources allow and community needs dictate, they may provide a number of other services, including legal assistance, counseling, and companion services. They may provide services to any person aged 62 years or older without a means test, but there is pressure for Triple-As to serve those at highest risk of institutionalization and to apply a sliding scale based on the client's ability to pay. Triple-A agencies do not require physician supervision and are prevented from providing medical care. This restriction is consistent with the nonmedical nature of LTC needs and assures agencies some flexibility, but may encourage duplication and fragmentation.

Another home care service is the Personal Care Attendant (PCA) service for those with major disabling conditions. PCAs are independent contractors who help with medical, social, ADL, and IADL needs. They are recruited, hired, trained, supervised, and when necessary fired by their disabled employers. There is some interest in making PCA services available to older people who can either manage their own affairs or have friends or relatives to manage on their behalf. However, little progress has been achieved to date.

Long-Term Care Financing

An estimated $32 billion was spent on institutional LTC in 1982 (R. Gibson et al., 1983). There is no estimate of total expenditures on noninstitutional LTC, but in 1983 Medicaid spent $597 million and Medicare $1.5 billion on home health care (Doty et al., 1985).

Figure 6.5 shows that almost half of all institutional LTC expenditures are paid from personal resources. The vast majority of the remainder comes from the state-federal Medicaid program.

Figure 6.5
Sources of Nursing Home Funds (1984—Total = $32.0 Billion)

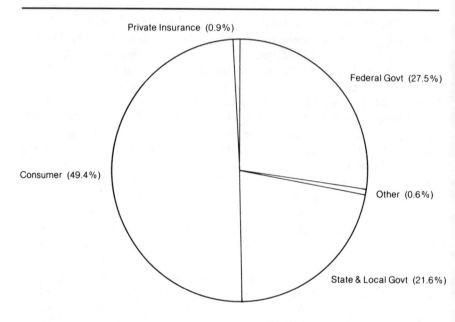

Private Insurance (0.9%)

Federal Govt (27.5%)

Consumer (49.4%)

Other (0.6%)

State & Local Govt (21.6%)

LTC accounts for a large part of total Medicaid expenditures. Older adults represent about 16 percent of Medicaid recipients, but institutional LTC accounts for about 35 percent of Medicaid expenditures, higher even than acute hospitals (K. R. Levit et al., 1985). Many nursing home residents are eligible for Medicaid at the time of admission; most of the others "spend down" (i.e., deplete their resources and become eligible) within a relatively short time. One state study found that about three-quarters of nursing home residents were Medicaid recipients at the time of the survey, while only half had been eligible at the time of their admission (Commonwealth of Massachusetts, Department of Public Health, 1986).

Smaller proportions of public funds for LTC come from a variety of other sources. Medicare pays some of the costs of medically necessary SNF care and all costs of medically necessary home health care. Title XX of the Social Security Act provides block grants that states may use for a variety of social services, including home care for older people. The Older Americans Act (NASUA, 1982) provides funds for Area Agencies on Aging to provide LTC services. The Veterans Administration also provides funds for LTC. The federal Department of Education provides funding for PCA services for working people. Finally, private insurance plans pay for less than 1 percent of LTC in the United States.

There is widespread concern about Medicare's relatively small role (less than 2 percent in 1985) in the funding of LTC. In fact, one source has characterized Medicare as having made an "unkept promise" to older adults (A. Stein, 1985).

Virtually all LTC funding is on a fee-for-service basis, although different funding sources pay for LTC in different ways. The two primary ways are the charge basis (in which the provider sets the rate) or the cost basis (in which the payer sets the rate). Private payment by recipients and their families is usually on a charge basis. Third party payers like Medicaid, Medicare, and most private insurance companies reimburse for the care provided based on a percent of the providers' usual and customary costs (or occasionally a cost-plus basis). The third party payers reimburse a fraction (and sometimes a premium) based on reasonable actual costs in providing care. Medicare has recently put upper limits on the amounts it will reimburse for home health care, regardless of cost.

Medicaid uses a variety of rate-setting mechanisms (R. A. Desonia and K. M. King, 1985). In general, Medicaid reimburses on a fee-for-service basis, with rates set on the basis of a proportion of retrospective costs. Many states also set reimbursement limits for each level of care. Medicaid is usually the least provident funding source, and as a result Medicaid recipients are among the least financially attractive clients. Therefore, providers have strong incentives to select those who have relatively light care needs.

A small number of state Medicaid programs have tried to change the basis of Medicaid reimbursement for LTC to prospective payment. There is little evidence of the effects of prospective payment upon either costs or quality of care, but considerable pressure exists to expand prepayment.

Quality Assurance in Long-Term Care

As the societal and individual costs of LTC are high and increasing very rapidly, there are substantial concerns about the quality and appropriateness of LTC. Periodic nursing home scandals highlight these concerns. Even in the absence of scandals, there is a widespread perception that too many LTC providers offer only a mediocre standard of care.

What constitutes high-quality LTC? Process measures are relatively straightforward, but not necessarily meaningful. It is common, for example, to assess the extent to which nursing homes comply with federal, state, or local life-safety occupancy codes, standards of drug prescribing and administration, hours of skilled nursing care per resident, and frequency of physician visits. (See Table 6.2.) However, none of these factors really provide insights into the nature of care in nursing homes. That is, within the limits imposed by their conditions, are residents happy? Do they feel secure?

Outcome measures of quality of LTC are even more elusive. What constitutes a desirable LTC outcome? Is it prolongation of life? Death with dignity? Resident satisfaction? Residents' family members' satisfaction? Restored physical, intellectual, or emotional function? Delayed physical or emotional decline? Under certain circumstances each of these factors may be an appropriate indicator of quality, but none is always and necessarily so. Moreover, all of them are extremely difficult to measure.

ISSUES FOR THE FUTURE

Projected Need for Long-Term Care Services

National data indicate that nursing homes are filled to about 95 percent of their capacity and that 75 percent maintain formal waiting lists. Consequently people are hospitalized who no longer require acute care, but are awaiting LTC placement. Also, a 1975 statewide study of noninstitutionalized people aged 65 or older found 5 to 7 percent with unmet needs for LTC support (L. G. Branch and F. J. Fowler, 1975).

Unfortunately, there is no clear measure of unmet needs for LTC, and no formula to project future need, or for the proper mix of institutional and home care. Therefore, it is only possible to project future LTC supply on the basis of current demand. Fox has projected that by 2030 there will be nearly 3 million nursing home residents (Fox, 1981). He has applied current age-specific utilization rates to population projections that are flawed for three reasons. First, age-specific utilization may change as other factors change; second, they fail to account for current unmet need; and third, they fail to take into account inappropriate excessive utilization.

It is feared that people will use LTC if the supply is increased simply because LTC is available. It is also feared that availability of LTC services will discourage informal care givers from providing care. No evidence supports either of these notions, and there is substantial evidence to the contrary. Older adults fear placement in nursing homes and go to extraordinary efforts to avoid it, and families make heroic efforts to maintain their older or severely impaired relatives at home. Nonetheless, the concerns are tenacious.

Contemporary Trends and Problems in Long-Term Care

There is an impressive array of problems associated with LTC: inadequate supply of institutional and home-based services; high and rapidly increasing system and individual costs; inadequate provider reimbursement; perverse reimbursement incentives; inappropriate reimbursement mechanisms; and serious questions about the quality and appropriateness of care. There are a number of recent developments; some may remedy some of the problems in the long run, but most mean even greater short-term stress and uncertainty.

Most important is the recent change in Medicare reimbursement for acute hospital care from hospital-specific rates based on retrospective costs to national fixed payments based on diagnosis. This change is called *Diagnosis*

Related Groups (DRGs) (American Medical Association, 1984). As a result of DRG reimbursement, acute hospitals have powerful financial incentives to discharge Medicare patients quickly and to minimize the number of patients recuperating or awaiting LTC placement in hospitals. Although there are no systematic data, there is fear that because of these "quicker and sicker" discharges, a greater number of Medicare recipients will require intensive, "short-term" LTC (K. N. Lohr et al., 1985). Since federal DRG legislation (PL 98–21 of 1983) provides no funds for additional LTC (nor for the collection of data on DRGs' impact on LTC), the effect of this reimbursement method, while difficult to measure, may be profound.

Another important problem concerns the diminishing supply of personnel, particularly nonskilled and semi-skilled personnel (homemakers, home health aides, nursing home aides, and personal care attendants) who provide the great majority of paid LTC. Historically these jobs have been unattractive because they offer low pay, few fringe benefits, difficult working conditions, and few career tracks. Owners and administrators argue that reimbursement levels are too low to permit better conditions. Unions generally have been unable to organize LTC workers, most of whom are poorly educated, female, and minority group members, so there has been little pressure from organized labor. Paradoxically, the personnel supply worsens with a better economy. With lower levels of unemployment, unskilled and semi-skilled workers can find better-paying jobs in other sectors and are less attracted to LTC.

Effects of a third major trend, incorporation of LTC into large organizations, are more ambiguous. This process takes two forms: growth of proprietary chains of nursing homes and home health agencies; and vertical integration of both proprietary and nonprofit health care organizations. The impetus for this process comes from a variety of factors: economies of scale; management efficiencies; and the need for access to large-scale, capital markets. The process of vertical integration has additional impetus from DRGs. Hospitals want ambulatory facilities as sources of patient referrals and LTC services to facilitate earlier discharges of patients whose reimbursement is based upon DRGs (Committee on Nursing Home Regulation, 1986; J. R. Lave, 1985).

There are concerns about both processes. Proprietary agencies could exploit third-party reimbursement to maximize profits. Larger scale organizations could compromise the quality of care in the interest of greater profits and efficiency. Corporate LTC could deal unfairly with labor, and national organizations may be insensitive to local needs. On the other hand, these processes may represent opportunities to address some problems because hospitals and corporations generally have greater management sophistication, greater financial resources, better public relations, and stronger political constituencies than home health agencies and nursing homes.

Remedies and Reforms

Although LTC faces an increasing array of problems, there are also proposals for fundamental financial and administrative reform. The proposals differ in scope and comprehensiveness. Most entail either or both of two principles: (1) centralization and coordination of all health services (managed care); and (2) prepayment for services.

The most popular prepayment proposal is Long-Term Care Insurance, either private individual insurance or public contributory programs with contributions from subscribers, employers, and general tax revenues, a so-called Title XXI of the Social Security Act (M. R. Meiners, 1984). Only a small number of insurance companies write LTC policies, most of which provide limited coverage. There is a growing interest in LTC insurance by the insurance industry, by state insurance commissioners, and by the American Association of Retired Persons. The industry concerns about benefit levels, costs of premiums, exclusion, adverse selection, and uncertain actuarial data suggest that such a development may be tentative and slow.

There are proposals to provide recipients with fixed value "vouchers," which they could "redeem" with providers of their choice. Providers who could offer lost-cost services would realize a profit; higher-priced providers would suffer financial losses (P. Youket, 1981).

A third proposal would replace nursing home reimbursement based on historic costs and level of care, with reimbursement based on resident outcomes. In outcome-based reimbursement, each resident would have specific goals and an individualized care plan. Nursing homes would be reimbursed according to their ability to meet the goals (R. L. Kane et al., 1983).

Some managed care proposals entail the channeling of existing public funding from Medicaid, Title XX, the Administration on Aging, and in some cases Medicare to agencies whose employees act as "managers" to assure that recipients get the kinds and amounts of LTC they need on a fee-for-service basis. The National Channeling experiment from 1980 to 1985 combined the resources of Triple-A agencies and home health care agencies to provide comprehensive community-based LTC (J. J. Callahan, 1981).

Other managed care proposals incorporate prepayment so that agencies and case managers have the ability to coordinate services and incentives to reduce costs. The most prominent examples are Social/Health Maintenance Organizations (S/HMOs), which provide comprehensive acute and ambulatory services on a prepaid basis, and limited institutional and home-based LTC (C. Harrington and R. T. Newcomer, 1985).

Continuing Care Retirement Communities (CCRCs, also known as Life Care Communities) are another comprehensive form of prepaid managed LTC (L. G. Branch, 1987). Although there have been a number of recent changes in continuing care contracts, CCRCs have traditionally offered their residents lifetime housing, utilities, amenities, some social services, LTC,

Table 6.3
Continuing Care Retirement Communities Endowment Fees and Monthly Fees, 1985

Unit	Endowment Fee		
	Lower Quartile	Median	Upper Quartile
Studio	$18,500	$24,500	$35,000
1 Bedroom	$33,365	$45,000	$56,750
2 Bedrooms	$55,175	$71,108	$78,800
3 Bedrooms	$55,229	$75,581	$96,000

Unit	Monthly Fee		
	Lower Quartile	Median	Upper Quartile
Studio	$ 530	$ 599	$ 700
1 Bedroom	$ 602	$ 700	$ 905
2 Bedrooms	$ 682	$ 829	$ 1,093
3 Bedrooms	N/A	N/A	N/A

Source: Laventhal and Horvath, *Lifecare Retirement Center Industry 1985* (Philadelphia: Laventhal and Horvath, 1985).

and in some cases ambulatory and acute health care, in exchange for a substantial endowment (entrance) fee and monthly continuing fees (Alpha Center, 1984). National average endowment and continuing fees for CCRC units of different sizes appear in Table 6.3. Data indicate that CCRCs serve older adults whose age and sex profiles resemble those of nursing home residents; i.e., about three-quarters of the residents are females, with a median age of about 79 (Laventhal and Horvath, 1985).

LTC in the United States faces serious challenges and has major opportunities. The challenge is to provide options for appropriate and humane LTC to everyone in need at a reasonable cost. The opportunity is to do so before there is an overwhelming need.

REFERENCES

Alpha Center (1984). Long Term Care Alternatives: Continuing Care Retirement Communities. *Alpha Centerpiece*. Bethesda, Md.: Alpha Center.

American Medical Association (1984). *Diagnosis-Related Groups and the Prospective Payment System*. Chicago, Ill.: American Medical Association.

Anderson, D. W., and McLaurin, R. L. (1980). Report on the National Head and Spinal Cord Injury Survey. *Journal of Neurosurgery, 53*, 51–543.

Branch, L. G. (1987). Continuing Care Retirement Communities: Self-Insuring for Long-Term Care. *Gerontologist, 27*, 4–8.

Branch, L. G., and Fowler, F. J. (1975). The Health Care Needs of the Elderly and Chronically Disabled in Massachusetts. *Survey Research Program Monograph*. Boston: Commonwealth of Massachusetts.

Branch, L., and Stuart, N. (1984). A Five-Year History of Targeting Home Care Services to Prevent Institutionalization. *Gerontologist, 24*, 387–91.

Callahan, J. J. (1981). A Systems Approach to Long-Term Care. In J. J. Callahan and S. S. Wallack, eds., *Reforming the Long-Term Care System*. Lexington, Mass.: Lexington Books.

Callahan, J. J., and Wallack, S. S. (1981). *Reforming the Long-Term Care System*. Lexington, Mass.: Lexington Books.

Committee on Nursing Home Regulation, Institute of Medicine (1986). *Improving the Quality of Care in Nursing Homes*. Washington: National Academy Press.

Commonwealth of Massachusetts (1986). Department of Public Health, Unpublished data.

Desonia, R. A., and King, K. M. (1985). State Programs of Assistance for the Medically Indigent. *Intergovernmental Health Policy Project*, Washington: George Washington University.

Doty, P., Liu, K., and Wiener, J. (1985). An Overview of Long-Term Care. *Health Care Financing Review, 6*, 69–78.

Feller, B. (1983). *Americans Needing Help to Function at Home: Advance Data*. U.S. Department of Health and Human Services, Public Health Service, 92(2) (September 14).

Fox, P. D. (1981). Long-Term Care: Background and Future Directions. *Health Care Financing Administration Working Paper*. Baltimore, MD: U.S. Department of Health and Human Services.

Fries, J. (1980). Aging, Natural Death, and the Compression of Morbidity. *New England Journal of Medicine, 303*, 130–35.

Gibson, R., Waldo, D., and Levit, K. (1983). National Health Expenditures, 1982. *Health Care Financing Review, 5*, 1–32.

Greenblatt, M., and Norman, M. (1983). Deinstitutionalization: Health Consequences for the Mentally Ill. *Annual Review of Public Health, 4*, 131–54.

Harrington, C., and Newcomer, R. J. (1985). Social/Health Maintenance Organizations: New Policy Options for the Aged, Blind and Disabled. *Journal of Public Health Policy*, 204–222.

Kane, R. L., Bell, R., Riegler, S., Wilson, A., and Keeler, E. (1983). Predicting the Outcomes of Nursing Home Patients. *Gerontologist, 23*, 200–206.

Lave, J. R. (1985). Cost Containment Policies in Long-Term Care. *Inquiry, 22*, 7–23.

Laventhal & Horvath (1985). *Lifecare Retirement Center Industry 1985.* Philadelphia: Laventhal & Horvath.

Levit, K. R., Lazenby, H., Waldo, D. R., and Davidoff, L. M. (1985). National Health Expenditures (1984). *Health Care Financing Review, 7,* 1–35.

Lohr, K. N., Brook, R. H., Goldberg, G. A., Chassin, M. R., and Glennan, T. K. (1985). *Impact of Medicare Prospective Payment on the Quality of Medical Care.* Santa Monica, Calif.: Rand Corporation.

Manton, K. (1982). Changing Concepts of Mortality and Morbidity in the Elderly Population. *Milbank Memorial Fund Quarterly, 60,* 183–244.

Manton, K., and Soldo, B. (1985). Dynamics of Health Changes in the Oldest Old: New Perspective and Evidence. *Milbank Memorial Fund Quarterly, 63,* 206–285.

Meiners, M. R. (1984). *The State of the Art in Long-Term Care Insurance.* Washington: National Center for Health Services Research.

Meyers, A., Feltin, M., Master, R., Nicastro, D., Cupples, A., Lederman, R. I., and Branch, L. G. (1985). Rehospitalization and Spinal Cord Injury: Cross-Sectional Survey of Adults Living Independently. *Archives of Physical Medicine and Rehabilitation, 66,* 232–36.

National Association of State Units on Aging (1982). *An Orientation to the Older Americans Act.* Washington: NASUA.

Rosenwaike, I. (1985). A Demographic Portrait of the Oldest Old. *Milbank Memorial Fund Quarterly, 63,* 187–205.

Schneider, E. L., and Brody, J. A. (1983). Aging, Natural Death, and the Compression of Morbidity: Another View. *New England Journal of Medicine, 39,* 854–56.

Sirrocco, A. (1985). An Overview of the 1982 National Master Facility Inventory Survey of Nursing and Related Care Homes. *Advanced Data From Vital and Health Statistics, 111,* DHHS Pub. No. (PHS) 85–1250.

Soldo, B., and Manton, K. (1985). Changes in the Health Status and Service Needs of the Oldest Old: Current Patterns and Future Trends. *Milbank Memorial Fund Quarterly, 63,* 286–323.

Stein, A. (1985). Medicare's Broken Promise. *New York Times Magazine* (February 17).

U.S. General Accounting Office (1983). *Medicaid and Nursing Home Care: Cost Increases and the Need for Services Are Creating Problems for the States and the Elderly.* Washington: Government Printing Office.

Verbrugge, L. (1984). Longer Life but Worsening Health? Trends in Health and Mortality of Middle-Aged and Older Persons. *Milbank Memorial Fund Quarterly, 62,* 475–519.

Youket, P. (1981). Previous Analyses of Market Reform Options for Long-Term Care. In J. J. Callahan and S. S. Wallack, eds., *Reforming the Long-term Care System.* Lexington, Mass.: Lexington Books.

SUMMARY

These chapters underline the need for thorough policy analysis, innovative policy development, and the political determination to implement and integrate health care systems that include long-term care programs. The lack of data within both countries bears witness to the lack of integration in either country. Specific to long-term care itself, a start must be made to develop standardized uniform definitions and comparable data across state and provincial jurisdictions. One would hope that such development could be sufficiently broad to enable cross-national comparisons of long-term care between these countries. Currently, that is almost impossible and at a very rudimentary level it defies useful analyses.

For the preservation of our long-term care givers on both sides of the border, gerontologists must develop greater understanding of the epidemiology of women's health status and conditions. It is essential to learn what health risks we place on women within the formal health care occupations, within the informal care-giving community, and the interaction of these two facets of risk for a very large segment of our female, paid and unpaid, labor force. Any attempt to project or predict the nature of long-term care service demands over the next decades without this knowledge will be faulty and totally inadequate for planning. This increased knowledge should generate changes in our training programs as well.

The other major area requiring further research within and between Canada and the United States is the analysis of the impact of change in one component of the health care system on all other components of the system, including the informal support component. For example, we must know what impact prospective payment to hospitals based on DRGs (Diagnostically Related Groups) has on long-term care institutions and family care givers if we are to understand the financing of health care, the choices available for service utilization, and ultimately the type and quality of care being delivered to older Canadians and Americans. Failing such analyses, policy decisions will remain largely uninformed, compartmentalized, and in all probability both inefficient and cost-ineffective.

IV

THE CHRONIC MENTALLY ILL

The conditions facing older chronic mentally ill persons in both countries have received mass media and public attention. Such problems as benefit cutoffs, homelessness, and abuses found in nursing homes and community care facilities have received harsh critiques from scholars, journalists, and public officials. The similarities between Canada and the United States are readily evident from the content of these chapters. Variations exist between countries, in the numbers of people who are classified as older chronic mentally ill, the systems of care, and the public policies governing program design and resource distribution.

Colin M. Smith and Nancy J. Herman, as well as Joan Hashimi, note the dilemma of defining the population's parameters. Definitions vary greatly within and between the two countries. The Canadians report on data from Saskatchewan because numerous studies on patient discharge outcomes spanning several decades have been conducted within that province. Hashimi refers to a two-state comparison, contrasting New York and Wisconsin. Historically to the present, two separate state approaches have been operative. New York relied on a state hospital system conceptualized according to a hospital district model encompassing both acute and chronic care. Wisconsin departed from this plan with a county hospital arrangement providing a cost-sharing plan between the state and counties for county-based care of chronically impaired individuals.

Early phases of mental health care in both countries note the slow progress toward institutional reform. Smith and Herman discuss the influence of specific reforms instituted within Saskatchewan that were later followed by other provincial plans to improve care. The United States author constructs a historic summary of reforms starting with the colonial period and moving to the time after World War II. The points of rapid deinstitutionalization, aproximately timed in both countries, are considered. Saskatchewan took the Canadian lead during 1963–66. There was an uneven pattern of state hospital discharge in the United States with some states moving more quickly than others. The rate of progress was based on available finances.

Hashimi overviews the national effort to design systems of care. Professional and political attention over the breakdown of aftercare reached a high point in the late 1970s. The community mental health center system along with private clinics and centers has been judged somewhat successful for acute treatment, but it has been an abhorrent failure in providing care to chronic patients. Standard services from mental health centers have left, and continue to leave, large gaps in the community-based support of older chronic patients. Lack of community care has forced nursing homes to become the placement location for patients who are able to gain admission to them.

Smith and Herman question whether deinstitutionalization was a real outcome or whether older chronic patients were merely reinstitutionalized into alternative settings. The rapid expansion of special care homes in the community has parallelled the declining census of mental hospitals. The principle of normalization — a Scandinavian approach initially conceived for the mentally retarded—has gained acceptance in Canada. That principle coexisted with a trend toward greater psychiatric care provision in general hospitals. Since such hospitals have been found to have the capacity to care for all types of psychiatric patients, they are judged more acceptable as treatment settings, and are financed by cost-sharing between provincial governments and the federal government. This care trend is only now being seriously considered by United States mental health planners.

Older chronically impaired individuals suffer from stigma, poor housing, lack of basic living skills, unemployment, and poverty. The limited aftercare available hinders their functioning and lowers their satisfaction with community life. These are common problems in both countries as discharged patients have scattered to urban and rural areas. Similar treatment innovations that apply comprehensive case management and patient education have been created in both countries to eliminate certain community aftercare problems. Among these problems we find the lack of skills preparation, no phased transitional experiences from hospital to community, and unevaluated applications of different treatment models.

CHAPTER 7

The Chronic Mentally Ill in Canada

Colin M. Smith and Nancy J. Herman

INTRODUCTION

This chapter looks at historical and recent changes in the care and management of the chronic elderly mentally ill. The focus is deinstitutionalization—with particular attention to the Province of Saskatchewan because of its detailed reporting of deinstitutionalization and its sequelae. The authors include some ethnographic data on the posthospital experiences of eighty-five elderly, chronic ex-mental patients residing in communities in southern Ontario in an attempt to document their experiences in community-based residency after hospital discharge.

A Backwards Glance at History

Canada experienced in the nineteenth century a rise in concern for the disadvantaged paralleling that in Europe and the United States, together with the building of massive institutions. In the latter half of the century, disenchantment with the huge monoliths grew. Economic downturns, coupled with a flood of admissions as a result of immigration, unemployment, and other causes, resulted in increasing overcrowding, deplorable conditions, and the growth of therapeutic nihilism. In 1918 Canada's National Committee for Mental Hygiene was formed, and many institutions and programs were surveyed under its authority.

Conditions in the Province of Saskatchewan were grim, and they were duplicated across Canada. Between 1932 and 1946 the number of patients in mental institutions rose from 3.17 to 4.00 per 1,000 population. Two distinct populations of the elderly were involved: first, admission elderly were usually victims of organic brain disorders (Alzheimer's disease, multi-infarct dementia, etc.) whereas long-term residents grown old in hospital were mostly suffering from functional disorders, mainly schizophrenia. Over the next two decades the chances for discharge improved steadily, but there was a considerable long-stay population being generated. After 1946 a slight decline occurred in the total mental hospital population, but this was followed by a rise to the maximum figure of 4.25 in 1955. A slow fall then commenced, reaching 3.70 in 1960 and, gathering momentum, attaining 2.8 in 1970 and a lowly 0.7 in 1980–81 (Statistics Canada, Mental Health Statistics 83–205, 83–208). It continues to decline.

Deinstitutionalization or Reinstitutionalization?

Canada experienced a proliferation of special care homes (i.e., nursing or extended care homes) accompanying the decline of the mental institutions. Further, some mental institutions were reclassified as special care homes with a straight transfer of patients (C.M. Smith, 1971; 1979). Because of classification and reporting differences, it is difficult to enumerate precisely the number of persons in Canadian special care homes. In Saskatchewan, where more precise figures are available, a clearer picture emerges. Between 1962 and 1985 the number of special care home beds jumped from 2,178 to 8,814. Meanwhile, the number of persons of the 65 + age group in mental hospitals dropped from 1,273 in 1962 to 75 in 1985. The total percentage of older (65 +) institutionalized persons had increased from 2.84 percent in 1962 to 7.08 percent in 1985 (percentages expressed in relation to total numbers of 65 + citizens). In the interval the absolute number of persons of 65 + had risen from 84,367 to 124,496—from 9 percent to 12.09 percent of the total population. The elderly have certainly not been deinstitutionalized unless that term is applied strictly to the decline in numbers in mental hospitals.

Patients with functional mental disorders were not seen as the most desirable candidates for nursing homes, and usually had to make out as best as they could in the community or through short-term admissions to general hospital units. Although the number of chronically mentally ill of all ages in the community has greatly increased in recent years, their exact number is unknown. The main problem has been failure to define this population in a shareable, reliable objective way.

A. Richman (1985) looked at the declining use of mental hospital beds throughout the country and found that there was actually a higher proportion of the elderly in mental hospitals at the end of the 1956–1976 period. Although the total number of patients decreased by 60 percent, the elderly did so by only 49 percent. There is no logical justification for this, as the elderly often have multiple physical disabilities that are more appropriately cared for in general hospitals when hospitalization is required. Using Ontario data, Richman also makes the point as does B. Liptzin (1984) that elderly patients are underserved through the private sector in relation to their numbers in the population. In 1978–79 persons of 65 + made up 8.9 percent of the population of Ontario but generated only 4.4 percent of the payments.

The Province of Saskatchewan emptied its mental hospitals much more rapidly than other parts of Canada during the 1960s. In this period, the rapid growth of the nursing home beds, together with enhanced funding from the Canada Assistance Plan, made this possible. The same basic team cared for the patient in hospital and community—a better system—and in the early years active research studies were carried out. The Weyburn Hospital was one of the very few places to conduct follow-up studies on discharged psychiatric patients. The dearth of studies on the post-discharge conditions is a serious deficiency in contemporary community psychiatry in Canada.

In Saskatchewan a number of principles had been formulated (C. M. Smith, 1969; 1971) that eased the transition from hospital to community. These were good follow-up, continuity of care, specially trained staff, sensitivity to social stresses, the creation of a truly therapeutic environment, readmission where necessary, public education, and research studies. The importance of community involvement, a cybernetic model, nonzero sum resolutions of conflicts and concerns for people were all stressed. While such ideals were imperfectly realized in practice, they served as useful guidelines in a relatively trouble-free system.

The Toronto group (Community Resources Consultants, 1981; D. Wasylenki et al., 1985) added a valuable dimension to previous follow-up studies by looking at estimated and met needs in five separate dimensions as well as outcomes. They examined perceived and met needs in the five dimensions of medical therapeutic, social recreational, vocational educational, housing, and financial needs. Only the medical therapeutic needs were fairly well met. The other needs were dealt with poorly, particularly the social recreational component. The two year outcome showed a high readmission rate (62 percent) with many serious deficiencies in housing, employment, social, recreational, and financial areas. Similar concerns with regard to the "disabled" were raised in the comprehensive report of the Mental Health Survey in British Columbia (1979).

Causes and Effects of the Mental Hospital Decline

Attempts to describe a single cause of mental hospital decline are likely to remain fruitless. Many concepts, including those offered by Ralph (1983) such as the benevolent government, the mental health lobby, social control, and labor factors are interesting to discuss but not necessarily testable. In Canada there were a number of specific factors which accelerated the decline of the monoliths.

General hospitals were much more popular with staff and patients. A number of studies emanating from Saskatoon (C. M. Smith and D. G.

McKerracher, 1964) had established that the general hospital could handle all types of psychiatric patients. General hospital care became a universally insured service in Saskatchewan in 1946 and in the rest of Canada from 1957 to 1961. The insuring of physicians' services began in Saskatchewan in 1962 and had spread nationally by 1968. Thus financial barriers to psychiatric treatment in general hospitals had been removed. B. Liptzin (1977; 1984) has provided two useful summaries of the differences between the Canadian and U.S. systems, including the implications for the elderly.

Health is a provincial responsibility in Canada, but the federal government exercises a major influence by its spending power. The costs of general hospital and physicians' services were shared roughly 50:50 by provincial and federal governments. However, mental hospitals were not cost-shared, and this virtually sealed their doom. The Canada Assistance Plan (1966) was a similar cost-sharing venture in the fields of welfare and rehabilitation, and this made it much easier to discharge long-term patients without means into the community. Accordingly, the number of approved homes in the community rose sharply after 1966. In Saskatchewan, for example, there were 124 "approved" homes for ex-patients in 1965 (Ad Hoc Committee Report, 1966). By 1970 the number of approved homes was 404, and the number continued to rise to a maximum of 496 in 1971, falling gradually thereafter to 408 in 1984. Approved homes are simply small private homes subject to government regulations regarding standards and are supposed to provide a more familylike atmosphere for patients.

At first few lamented the passing of the mental hospitals, but soon there were problems. Patients were too often discharged without adequate services. Some landed in jails or ghettos (A. E. Lehman et al., 1982; Committee of Enquiry, 1984; M. Borzecki and J. S. Wormith, 1985). The issue of homeless and chronic mental illness soon drew many criticisms throughout Canada. Meanwhile, a new type of chronic mental patient has been described—one who has never been institutionalized (B. Pepper et al., 1982). And a Canadian Psychiatric Association position statement (J. A. Watt and N. el-Guebaly, 1981) lamented the fact that a new segregation of the mentally ill had taken place—in our downtown ghettos. Despite many problems, the outcome of deinstitutionalization in Canada has been less unfavorable than in the United States. J. A. Talbott (1985), a past president of the American Psychiatric Association, evaluated the mental health services in Saskatchewan as superior to those available throughout most sections of the United States.

Clearly there is no cause for complacency anywhere. Systematic, objective research studies are needed of the effects of deinstitutionalization on the patients, their relatives, and the community at large. Attention will now turn to a consideration of the posthospital everyday worlds of Canadian chronic elderly ex-psychiatric patients. The remainder of the chapter deals with the meanings that clients of the psychiatric system associate with their deinstitutionalization experiences and suggest where improvements are most needed from the client perspective.

THE CLIENTS SPEAK—AN ETHNOGRAPHIC ANALYSIS

To learn the meanings that the chronic elderly ex-patients defined as important and real, a qualitative and inductive methodological approach was adopted by one of the authors N.J. Herman (1987). Specifically, the findings discussed here are based on three and one-half years of participant observation, informal and semi-formal interviewing with a sample of eighty-five chronic elderly former patients living in various communities in southern Ontario. Data were collected between 1981 and 1984 from persons 55 years and older. The stratified random sample included people discharged from psychiatric wards in general hospitals. Their shared characteristic of "chronic" status was reflected in the continual pattern of hospitalization of two years or more with five or more admissions. Descriptive data on the nature of the posthospital experience were gathered in different community environments regarding the stigma of mental illness, inadequate housing, lack of basic living skills, poverty, unemployment, and problems with psychiatric aftercare resources.

Coping Strategies to Manage Stigma

Numerous problems lie ahead for older individuals attempting to return to a conventional life after long-term hospitalization. In short, ex-deviants discover upon their discharge that not only are there no such ritualistic ceremonies to "transfer them back" to their old conceptions of normality but rather that they possess a mark—a stigma or blemish that serves as a threat to their social statuses as "normal" societal members. Stigma, although having an objective basis in the "real world," may also be conceptualized as a subjective feeling arising from a person's perception of self as possessing some discreditable attribute or condition.

Examination of the data indicates that for the majority of the chronic elderly ex-psychiatric clients, the stigma of mental illness is conceived of in negative terms, as representing some sort of personal failure to measure up to the rest of society. The data indicate that ex-patients learn that they possess a stigmatizable attribute through direct posthospital experiences with others who reject and disapprove of them; through their subjective perceptions of how they are viewed, or through both these experiences in combination. Friends and relatives "taught" these older people about the stigma associated with their institutional history. In extreme cases some in the sample experienced blatant rejection from their closest family ties.

While many chronic elderly ex-psychiatric patients discover the social meaning of their "failing" through direct negative experiences with "normals" in the community after hospitalization, still others learn such information through their acquired knowledge of societal attitudes toward mental patients and mental illness in general. Collected data indicate that these people learn and internalize, early in life, stereotypical images of normality and mental illness—images that are constantly reaffirmed in ordinary social discourse. Incorporating the stereotypes provide these ex-patients with self-definitions of discreditability. Through different routes most of the individuals in this sample had come to realize that they possess a stigmatizable attribute making reintegration seem improbable, if not impossible.

Those interviewed felt that as a result of the stigma of mental illness, they are viewed by society as "unwanted clients." Over 90 percent of these persons, upon discharge, received neither support from family or prior friends without a psychiatric history, and the other 10 percent felt their support to be weak and inconsistent from one or two family members. A small number of patients were offered financial support and/or emotional support, but such reports were rare. In effect then, the data indicate that the elderly chronic ex-patients are alone in the community, often feared, hated, and ridiculed. Feelings of isolation, loneliness, and abandonment are common among these older men and women.

One strategy, termed here as *institutional retreatism*, is frequently adopted by this type of client. Such persons have experienced stigmata of various sorts and feel estranged from the larger society. Feelings of stigma can produce an institutional retreatism response. People described their active seeking of ways to return to the psychiatric hospital from which they were discharged—to their "home," their secure environment where needs were met, no responsibility demanded, and a place with a familiar role and status. Elderly ex-patients have often developed the capacity to manipulate the community environment and provoke return to hospital.

Another strategy is *societal retreatism* manifested in self-segregation, whereby individuals remain in the community, but actively retreat to its outermost fringes. By so doing, they are able to avoid what they conceive to be potentially stigmatizing reactions. The highly isolated living situations are viewed as preferable to running the risk of confronting the rejection found when they are visible to the community. A final strategem is that of *capitulation*. Such a negative response is generally employed when other coping has failed and in its ultimate expression leads to suicide as observed in two of the eighty-five study subjects.

The extreme coping responses should not mask the more generalizable realities. The posthospital lives of chronic elderly ex-patients are filled with sorrow and despair. Upon experiencing stigma with respect to family, friends, and community and/or anticipating further stigmatization from others, the elderly chronics either withdraw to marginal locations, take steps to ensure rehospitalization, or succumb to a range of other behaviors, many of which are harmful.

Deficits in Community Resources

Discussions with the direct questioning of subjects about the range of community resources encountered at time of discharge explained much about client service satisfaction and utilization experiences. Most ex-patients ended up in facilities such as boarding homes, nursing homes, homes for special care, lodging and rooming houses. While the mental health professionals view such facilities as cost-efficient and effective alternatives to institutionalization, the majority of chronic elderly ex-patients conceive of these in a negative manner. Specifically, one such problem with these housing facilities is their structural components. From the client perspective, the aftercare facilities in which they are placed are merely another form of institutionalization on a smaller scale. Ex-patients must comply with a set of rules and regulations, controlled by a set of authorities and the social environment that emphasizes dependency.

Boarding homes typically operate in a relatively similar manner, allowing for little variation in occupants' daily routine. When commenting about these settings, subjects expressed a mixture of outrage, resentment, and distress regarding living conditions. Incidents of exploitation were also mentioned, perhaps with greater risks for females. Few perceived much if any therapeutic benefit from these settings, leading one to conclude that custodial environments dominate.

Reported inability to carry out daily tasks necessary to live in the community is also a barrier. Some ex-patients, following a long-term institutionalization wherein their basic needs were met, find great difficulty in carrying out everyday routine affairs. Others, although hospitalized for short durations on a number of occasions in general hospital facilities, also lack such skills resulting from patterns of earlier socialization. Many are unable to cook for themselves, to budget their disability or old age pensions, to use public transportation effectively, and to make everyday decisions.

Despite attempts at reacquiring basic social living skills through various "day care" programs, many older persons become quickly frustrated and admit defeat. The impact of retraining regimes in the hospital discharge phase needs to be fully examined, especially for the older psychiatric patients for whom the programs for much younger patients may simply not apply. Therapeutic and rehabilitative offerings for the geriatric population leave room for great improvements.

Poverty is a common misfortune. Over 95 percent of the sample face poverty as a condition of daily life. Most of them exist on some form of disability pension that is quickly gone to pay rent or its equivalent. For those who depend on restaurants either because they cannot or will not cook or have no place to cook, money for eating runs short. In response to their lack of money, some attempt to sell their medications on the streets. Selling, losing, or failing to take medications can institute another set of risks that are probably greatest among the most isolated and retreated of the population.

Many former patients in advanced age (normal retirement age in the general population) seek jobs after discharge in nonsheltered settings. As E. C. Hughes (1958) notes, there is no more important claim to status, prestige, and identity than an individual's job (especially for older men). Although many in the sample desire to enhance their self-esteem by working in some type of nonsheltered employment, all are virtually unable to secure such jobs. Factors such as age, lack of skills, loss of skills, and the stigma of their illness history impede or preclude employment. The "sheltered workshops" for the mentally handicapped could well be the only source for work; however, many times tasks are considered menial and sometimes degrading or for low wages. Such forms of employment are accepted when ex-patients are unable to secure work in nonsheltered settings, in an effort to acquire additional income and enhanced self-esteem. However, persons discover the pay is only minuscule, and the jobs reinforce negative self-conceptions and identities.

A final problem expressed in interviews related to the various psychiatric aftercare facilities, such as community psychiatric services, support groups, the Mental Health Association, etc. Examination of the data indicate that approximately one-third of the sample expressed feelings of anger and frustration regarding their ability to locate such aftercare facilities. Taking the initiative to find these problems is especially difficult without adequate information to help facilitate a direct and prompt contact. Just as awareness and inability to locate these programs present problems for some, others express problems with the quality of the aftercare. Overcrowding, programmatic orientations, and staff attitudes contribute to lower client satisfaction with these aftercare services.

Discussion of Findings

Community care of the chronically mentally ill has been bedeviled by two assumptions, often unstated: (1) that it is cheaper than hospital care; and (2) that it is mainly a matter of delivering better medical and nursing services outside a hospital. Neither is valid on the bases of present data. Costing is beset with all kinds of difficulties—populations to be compared, standards for hospital and community care, the costing of many subsystems, placing a value on the burden to relatives, etc. W. A. Casswell, et al. (1972) tentatively estimated the costs of community care as 39 percent of that of mental hospital care in a Canadian sample of 458 chronic mental patients (41 percent aged 65 and over). However, these workers freely admitted that a vast amount of operational research was needed. The complex financial problems involved remain unanswered at present, but there is little doubt that the mirage of decreased costs was politically attractive.

The primacy of medical and nursing care was seldom explicitly stated but often dominated the thinking of health professionals. In fact, medical care was on the whole better delivered than components related to housing, vocational, education, financial, social, and recreational services. Yet it is abundantly clear that adequate care in the community cannot be offered by a mental health system working in isolation from other agencies.

The importance of stigma has been stressed in this chapter. Its reduction is not easy. Over a period of thirty years the problems facing Canadians have been recognized (E. Cumming and J. Cumming, 1957; C. D'Arcy, 1981; M. J. Dear and S.M. Taylor, 1982; Hutchison, et al., 1985). The implementation of innovative strategies to cope with stigma for the different cohorts of chronic mentally ill has not advanced systematically throughout Canada. This is one of the clear social policy and programmatic needs evident from the presented data. Other areas are also critical: good leadership to assure that the sickest patients are offered highest quality care rather than the reverse (C. M. Smith, 1975); more attention paid to the priorities recommended by mental health service consumer groups; better programs for teaching the essential life skills for community residency; housing development strategies that can impact on the needs of all homeless people; better integration of the mentally handicapped into mainstream employment; increased home care options that can serve the mentally impaired older population; systems that assure continuity of care, such as the one available in Saskatchewan; and a policy that assures adequate fiscal resources to follow the patient from hospital to the community (E. F. Torrey and S. M. Wolfe, 1986).

In many parts of Canada progress has been made in the delivery of better community care, but much remains to be done, and continuing pressure must be exerted to ensure that all persons who require high quality care actually receive it. The authors extend their appreciation to Elizabeth Troyer, head of research for the Saskatchewan Senior Citizens' Provincial Council for her reading of and helpful suggestions for this chapter.

REFERENCES

Ad Hoc Committee (1966). The Report of the Ad Hoc Committee on the Resettlement of Mental Hospital Patients to the Minister of Public Health (Saskatchewan). (June 27).

Borzecki, M., and Wormith, J. S. (1985). The Criminization of Psychiatrically Ill People: A Review with a Canadian Perspective. *Psychiatric Journal University of Ottawa*, 10, 242–47.

Casswell, W. A., Smith, C. M., Grunberg, F., Boan, J. A., and Thomas, R. F. (1972). Comparing Costs of Hospital and Community Care. *Hospital and Community Psychiatry*, 23, 17–20.

Committee of Enquiry (1984). The Legislation of Concern. Regina, Saskatchewan: Mental Health Association.

Community Resources Consultants of Toronto (1981). *Psychiatric Aftercare in Metropolitan Toronto*. Toronto: Clarke Institution of Toronto.

Cumming, E., & Cumming, J. (1957). *Closed Ranks*. Cambridge, Mass: Harvard University Press.

D'Arcy, C. (1981). Opened Ranks: Blackfoot Revisited. In Coburn D'Arcy, New and Tarrana, eds., *Health and Canadian Society*. Canada: Fitzhenry and Whiteside.

Dear, M. J., and Taylor, S. M. (1982). *Not on Our Street—Community Attitudes to Mental Health Care*. New York: Methuen.

Herman, N. J. (1987). " 'Mixed Nutters' and 'Looney Tuners,' The Emergence, Development, Nature and Functions of Two Informal Deviant Sub-Cultures of Chronic Ex-Psychiatric Patients." *Deviant Behavior*, 8, 235–58.

Hughes, E. C. (1958). *Men and Their Work*. Glencoe, Ill.: Free Press.

Hutchinson, P., Lord, J., Savage, H., and Schnarr, A. (1985). *Listening to People Who Have Directly Experienced the Mental Health System*. Toronto: Canadian Mental Health Association.

Lehman, A. E., Ward, N. C., and Linn, L. S. (1982). Chronic Mental Patients—The Quality of Life Issue. *American Journal of Psychiatry*, *139*, 1271–76.

Liptzin, B. (1977). The Effects of National Health Insurance on Canadian Psychiatry. *American Journal of Psychiatry*, *134*, 248–52.

Liptzin, B. (1984). Canadian and U.S. Systems of Care for the Mentally Ill Elderly. *Gerontologist*, *24*, 174–78.

Mental Health Planning Survey (John Cumming, Director) (1979). Report of the Mental Health Planning Survey British Columbia (May).

Pepper, B., & Ryglewicz, H., eds. (1982). *The Young Adult Chronic Patient*. San Francisco: Jossey-Bass.

Ralph, D. (1983). *The Rise of Community Psychiatry*. Montreal: Black Rose Books.

Richman, A. (1985). Use of Psychiatric Services by the Elderly in Canada, *30*, 89–97.

Smith, C. M. (1969). Measuring Some Effects of Mental Illness on the Home. *Canadian Psychiatric Association Journal*, *14*, 97–104.

Smith, C. M. (1971). Crisis and Aftermath: Community Psychiatry in Saskatchewan 1963–1969. *Canadian Psychiatric Association Journal*, *16*, 65–76.

Smith, C. M. (1975). Three Challenges. *Canadian Psychiatric Association Journal*, *20*, 501–512.

Smith, C. M. (1979). From Hospital to Community. *Canadian Journal of Psychiatry*, *24*, 113–20.

Smith, C. M., and McKerracher, D. G. (1964). The Comprehensive Psychiatric Unit in the General Hospital. *American Journal of Psychiatry*, *121*, 52–57.

Statistics Canada. Annual Reports of Mental Institutions, Fourth to Fourteenth Reports (1935–45); Mental Health Statistics 1963, vols. 1 and 2, 83–204 and 83–208; Mental Health Statistics 1976, vol. 2, 83–208; Mental Health Statistics 1980–81, vol. 3, 83–205; Mental Health Statistics 1980–81 and 1981–82, 83–204; Selected Tables from Annual Return of Special Care Facilities 1981–82, 83-X-201; National Health Division, Statistics Canada, Ottawa.

Talbott, J. A. (1985). Some Assorted Nits and Picks. *Psychiatric News, Newspaper of the American Psychiatric Association* (March 1).

Torrey, E. F., and Wolfe, S. M. (1986). *Care of the Seriously Mentally Ill.* Washington: Public Citizen Health Research Group.

Wasylenki, D., Doering, P., Lancee, W., and Freeman, S. J. J. (1985). Psychiatric Aftercare in a Metropolitan Setting. *Canadian Journal of Psychiatry, 30,* 329–336.

Watt, J. A., & el Guebaly, N. (1981). The Chronic Patient: The Position of the Canadian Psychiatric Association. *Canadian Journal of Psychiatry, 26,* 494–501.

CHAPTER 8

United States Elders with Chronic Mental Disorder

Joan Hashimi

Examination of supportive social welfare provision for older chronically mentally disabled adults most properly begins with a definition of that population and an examination of how care systems have evolved. This chapter begins with a section documenting two distinct types of chronicity and continues with a history of treatment of mental disorder in the United States. It will then describe what is known about the dimensions of the current older long-term chronic populations, their locus of treatment, major treatment and social provisions, and possible future service trends.

DEFINING CHRONIC MENTAL DISORDER

The chronically mentally disabled population includes those individuals who have mental disorders that "erode or prevent the development of their functional capacities in relation to . . . self-care, self-direction, interpersonal relationship . . . and that erode or prevent the development of their economic self-sufficiency" (Department of Health and Human Services, 1980, pp. 2–7). To discuss the psychiatric needs of an older chronic population it is necessary to distinguish between two groups, those who have experienced chronic mental disability for most of their adult lives (CMD) and those who are experiencing an organic mental disorder relatively late in life (OMD). This differentiation is important in the determination of service needs and resources. Most individuals with CMD have reached a plateau in the development of that disorder by mid-life. The level of disability is likely to be relatively stable until and unless it is complicated by the additional development of organic mental disorders and/or other physical disorders that lead to physical disability. If these elders do remain stable, their care needs can be met in less restrictive community settings and self-care may be maintained and/or improved. On the other hand, elders with organic mental disorders can be expected to deteriorate progressively. For these elders one might hope to maintain independent functioning as long as possible, but the condition will grow continuously worse and lead to a need for total nursing care (D. E. Gelfand and J. Berman, 1984).

The resources that elders in these two groups possess are likely to be quite different. The long-term CMD are less likely to have involved family members (the long period of hospitalization has dissolved family ties); they are unlikely to have established work records that provide access to social insurances; and they have a greater probability of dependence on means-tested income assistance programs and social and recreational activities through social service programs. On the other hand, the OMD are more likely to have access to social insurance programs, have family resources, and need services for families to help them cope in their care-giving responsibilities.

HISTORY OF SOCIAL PROVISION FOR THE MENTALLY DISABLED

The Colonial Period

In early eighteenth-century America institutions were developed to house vagabonds, idle persons, runaways, and drunkards, and to this mix were added the insane. In urban areas economic dependents were housed in almshouses, and the rural mentally ill were auctioned off. Mental disorder was seen as an affliction or possession, and abusive treatment was frequent (A. Deutsch, 1949). The chronically mentally disabled elders fared no better than their younger mentally disabled counterparts. D. H. Fischer (1978) states that "old age seems actually to have intensified the contempt visited upon a poor man.... Unattached old people often met with much brutality." Whenever public provision was made it was usually for the purpose of safeguarding the community (Deutsch, 1949).

Although most of those with mental disorder were minimally provided for by their families or in institutions that housed paupers and the sick, there were a very few, more specialized institutions. Pennsylvania Hospital, established in 1751, housed both the physically ill and those with mental disorders. The first mental hospital in the United States was established in Williamsburg, Virginia, in 1773; however, even here cruelty and neglect of patient care was the rule (P. V. Lemkau, 1982). Treatments included purging, bleeding, induced vomiting, blistering, near drowning, spinning in a chair, and an early form of electric shock. "All, it would appear, were planned as means of driving from the body some evil spirit or toxic vapor" (Joint Commission on Mental Illness and Health, 1961). It was common belief that the insane, like animals, could support indefinitely the miseries of existence. They were thought to be "insensitive to the extremes of hot and cold and the pangs of hunger" (A. Rosenblatt, 1984).

Since life expectancy was considerably lower, fewer people survived into old age, OMD was less frequent. Those individuals that developed dementia were more likely to die before they reached the very debilitated states.

The Nineteenth Century

The building of a few hospitals specifically for the mentally ill in the first quarter of the nineteenth century hardly began to meet the needs of the numbers of mentally ill needing attention (Deutsch, 1949). Moral treatment (as opposed to medical) was developed as a new possible approach. It was based on an assumption that favorable environmental conditions would lead to the amelioration of mental disorder, resembling today's concepts of milieu therapy (J. P. Morrissey and H. H. Goldman, 1984). It consisted of mild and kindly treatment; minimal use of restraint; using exemplary staff behavior to serve as a model for the patients; a warm, familial atmosphere; and occupational and recreational therapy, exercise, amusement, and games (Joint Commission on Mental Illness and Health, 1961; Morrissey and Goldman, 1984). While the treatment provided in these small institutions was excellent, it was available to only a few and its success seems to be associated with carefully select patients with acute rather than chronic disorder (Morrissey and Goldman, 1984).

In the 1840s an advocate, Dorothea Dix, arose for the chronic mentally disabled. She lobbied nationwide for state institutions and convinced state legislators to accept responsibility. A principle objective of her advocacy was to establish state rather than local responsibility and to centralize specialists in fewer institutions for better therapeutic care (Lemkau, 1982). Thirty state hospitals were built in which, she had hoped, moral treatment would be provided. However, this period of state hospital development occurred at the time of developing industrialization and massive immigration. Demands for admissions grew rapidly, and states increased the sizes of the institutions (Deutsch, 1949; Group for the Advancement of Psychiatry, 1978; Morrissey and Goldman, 1984). Faced with increasing demand that could not be accommodated, the institutions gave priority to acute cases.

Opinions were divided on how to provide for all the mentally ill. Two distinct public sector approaches emerged:

State care (the predominant pattern that was identified as the *New York Plan*). In 1890 in New York legislation provided that hospital districts be set up under state auspices, and that a hospital be established in each district to provide for all patients, thus ending a separation between acute and chronic care.

County care (a minority system identified as the *Wisconsin Plan*). The county care system provided for acute care state hospitals and a cost-sharing plan between state and county to provide for county-based care for chronic conditions. Acute and chronic cases were thus separated in different institutions (Deutsch, 1949).

To avoid the crowded public institutions, smaller private facilities for the affluent were established. Thus began what was to become the two-class system of psychiatric care at the core of the reform movement a hundred years later. By the 1870s the function of the state hospital was set; it offered minimal care for the greatest number at the lowest cost (Morrissey and Goldman, 1984).

The Recent Past

The deviation from purpose of the mental hospitals was brought to public attention by journalistic accounts. Clifford Beers (1908), who had been a mental patient in a state hospital, recovered and wrote *The Mind That Found Itself*. In this account he exposed the scandalous conditions of the state hospitals. With other advocates he founded in 1909 the National Committee for Mental Hygiene, which worked to "revive the notion of treatability of mental disorder, especially by early intervention with acute cases" (Morrissey and Goldman, 1984). As a result, a few acute care hospitals were built and some out-patient clinics and child guidance centers were developed, but they did not meet the treatment needs of the chronically disabled.

Responsibility for the care of CMD was largely a state responsibility. "Local officials, however, began to recognize the advantages in redefining insanity to include aged and demented individuals. By transferring such patients from local almshouses to the state hospitals, fiscal burdens associated with their care were shifted from local to state auspices" (Morrissey and Goldman, 1984). This provided relief for local almshouses that were primarily housing elders (Fischer, 1978). The daily census of state hospitals increased from 150,000 in 1903 to 512,500 in 1950—a growth rate double that of the growth of the U.S. population (Morrissey and Goldman, 1984).

In the 1940s public exposés of scandalous conditions within the state hospitals and rising cost burdens brought demands for change (Deutsch, 1949). In 1946 the National Mental Health Act created the National Institute for Mental Health (NIMH) to stimulate research. The Mental Health Study Act of 1955 established the Joint Commission on Mental Illness and Health to examine the plight of the mentally ill in the United States. The Joint Commission made their report in 1961 in *Action for Mental Health* recommending creation of community clinics for acutely ill, psychiatric units in general hospitals, and new, smaller state hospitals for acute disorder. A goal of the community mental health movement (CMH) was to bring to an end the dual mental health resource tracts existing for the rich and the poor (F. Chu and S. Trotter, 1974). To "save the patient from the debilitating effects of institutionalization" (Joint Commission on Mental Illness and

Health, 1961), it was recommended that the acute patient be returned to community life for treatment. Chronicity was seen as an avoidable outcome of long-term hospitalization. If long-term hospitalization could be prevented by early discovery and treatment, chronicity would be a thing of the past (Joint Commission on Mental Illness and Health, 1961; Group for the Advancement of Psychiatry, 1978; H. R. Lamb, 1984; C. A. Taube et al., 1983). Enthusiasm for the possibilities of the new drugs for new acute cases was still high.

The plight of the older chronic patients was largely ignored, however. They were accepted as custodial care patients, a final generation of patients that would not be repeated. This CMH ideal (and the possibility that community care would be less expensive) helped to get public and legislative acceptance for a focus on out-patient care through Community Mental Health Centers. What was ignored at this time was the less positive experience of the British with this new model, i.e., the continuing development of chronicity without hospitalization (Group for the Advancement of Psychiatry, 1978).

One cannot ignore the part played, in this shift in elder populations, by newly emerging financing mechanisms. The establishment in 1965 of Medicaid and the inclusion in 1963 of psychiatric disability under the Permanently and Totally Disabled category (later SSI) provided the states with a financial incentive to move older, psychiatrically stabilized patients from the state hospitals (which were state-funded) to nursing homes or board and care homes with federal funding (Group for the Advancement of Psychiatry, 1978; Lamb, 1984; Taube et al., 1983). States were able to pass chronic care costs to the federal government as they had been passed from local responsibility to state hospitals.

PREVALENCE OF CHRONIC MENTAL DISABILITY

The chronically mentally disabled are found in nursing homes; board and care homes; federal, state, and county mental hospitals; psychiatric wards of general hospitals; living with their families; living in isolated SROs (single room occupancy, often debilitated transient hotels); and living on the street or in temporary shelters (D. Mechanic, 1980). Because they are dispersed and often outside the network of treatment facilities, one must accept estimation of prevalence rather than firm counts of the CMD and OMD. In the publication Toward a National Plan for the Chronically Mentally Ill, which was developed by the Steering Committee on the Chronically Mentally Ill (Department of Health and Human Services, 1980), estimates were made by using information on institutional placement and on the use of treatment facilities and income maintenance programs for the disabled. These data indicate that there are between 1,700,000 and 2,400,000 chronically mentally ill in the United States, 750,000 of whom are in nursing

Table 8.1
Patients 65 and Older Placed in State and County Mental Hospitals,
Private Hospitals, and Nursing Homes in 1950, 1969, 1973, and 1980

	1950[1]	1969[2]	1973[3]	1980[4]
State & County Mental Health	141,346	111,420	70,615	36,997
Private Mental Health	N/A	2,460	1,530	383,376
Nursing Homes	N/A	96,415	193,900	383,376

Source: [1]M. Kramer, *Psychiatric Services and the Changing Institutional Scene 1950–1985,*
    DHEW Pub. No. ADM. 77–433 (Rockville, Md.: KHEW/PHS, 1977).
[2]The President's Commission on Mental Health, *Report to the President from the President's
    Commission on Mental Health,* vol. 1 (Washington: Government Printing Office, 1978).
[3]1980 U.S. Census.

homes, including people in skilled nursing facilities and intermediate care homes. Of this 750,000, 400,000 are diagnosed as "senility without psychosis." They were included in this count since "they represent a population who would have been admitted to state hospitals in the preinstitutionalization era" (Department of Health and Human Services, 1980).

In data taken from the *Report to the President from the President's Commission on Mental Health* (1978) and the 1980 census data, one can see that between 1950 and 1980 those 65 years and older are much less likely to be placed in mental hospitals and more likely to be placed in nursing homes. Table 8.1 shows the distribution of patients in these facilities.

There is no state in which the resident population in mental hospitals has not lowered significantly. But variations in state politics have led to differences in the rates of change (K. Minkoff, 1978). The degree to which nursing homes have replaced the mental hospital for the psychiatrically impaired in general and more specifically for those over 65 is not uniform in all states. For example, in comparing Wisconsin and New York we see that the ratio between those in state hospitals and homes for the aged varies from .13 in New York to .023 for Wisconsin.

Prevalence of any disorder is related to incidence and duration. Duration is a critical factor in understanding the expectation that the numbers of CMD and OMD will increase in the coming years. It has long been known that individuals with serious long-term mental disorders had higher mortality rates than those for the general population (G. Haughland et al., 1983; Task Panel Reports, 1978; S. F. Yolles and M. Kramer, 1969). Anything that can be done to modify conditions leading to early death will increase duration of disorder and thus increase prevalence. Advances in medical technology have in fact brought about an increase in length of life for many (M. Kramer, 1982). Improving public health practices have led to better levels of environmental sanitation and control of infectious disease; improved medical care and diet for the hospitalized mentally ill has led to a reduction of their mortality rate (Task Panel Reports, 1978). In a study of the prevalence of Alzheimer's disease in Sweden it was suggested that in the past its victims were more susceptible to pneumonia and frequently died in the early stages of this disorder (E. M. Gruenberg, 1980). Now pneumonia is more successfully treated and as a result, in the study populations, there was a rising prevalence of Alzheimer's disease. Because of increases in the populations at risk and the duration of chronic mental disorder, one can anticipate rising prevalence figures. Kramer (1982) provides data of 1980 incidence rates and projections to 2005.

SYSTEMS OF CARE

The systems of care for the CMD are in one sense quite limited. While a variety of model programs have creatively sought to enhance the potential for self-care and independence of the CMD, these programs are limited in size, leaving the vast majority of persons without any service or only minimal service. Most chronically mentally disabled elders are cared for at home, in nursing homes, in board and care homes, and in state, county, and city mental hospitals. Some are not cared for at all; these people are located in single room hotels or worse as part of the urban homeless. However, while approximately 30 percent of the homeless have been estimated to be chronically mentally disabled, they tend to be young or middle-aged. A New York study gave 36 as the median age for their study group. Another study in Philadelphia reported 67 percent of a shelter population under 50 (A. A. Arce and M. J. Vergare, 1984). It would appear that few CMD or OMD elders would be within this group.

The failure of existing systems to deal adequately with the CMI population has been amply described (Department of Health and Human Services, 1980). Many CMD remain in mental hospitals for want of a more appropriate placement while others have been discharged into the community without appropriate service provision (J. E. C. Turner, 1978). Those who are chronically impaired and have remained in state hospitals may well be the best off (Gruenberg, 1982; Minkoff, 1978).

The Nursing Home

The most likely current placement of the CMI elder is the nursing home. Only some residents have a primary diagnosis of mental disorder; many

Table 8.2

Incidence of Mental Disorder for 1980 and Estimates for 2005

	White		Black	
	1980	2005	1980	200
Total Population	191,581,000	225,186,000	30,578,000	42,416,000
Serious Mental Disorder (1%) (excluding Senile Dementia)	1,915,000	2,251,060	305,780	424,160
Schizophrenia Annual incidence under care per year	135,150 943,571	141,565 1,119,607	47,665 211,269	66,308 332,275
Senile Dementia Point Prevalence 65+	1,901,154	2,735,873	182,857	314,896
Admissions to Psychiatric Facilities	3,200,363	3,749,944	648,003	985,741
Residents in Nursing Homes	1,228,769	1,800,705	67,872	96,145
	65-69	70-74	75-79	80+
Prevalence rates for Senile Males	1.71	3.58	7.16	24.7
Dementia vary by age and sex Females	1.64	6.14	13.80	22.50

Source: M. Kramer, The Continuing Challenge: The Rising Prevalence of Mental Disorders, Associated Chronic Diseases, and Disabling Conditions, in M. O. Wagenfeld, P. V. Lemkau and B. Justice, eds., *Public Mental Health: Perspectives and Prospects.* (Beverly Hills, Calif.: Sage Publications, 1982), 103–130.

others appear depressed and withdrawn, agitated and nervous, or abusive and aggressive. Between 43 percent and 75 percent of nursing home residents have prescriptions for psychotropic drugs (E. Hing, 1981).

Ninety percent of direct care service in the nursing home is delivered by low-paid untrained aides. Direct care staff are uncomfortable with and have difficulty managing behavioral problems. A study by R. B. Teeter et al. (1976) suggested that nursing home staff showed negative or inappropriate attitudes (hostility and infantilization) toward residents with psychiatric disturbances. H. M. Waxman et al. (1985) suggested psychotropic drugs are used to control behavior and management problems, but because of the drug use iatrogenic illness is common. This situation is particularly distressing for the residents admitted specifically for mental disorder, who are often younger than most residents (35 percent are under 65). As a special group they often do not fit into nursing home routine since the primary focus of the nursing home is care for physical disability. They often exhibit behavioral problems and are given gradually increased medications. These long-term residents tend to regress over time, exhibit decreased levels of activity and decreased independence (Minkoff, 1978).

The State Hospital

Although the locus of institutionalization has shifted dramatically from the state hospital to the nursing home, the state hospital is still the institution that cares for the most difficult of the older chronic psychiatric patients (L. D. Ozarin, 1982; Taube et al., 1983). There appears to be a new build-up of long stay persons in the state hospital census figures for the years 1975 through 1979. Taube et al. (1983) noted that during that four-year period there was shift from discontinuations being more numerous than additions. When the number of deaths in the hospital were computed in, the hospital was still losing in census, but the trend over time was for the death rate to drop. There had been a 40 percent reduction between 1971 and 1979. Since life threat to this venerable population is being reduced, one might expect the death rate to continue dropping. Then the actual increase in a residual state hospital population may become visible. What does seem evident is that at every turn the mental health systems refill with the CMD for whom there is no effective treatment or the resources to apply what is known to maximize potential for independent living.

The extent to which the state hospitals will recycle as dominant treatment facilities will rest on political and economic realities, quite apart from treatment concerns. Many states have empty state hospital beds while also paying to hospitalize patients in general hospitals. With the excess state hospital bed capacity supported by state dollars and increasing limitations on Medicaid-supported alternatives, the result would seem to support a movement of reinstitutionalization (S. S. Sharfstein et al., 1984). Changes in Medicare reimbursement may reduce nursing home use. The more recent development of prospective payment schedules and set amounts schedules of reimbursement linked to diagnosis related groups (DRGs) may mean increased use of nursing homes as extended care facilities to provide care for residents with very high medical care needs. This potential shifting in purpose may mean the nursing home will become less receptive to providing care for the CMD elder.

Community Alternatives

The original intent of the deinstitutionalization movement was to emphasize community settings and to utilize the newly emerging CMHC. These centers, however, responded more to "new" patients than they did to the CMD. The huge expansion of episodes of care represented an opening of the public mental health system to the "worried well" rather than to the seriously disabled. The tremendous increase in expenditure in public mental health services circumvented the chronic populations (J. W. Thompson et al., 1982). Much of the cost of care for many CMD patients has shifted from mental health budgets to Medicaid and Medicare coverage.

Although most CMD did not receive mental health services, some were provided for in exemplary programs. In 1978 nineteen states and the District of Columbia received National Institute of Mental Health (NIMH) contracts through the Community Support Programs (CSP) (Love, 1984; Turner and Shifren, 1979). The community support system is defined as a network of service providers meeting the needs of a vulnerable chronic population. The CSP focuses exclusively on severely mentally disabled for whom long-term, twenty-four-hour care is unnecessary. Elderly persons are included unless their physical or mental condition requires nursing care (for all practical purposes the OMD are excluded). The initiative was launched because there had been no coherent federal policy for the CMD; responsibility for their care was fragmented; there was no systematic way to finance community programs; mainstream mental health agencies had no commitment to the CMD; and advocacy for this group was disorganized and ineffective (Love, 1984; Turner and Shifren, 1979). The CSS model includes client outreach, assistance with benefit applications, skills training, psychosocial rehabilitation, crisis and family intervention, and indefinite community support (Turner and Shifren, 1979).

"This program unquestionably generated a substantial amount of activity on behalf of the target population, particularly at the state level. Nevertheless, documenting the direct accomplishments of CSP has proven difficulty. . . . It is clear that CSP did not achieve its ultimate goal of improving the quality of life of the CMI" (Love, 1984). Many of the reasons behind this failure were political and economic. R. L. Okin (1985) states "The community based system is in many areas woefully underfunded, incomplete, fragmented, poorly monitored, and inaccessible to many patients." Community support has not proved to be less costly when including the costs of all public programs (W. W. Menninger, 1978; Sharfstein et al., 1978). To get a complete picture of cost, however, one must compare institutional cost with total community care costs to include services to coping families.

Public programs and their funding sources that are important in providing for the CMD and OMD elder are depicted in Figure 8.1. Many programs, services, or institutions may be supported by many different sources of

Figure 8.1
Programs Important in Care of Elders with Chronic Mental Disorder

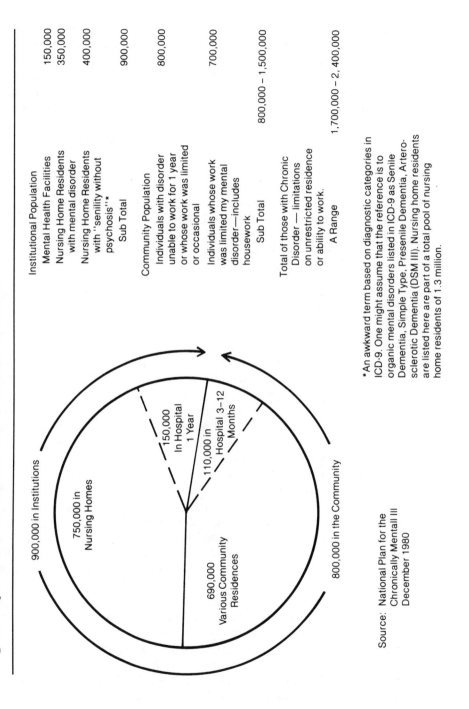

Institutional Population	
Mental Health Facilities	150,000
Nursing Home Residents with mental disorder	350,000
Nursing Home Residents with "senility without psychosis"*	400,000
Sub Total	900,000
Community Population	
Individuals with disorder unable to work for 1 year or whose work was limited or occasional	800,000
Individuals whose work was limited my mental disorder—includes housework	700,000
Sub Total	800,000 – 1,500,000
Total of those with Chronic Disorder — limitations on unrestricted residence or ability to work.	
A Range	1,700,000 – 2,400,000

*An awkward term based on diagnostic categories in ICD-9. One might assume that the reference is to organic mental disorders listed in ICD-9 as Senile Dementia, Simple Type, Presenile Dementia, Artero-sclerotic Dementia (DSM III). Nursing home residents are listed here are part of a total pool of nursing home residents of 1.3 million.

Labels within figure:
- 900,000 in Institutions
- 750,000 in Nursing Homes
- 150,000 In Hospital 1 Year
- 110,000 in Hospital 3–12 Months
- 690,000 Various Community Residences
- 800,000 in the Community

Source: National Plan for the Chronically Mentall Ill
December 1980

funding. A single person may be receiving services from a variety of programs which must be sought out separately. Clusters of services and programs tend to be utilized by different groups of elders. Middle-class elders have services supported by social insurances, religious and fraternal organizations, and private pay. The CMD are provided for in the psychiatric centers and clinics, and the OMD are seen as the concern of the medical community. To some extent however, the elder CMD are step children of all systems. The mental health programs are geared to younger CMD. While the array of services is extensive, the elder CMD is often included in any one of them only marginally.

While we are witnessing an increased use of mental health facilities, the increase in the use by the elderly is below increases in other age groups (S. Simson and L. B. Wilson, 1982; M. O. Wagenfeld and J. H. Jacobs, 1982). Indirect services focused on the elderly fare no better. While one-third of staff time was focused on consultation and education with agencies dealing with children, only 5 percent was associated to facilities for the elderly (Wagenfeld and Jacobs, 1982).

Overall Evaluation

There is much to be concerned about in our current "nonsystem" of public psychiatric care. Specifically, many elders have been transinstitutionalized, while much of the mental health dollars have stayed with state hospitals, and community services are badly fragmented (J. A. Talbott, 1985). In a recent document E. F. Torrey and S. M. Wolfe (1986) presented the results of an analysis by the public Citizen Health Research Group on services in the United States for those with "serious mental illness." States were ranked on the quality of in-patient and out-patient treatment programs and attractiveness of ward environment. The states were also judged on the basis of whether or not the services were improving; this depended on governmental leadership and willingness to make changes, and the existence of strong consumer groups, e.g., State Alliance for the Mentally Ill. The state listed as number one in this analysis was Wisconsin.

Wisconsin was cited particularly for a single nationally reputed county program. The state has dramatically reduced the number of in-patient beds, and those that remain are of high quality. Wisconsin's success is related to a long history of county responsibility. The eminence that Wisconsin has achieved is in spite of its ranking of twenty-eighth (out of fifty states plus the District of Columbia) in per capita income and fortieth in state mental health agency dollar expenditure per capita. Its eminence is due perhaps to its strong government and group advocacy leadership.

In this same analysis New York is ranked as twentieth-sixth for overall care. New York is still focusing on institutional development, and a relatively large share of its mental health dollars goes toward state hospital funding.

The care in these heavily funded institutions is described as poor; it is no longer an example of institutional excellence as it was when first described by Deutsch (1946). New York does have examples of good programs; Fountain House in New York City has long been example of outstanding programming for the CMD. The corresponding economic data for New York is that it ranks sixth in per capita income and second in per capita mental health expenditures. It has 27.7 psychiatrists per 100,000 people in the state as opposed to 9.1 in Wisconsin. What can be seen readily from these examples is that states vary considerably in economic resources, philosophy of care, care provision, and effective use of resources.

In contrast, programming for those with organic mental disorder is more diffuse, making interstate comparison difficult. There are limited special programs for treatment of organic disorders outside general medical facilities. Care is provided in families, in nursing homes, in day care centers, and through an assortment of home health services. These service provisions are not specific to organic mental disorder, but rather programs for older adults with disabilities related to diseases associated with aging. More recently there has been the development of private practicing psychiatrists specializing in geriatric care; consumer advocacy groups such as Alzheimer's Disease and Related Disorders Association; a growing public awareness, through media accounts, of disorders such as Alzheimer's disease; and mushrooming research studies directed toward understanding cause and cure of these disorders. The research being done is largely within the medical community rather than the psychiatric community.

CONCLUSIONS

Historical trends and changes in service provision continue. At each point of reform new care provisions are proposed. They are implemented for a small part of those needing services (those with acute disorders). Those left outside of this treatment network (those with chronic conditions that do not respond to the available treatments) become the examples of poor care to launch the new enthusiasm. A variety of treatments have been effective with many needing psychiatric care, but the treatment needs of those with chronic conditions, particularly elder CMD, have largely been ignored.

The scandalous conditions in institutions may seem the catalyst of program change, yet the true catalyst is often change in other governmental programs and policies shifting economic efficiency in one direction and then another (J. Rubin, 1984). The most critical change now is a decrease in the availability of federal funding. If this responsibility is left to state funding and control, there will be greater interstate differences and perhaps a greater use of state mental hospitals. Hopefully, limited Block Grant funds coming from the federal to state level will be used to keep operative existing community structures. It is doubtful that one will see new or larger sums of monies available in the short range.

For the older mentally impaired, new consideration might be given to how this population is to be thought of—as medically needy, as older, or as psychiatrically impaired. The issue is which service system should be responsible for their care. The elderly with organic mental disorder without intractable behavioral problems seem to fit more with medical programs. One is dealing with a physical disorder for which answers are being sought within medical research. In all respect these persons resemble the physically ill more than those with long-term mental disorders (H. H. Goldman et al., 1986). While we classify the organic mental disorder and emphasize the mental health care needs of this group, the mental health community provides little emphasis for them (Ahr and Holcomb, 1985). Historically, their classification as having a mental disorder was a device to transfer the responsibility of their care from local government to the state. In whatever way this issue might be resolved, one does see the pattern of divided responsibility as a reality.

The extent to which mental problems are linked to physical disorders suggests the advantage of cooperative linkage between the psychiatric and general health sectors (J. V. Coleman, 1982). This would be particularly beneficial to elders in that with advancing age most individuals have at least one chronic physical problem in addition to any psychiatric problems. It would seem more reasonable to have their needs met by a team that would include general health and psychiatric workers (Coleman, 1982). The beginning of this trend is possible if we include in health maintenance organizations (HMOs) (required in those that are federally funded) mental health clinical services (Coleman, 1982).

CMD patients without organic impairment should not be age-segregated from a treatment program from which they might profit. These clients can and do respond to treatment. For those clients who respond to special training programs, integration into the social and recreational activities provided to elders becomes a possibility. It is at this point that chronic mental disorder is a descriptor of a person, rather then becoming the whole person, thus leaving that individual free to participate as far as possible in the mainstream community.

REFERENCES

Ahr, P. R., and Holcomb, W. R. (1985). State Mental Health Directors' Priorities for Mental Health Care. *Hospital and Community Psychiatry*, 36, 39–45.

Arce, A. A., and Vergare, M. J. (1984). Identifying and Characterizing the Mentally Ill among the Homeless. In H. R. Lamb, ed. *The homeless mentally ill* (75–89). Washington: American Psychiatric Association.

Beers, C. (1908). *The Mind that Found Itself* (lst ed.). New York: Longmans, Green.

Chu, F., and Trotter, S. (1974). *The Madness Establishment*. New York: Grossman Publishers.

Coleman, J. V. (1982). Health/mental health integration. In M. O. Wagenfeld, P. V. Lemkau and B. Justice, eds., *Public Mental Health: Perspectives and Prospects* (238–63) (vol. 5, Sage Studies in Community Mental Health). Beverly Hills, Calif.: Sage Publications.

Department of Health and Human Services Steering Committee on the Chronically Mentally Ill (1980). *Toward a National Plan for the Chronically Mentally Ill* (DHHS Publication No. (ADM)81–1077). Washington: U. S. Department of Health and Human Services, Public Health Service.

Deutsch, A. (1949). *The Mentally Ill in America* (2nd ed.). New York: Columbia University Press.

Fischer, D. H. (1978). *Growing Old in America* (rev. ed.). NewYork: Oxford University Press.

Gelfand, D. E., and Berman, J. (1984). *The Aging Network: Programs and Services* (2nd ed.) (Vol. 8, Springer Series on Adulthood and Aging). New York: Springer Publishing.

Goldman, H. H., Feder, J., and Scanlon, W. (1986). Chronic Mental Patients in Nursing Homes: Reexamining Data from the National Nursing Home Survey. *Hospital and Community Psychiatry, 37*, 269–72.

Group for the Advancement of Psychiatry (1978). *The Chronic Mental Patient in the Community* (Publication No. 102, vol. 10). New York: Mental Health Materials Center.

Gruenberg, E. M. (1980). Epidemiology of Senile Dementia. In S. G. Haynes, M. Feinleib, J. S., Ross and L. Stallones, eds., *Epidemiology of aging: Proceedings of the Second Conference* (91–97). (NIH Publication No. 80–969). Washington: DHHS, Public Health Service.

Gruenberg, E. (1982), The Deinstitutionalization movement. In M.O. Wagenfeld, P. V. Lemkau, and B. Justice, eds., *Public Mental Health: Perspectives and Prospects* (264–87). (Vol. 5, Sage Studies in Community Mental Health). Beverly Hills, Calif.: Sage Publications.

Haughland, G., Craig, T. J., Goodman, A. B., and Siegel, C. (1983). Mortality in the era of deinstitutionalization. *American Journal of Psychiatry, 140*, 848–52.

Hing, E. (1981). *Characteristics of Nursing Home Residents, Health Status, and Care Received: National Nursing Home Survey 1977*. (DHHS Publication # (PHS)81–1712). Hyattsville, Md.: U.S. Department of Health and Human Services, Public Health Service.

Joint Commission on Mental Illness and Health (1961). *Action for Mental Health*. New York: Science Editions, Basic Books.

Kramer, M. (1977). *Psychiatric services and the changing institutional scene 1950–1985*. (DHEW Publication No. (ADM)77–433). Rockville, Md.: Department of Health, Education, and Welfare, Public Health Service.

Kramer, M. (1982). The Continuing Challenge: The Rising Prevalence of Mental Disorders, Associated Chronic Diseases, and Disabling Conditions. In M. O. Wagenfeld, P. V. Lemkau and B. Justice, eds., *Public Mental Health: Perspectives and Prospects* (103–130). (Vol. 5, Sage Studies in Community Mental Health). Beverly Hills, Calif.: Sage Publications.

Lamb, H. R. (1984). Deinstitutionalization and the Homeless Mentally Ill. *Hospital and Community Psychiatry*, 35, 899–907.

Lemkau, P. V. (1982). The Historical Background. In M. O. Wagenfeld, P. V. Lemkau, and B. Justice, eds., *Public Mental Health: Perspectives and Prospects* (16–29). (Vol. 5, Sage Studies in Community Mental Health). Beverly Hills, Calif.: Sage Publications.

Love, R. E. (1984). The Community Support Program: Strategy for Reform? In J. A. Talbott, ed., *The Chronic Mental Patient: Five Years Later* (195–214). Orlando, Fla.: Grune & Stratton.

Mechanic, D. (1980). *Mental Health and Social Policy* (2nd ed.). Englewood Cliffs, N.J.: Prentice-Hall.

Menninger, W. W. (1978). Economic Issues Involved in Providing Effective Care for the Chronic Mental Patient. In J. A. Talbott, ed., *The Chronic Mental Patient: Problems, Solutions, and Recommendations for a Public Policy* (151–56). Washington: American Psychiatric Association.

Minkoff, K. (1978). A Map of Chronic Mental Patients. In J. A. Talbott, ed., *The Chronic Mental Patient: Problems, Solutions, and Recommendations for a Public Policy* (11–37). Washington: American Psychiatric Association.

Morrissey, J. P., and Goldman, H. H. (1984). Cycles of Reform in the Care of the Chronically Mentally Ill. *Hospital and Community Psychiatry*, 35, 785–93.

Okin, R. L. (1985). Expand the Community Care System: Deinstitutionalization Can Work. *Hospital and Community Psychiatry*, 36, 742–45.

Ozarin, L. D. (1982). Mental Health in Public Health: The Federal Perspective. In M. O. Wagenfeld, P. V. Lemkau, and B. Justice, eds., *Public Mental Health: Perspectives and Prospects* (30–45). (Vol. 5, Sage Studies in Community Mental Health). Beverly Hills, Calif.: Sage Publications.

The President's Commission on Mental Health (1978). *Report to the President from the President's Commission on Mental Health*. (Vol. 1). (Stock No. 040-000-00390-8). Washington: Government Printing Office.

Rosenblatt, A. (1984). Concepts of the Asylum in the Care of the Mentally Ill. *Hospital and Community Psychiatry*, 35, 244–50.

Rubin, J. (1984). Developments in the Financing and Economics of Mental Health Care. In J. A. Talbott, ed., *The Chronic Mental Patient: Five Years Later* (269–79). Orlando, Fla.: Grune & Stratton.

Sharfstein, S. S., Frank, R. J., and Kessler, L. G. (1984). State Medicaid Limitations for Mental Health Services. *Hospital and Community Psychiatry*, 35, 213–15.

Sharfstein, S. S., Turner, J. E. C., and Clark, H. W. (1978). Financing Issues in the Delivery of Services to the Chronically Mentally Ill and Disabled. In J. A. Talbott, ed., *The Chronic Mental Patient: Problems, Solutions, and Recommendations for Public Policy* (137–50). Washington: American Psychiatric Association.

Simson, S., and Wilson, L. B. (1982). Meeting the Mental Health Needs of the Aged: The Role of Psychiatric Emergency Services. *Hospital and Community Psychiatry*, 33, 833–36.

Talbott, J. A. (1985). The Fate of the Public Psychiatric System. *Hospital and Community Psychiatry*, 36, 46–50.

Task Panel Reports: Submitted to the President's Committee on Mental Health

(1978). (Volume 2, Appendix). (Stock No. 040–000–00391–6). Washington: Government Printing Office.

Taube, C. A., Thompson, J. W., Rosenstein, M. J., Rosen, B. M., and Goldman, H. H. (1983). The "Chronic" Mental Hospital Patient. *Hospital and Community Psychiatry, 34*, 611–15.

Teeter, R. B., Garetz, F. K., Miller, W. R., and Heiland, W. F.(1976). Psychiatric Disturbances of Aged Patients in Skilled Nursing Homes. *American Journal of Psychiatry, 133*, 1430–34.

Thompson, J. W., Bass, R. D., and Witkin, M. J. (1982). Fifty Years of Psychiatric Services: 1940–1990. *Hospital and Community Psychiatry, 33*, 711–21.

Torrey, E. F., and Wolfe, S. M. (1986). *Care of the Seriously Mentally Ill: A Rating of State Programs.* Washington: Public Citizen Research Group.

Turner, J. E. C. (1978). Philosophical Issues in Meeting the Needs of People Disabled by Mental Health Problems: The Psychosocial Rehabilitation Approach. In J. A. Talbott, ed., *The Chronic Mental Patient: Problems, Solutions, and Recommendations for a Public Policy* (65–72). Washington: American Psychiatric Association.

Turner, J. E. C., and Shifren, I. (1979). Community Support Systems: How Comprehensive? In L. I. Stein, ed., *Community Support Systems for the Long-Term Patient.* (New Directions for Mental Health Services, a quarterly sourcebook) (1–13). San Francisco: Jossey-Bass.

Wagenfeld, M. O., and Jacobs, J. H. (1982). The Community Mental Health Movement: Its Origins and Growth. In M. O. Wagenfeld, P. V. Lemkau, and B. Justice, eds., *Public Mental Health: Perspectives and Prospects* (46–88). (Vol. 5, Sage Studies in Community Mental Health). Beverly Hills, Calif.: Sage Publications.

Waxman, H. M., Klein, M., and Carver, E. A. (1985). Drug Misuse in Nursing Homes: An Institutional Addiction? *Hospital and Community Psychiatry, 36*, 886–87.

Yolles, S. F., and Kramer, M. (1969). Vital Statistics. In L. Bellack and L. Loeb, eds., *The Schizophrenic Syndrome.* New York: Grune & Stratton.

SUMMARY

Several conclusions can be drawn about the services to older chronic mentally ill people that transcend both countries. First is the need to realize that new cohorts of "older" chronic patients are rapidly accumulating to the point where they represent a critical group in each nation. Both chapters indicate that neither state nor provincial authorities have adequately prepared for the needs of this group. The very aged chronic mentally ill who have lived for years as nursing home patients are dying, while the younger patients who were discharged to the community during the 1960s and 1970s are now reaching old age. One implication of this is that the formal mental health system is attempting to move these individuals into the geriatric care system. It is doubtful whether this cost-containment strategy to reassign care responsibilities to another system will be acceptable or effective. The better solution would be to strengthen geriatric mental health as an integrated service link between local aging service centers and mental health programs.

The mental health system may be expected to assume greater involvement in the direct and sustained care of middle- and late-state Alzheimer's disease patients. While both countries are providing federal funding for basic research and special treatment programs, the number of people suffering the disease is increasing, but they face inadequate supportive assistance to meet long-term care needs. Current problems of large-scale patient management result from a lack of comprehensive planning. Is it realistic to expect that federal leadership is needed in both countries to formulate a national plan of care? Can provincial and state governmental units move beyond fragmented services and categorical funding to finance a range of community-based care supports and the appropriate in-patient care?

One can hope that the failures of caring for the very old chronic mentally ill population will not be repeated as new cohorts move into their aging cycle. A better care system also requires professionals with appropriate geriatric mental health knowledge and skills who can work with patients and the community to reduce the stigma, lack of community and in-patient treatment, family care burdens, and the devastating costs of patient maintenance. A final priority for both countries must be to continue the basic research necessary to fully and finally determine the causal factors associated with schizophrenia, depression, and Alzheimer's disease.

V

RURAL AGING

In both countries rural gerontology is an emerging area of interest. Increasing research on rural aging now provides both countries with greater understanding of the nonurban aging/aged populations. However, stereotypes and myths about rural life in Canada and the United States are entrenched. The typical urban dweller has, at best, vague images of the remote and isolated areas of her/his own state or province of residence. This mindset has transferred to mainstream gerontological research and policy analysis, and has caused urban conditions to be generalized, without foundation, to rural sectors. Both authors encourage greater attention by researchers to rural variables and their ongoing conceptual refinement if data results are to have greater explanatory significance for the aged in nonmetropolitan areas.

More recently than the United States, Canada has begun to accumulate data on the rural old. During the 1980s some significant first steps were taken by researchers to produce a foundation of new information about the population. While greater numbers of studies on rural aging are available for application in the United States, these data sets often lack methodological and conceptual consistency. Inconsistency among surveys in rural areas is a paramount problem for information collection, interpretation, and application. Census data, while an important data source for national and provincial/state human service planning, often differs from the data collected by individual scholars.

The chapters summarize key rural issues such as health status; health services; family relationship; and community participation of the old. Health care, the availability of both formal and informal resources, and barriers to informal helping are important concerns with overlapping implications for Canadian and United States service planning. Both authors question the simplistic debates over whether conditions are "better or worse" or resources are "more or less available" for urban and rural aged.

CHAPTER 9

Aging in Rural Canada

Anne Martin Matthews

Over a decade ago J. Simmons and R. Simmons observed that, despite such images of Canada as "bald prairie sweeping to bleak horizons, ... the crumpled rocks and straggly pines of the Shield, an Arctic waste stretching across the top of a continent, ... the real Canadian scene is a cityscape. ... Canadians and their activities are becoming more and more concentrated in a hundred or so urban areas which occupy less than one percent of the land area" (1974). They further noted that "an accurate map of most of the socioeconomic variables describing Canada would show a few dozen islands of intense activity and greater variation, separated by hundreds of miles of low density, homogeneous areas" (1974).

The focus of this chapter is on the characteristics of the elders and the processes of aging in nonurban areas. Rural elders are not homogeneous, but they share the characteristic of living in a predominantly urban culture. Over two-fifths of the Canadian population (41.2 percent) live in cities of 500,000 or more population (Statistics Canada, 1982a). Although urban and rural elderly are quite similar, the rural elderly believe that their personal and environmental attributes are inherently different from those of people in urban society. This chapter explores the world of the rural elderly, focusing on demographic realities and examining health care utilization, social support, perceptions of quality of life, and transportation.

At the outset it is important to acknowledge the limitations imposed by the census definition of rural. The term *rural* is defined as that which is nonurban, i.e., places with a population of less than 1,000 residents. This definition, based on population size alone as the criterion for "rurality," fails to consider the character of rural life. Life in a town of 2,000 is typically more similar to life in a village of 500 than to a city of 25,000 inhabitants. The town, although urban by definition, is often decidedly rural in character. Many studies employ broader definitions of rurality than this census definition, adding to the confusion in that communities classified as rural by researchers may not be so by census definition. This definition differs from that used in the United States, where areas of less than 2,500 population are defined as rural. Thus definitional variation clearly limits the comparability of findings in each country.

DEMOGRAPHIC PERSPECTIVES

The drift of population from rural to urban areas constituted the most significant population shift of Canada's first century. In 1871, 80 percent of the population lived in rural areas, but improvements in agricultural technology and productivity increasingly made a surplus of farm workers. By 1976 the proportion of persons living in rural areas had fallen below 25 percent, and fewer than 5 percent of Canadians lived on farms. It is projected that the rural-urban distribution in Canada will remain relatively stable at this 25–75 percent split, for the immediate future (C. Lindsay, 1980).

Despite this long-term trend, rural areas have actually gained population in recent years—growing by 8.9 percent between 1976 and 1981, compared to a 5 percent increase of the urban population (Statistics Canada, 1982b). However, this overall growth rate masks considerable regional variation: 5.9 percent for the Atlantic region, 13.9 percent for Quebec, 5.7 percent for Ontario, 4.3 percent for the Prairie region (varying from 0.1 in Manitoba to 14.8 percent in Alberta), and 17.4 percent for British Columbia (Statistics Canada, 1984). This increase "does not imply a return to the farming way of life. Almost half the rural growth between 1976 and 1981 occurred in rural fringe areas of census agglomerations and census metropolitan areas. ... What some have termed as 'exurbia' has shown very fast growth in the 1976–1981 period" (Statistics Canada, 1984).

One must query whether the concept of *rurality* is still salient in Canadian society. G. Hodge and M. A. Qadeer observed that "in the minds of most Canadian city dwellers, towns and villages are, at best, an anachronism and probably destined for demise" (1983). They nevertheless conclude that "while the conventional rural-urban differences have eroded, new factors have come into play which distinguish small and large communities ... there are qualitative and threshold distinctions to be observed in dealing with them. Towns and villages may not be a separate universe, but they certainly are a distinct genre of the contemporary urban species" (1983).

Several features characterize this "separate universe" of small town and rural Canada: generally families are larger, birth rates are higher, outmigration is higher, labor force participation rates are lower, service sector employment is less important, income levels are lower, educational levels are lower, and access to communication media is lower (cf. R. Thompson, 1983). The geographic environment is typically characterized also by low population density and large distances between communities. Demographic maturity is also a distinct feature of rural populations. Table 9.1 illustrates the high concentration of elders in rural towns and villages.

Canada reports 21.9 percent of its elderly population living in rural areas, slightly more than one in five of its citizens aged 65 and over. A recent Health and Welfare Canada report states that "only 9.4 percent of the total population of large urban centres was age 65 and over in 1981.... Small towns, on the other hand, had an unusually large proportion of elderly persons in their populations. In towns with 1,000 to 2,499 people, 13.5 percent of the population was aged 65 or more..." (1983). Indeed, census data show that small towns had a larger than average proportion of persons aged 80 and over relative to their total population—3.1 percent compared to the national average of 1.9 percent (Health and Welfare Canada 1983).

There are significant regional variations. Rural farm areas, for example, had a rather low proportion of their population in the older age groups in 1981. Only one person in 20 in rural farm areas was at least 65 years old, and fewer than one in 100 were at least 80 (Health and Welfare Canada, 1983). In some communities in southern Ontario, however, concentrations of the aged are as high as 30 percent (Ontario Advisory Council on Senior Citizens, 1980). A report on rural districts in Ontario's north also indicates that many towns, villages, and townships have proportions of 10 percent to 25 percent of their populations over the age of 65 (Ontario Ministry of Northern Affairs, 1982). In some areas of British Columbia, proportions of the elderly range from 25 percent to 50 percent (Social Planning and Review Council of British Columbia, 1976).

Tables 9.1 and 9.2 illustrate interprovincial variability. For example, in Manitoba the proportions aged 65 and over average a staggering 22.6 percent for communities between 2,500 and 4,999 population (Conference Planning Committee, 1985), while in Ontario the largest concentrations of the aged are in small towns of 1,000 to 2,499 population, where they represent 16.1 percent of the inhabitants. Table 9.2 further illustrates the trend toward concentrations of the *very* aged in rural areas. In Manitoba 4.8 percent of the population of communities 1,000 to 2,499 were aged 80 and over, while for towns of 2,500 to 4,999, the proportion was 5.9 percent. The provincial average was 2.1 percent (Conference Planning Committee, 1985). Similarly in Ontario concentrations of the very old are highest in small towns of 1,000 to 2,499 and 2,500 to 4,999 population, but they do not exceed 3.8 percent.

Other sociodemographic characteristics distinguish the rural and urban elderly. There is an inverse relationship between community size and the ratio of men to women in the older population (R. Santerre, 1982; Saskatchewan Senior Citizen's Provincial Council, 1983). In 1976 urban areas of 500,000 or more residents had only 66 men per 100 women aged 65 and over, while rural nonfarm and the rural farm areas had more men than

Table 9.1
Distribution of the Population Aged 65 and Over by Urban-Size Groups, Rural NonFarm, and Rural Farm, Canada and Provinces, 1981

	CANADA		NFLD.	P.E.I.	NOVA SCOTIA	NEW BRUNSWICK	QUEBEC	ONTARIO	MANI-TOBA	SASKAT-CHEWAN	ALBERTA	B.C.
	N	%*	%	%	%	%	%	%	%	%	%	%
TOTAL	2,360,975	9.7	7.7	12.2	10.9	10.1	8.8	10.1	10.5	12.0	7.3	10.9
URBAN	1,842,950	10.0	7.6	14.8	10.9	11.2	9.2	10.2	12.4	12.5	7.3	11.8
500,000 +	938,600	9.4	-	-	-	-	9.1	9.5	11.6	-	6.5	11.4
100,000-499,999	261,135	10.2	8.9	-	8.4	-	8.7	10.1	-	9.4	-	17.4
30,000- 99,999	209,600	10.5	-	-	13.0	10.8	9.3	10.5	13.9	13.1	8.4	11.8
10,000- 29,999	154,800	9.9	6.4	14.9	12.3	10.7	8.0	11.6	9.3	14.7	7.0	9.5
5,000- 9,999	86,805	10.9	6.0	-	13.0	9.8	9.3	12.2	14.9	16.5	8.8	10.4
2,500- 4,999	98,385	12.3	8.4	-	14.7	16.4	10.3	13.9	22.6	18.9	10.5	11.8
1,000- 2,499	93,630	13.5	7.5	14.4	15.0	12.0	11.7	16.0	17.4	21.0	12.2	9.8
RURAL	518,025	8.8	7.8	10.6	11.0	9.1	7.6	9.3	10.5	11.3	7.3	7.7
NON-FARM	461,640	9.5	7.8	11.0	11.1	9.1	8.2	9.9	12.9	16.0	8.9	8.0
FARM	56,385	5.4	5.5	8.6	8.9	7.7	4.1	6.5	5.3	5.4	4.7	5.1

Source: Statistics Canada (1982), Census of Canada, Catalogue 92–901, Table 6.
*Percentages are hand-tabulated and refer to proportion of population of urban size groups and rural areas who were aged 65 and over in 1981.

Table 9.2
Distribution of the Population Aged 80 and Over by Urban-Size Groups, Rural NonFarm, and Rural Farm, Canada and Provinces, 1981

	CANADA N	%*	NFLD. %	P.E.I. %	NOVA SCOTIA %	NEW BRUNSWICK %	QUEBEC %	ONTARIO %	MANI- TOBA %	SASKAT- CHEWAN %	ALBERTA %	B.C. %
TOTAL	450,575	1.9	1.4	3.0	2.2	2.0	1.5	2.0	2.1	2.5	1.4	2.1
URBAN	365,435	2.0	1.4	4.2	2.2	2.4	1.6	2.1	2.7	2.9	1.5	2.5
500,000 +	178,425	1.8	-	-	-	-	1.5	1.9	2.4	-	1.3	2.4
100,000-499,999	53,175	2.1	1.8	-	1.6	-	1.4	2.0	-	2.1	-	4.3
30,000- 99,999	40,400	2.0	-	-	2.5	2.3	1.5	2.0	3.3	3.1	1.7	2.3
10,000- 29,999	31,450	2.0	1.2	4.1	2.3	2.0	1.4	2.5	2.1	3.3	1.8	1.8
5,000- 9,999	18,675	2.4	.9	-	2.7	2.2	1.8	2.8	3.3	4.0	2.0	1.8
2,500- 4,999	21,805	2.7	1.5	-	3.8	4.1	2.2	3.2	5.9	4.8	2.4	2.0
1,000- 2,499	21,510	3.1	1.3	4.5	3.7	2.8	2.4	3.8	4.8	5.3	2.9	1.9
RURAL	85,140	1.4	1.4	2.3	2.1	1.6	1.2	1.5	1.8	2.0	1.1	1.0
NON-FARM	77,685	1.6	1.4	2.3	2.1	1.6	1.2	1.7	2.4	3.1	1.5	1.0
FARM	7,455	.01	1.0	1.9	1.7	1.4	0.7	0.9	0.6	0.6	0.5	0.6

Source: Statistics Canada (1982), Census of Canada, Catalogue 92–901, Table 6.
*Percentages are hand-tabulated and refer to proportion of population of urban size groups and rural areas who were aged 80 and over in 1981.

women in the older population (Government of Canada, 1982). However, Hodge and Qadeer (1983) predict that "the sex ratio will fall, and the small settlements may increasingly become centres of elderly women". The rural aged are also more likely than the urban to be married (United Senior Citizens of Ontario, 1985); to be generally less well educated (Hodge and Qadeer, 1983); and to own their dwelling (United Senior Citizens of Ontario, 1985; J. Lin et al., 1972; Ontario Advisory Council on Senior Citizens, 1980).

The elderly widowed are also overrepresented in rural areas. Widows comprise 11.9 percent of women living in urban areas and 17.5 percent of women in rural areas. Among widowed rural women 92.7 percent reside in nonfarm areas, typically small towns and villages. The rural elderly are also more ethnically homogeneous than the urban. In one study 79 percent of the rural aged were of British origin (United Senior Citizens of Ontario, 1985).

There is some debate whether the rural aged are financially worse off than their urban counterparts. A report of the National Council of Welfare indicates no substantial variation in the risk of poverty for families living in different-sized communities. "Unattached individuals living in rural areas face the lowest risk of falling below the low-income line, while those in small urban areas (30,000–99,999) have the highest poverty rate" (1985).

Other research (Ontario Advisory Council on Senior Citizens, 1980) found that rural households with elderly heads have smaller family incomes than do urban. A Manitoba study also found that the mean monthly incomes reported by rural elders were consistently lower than those of urban elderly (E. Shapiro and L. L. Roos, 1984). Canadian poverty lines are adjusted by degree of urbanization and are higher in urban areas, therefore, a rural elder could have the lower income with only the urban resident being classified as "poor." A study of the socioeconomic status of 236 rural and 222 urban elders in southern Ontario found no significant differences in reported levels of personal or household income (A. Martin Matthews et al., 1984). While a larger proportion of rural than urban elders were still employed after age 60, their labor force participation did not lead to higher income levels.

Such debates mask significant regional differences in income levels throughout Canada. For over fifty years per-capita personal income in Ontario has been almost exactly double that in the provinces of Prince Edward Island and Newfoundland. These indicators of economic disparity are used most frequently to substantiate claims of "objective regional differences" across the country, and reflect the distinctive economic bases of regions and subregions wherein the elderly reside (R. Matthews, 1983).

METHODOLOGICAL AND CONCEPTUAL ISSUES IN COMPARISONS BETWEEN THE RURAL AND URBAN AGED

Only seven years ago V. W. Marshall noted that "research on Canada's rural aged is almost completely non-existent, and we can only speculate about the important differences which might persist on the basis of rural-urban variability" (1980). While there is as yet no comprehensive and extensive body of research on rural aging in Canada, Marshall's statement is no longer true. A recently published bibliography of research on rural aging in Canada (N. Ryan, 1985) lists no fewer than 135 papers and reports on the subject, with 68.5 percent of them appearing since 1980. The majority of these studies are small locally focused community surveys conducted by government and local planning agencies and approximately 25 percent report findings that permit some national generalizations. Studies focus either on physical locale influences on aging or elder experiences in rural versus urban settings. Most research has the latter focus, examining rural elder access to social and health resources.

Most Canadian studies focus *exclusively* on the rural elderly. Lack of a direct comparison of rural and urban elderly severely limits generalizability and restricts the utility of extant research in shaping the process of policy development. Such studies document rural characteristics, but do not contribute to an understanding of geographic environmental impact on the experience of growing older.

Other problems are created when researchers use vastly different definitions of rurality, further restricting comparability and generalizability. For example, research on elder transportation in rural Saskatchewan included all "rural" municipalities, small towns with a population of less than 600, and three larger towns with populations ranging from 1,500 to 5,000 (P. R. Grant, 1983; P. R. Grant and B. Rice, 1983). Another study included those towns which were "quite isolated, involved in forestry and other resource related industries" and with populations from 7,000 to 10,000 (J. Wallace, 1977). Documents from the Ontario Ministry of Municipal Affairs and Housing (1983) describe as rural those communities up to 5,000 population, and rural towns of 400 density per square kilometer. G. Hodge (1984) included towns and villages with populations ranging from 290 to 4,863. J. L. McGhee notes: "Because of differing conceptualizations of rurality employed in research studies, it is not possible to draw any definite conclusions about the overall extent of ... rural problems" (1983).

There is also more to being rural than current residence alone indicates. The concept of *earlier environmental history* is particularly salient in this regard. It is questionable what length of residency in a particular community is necessary for rural or urban categorization. However, rural settings primarily populated by the rural-reared will be potentially quite different from those with concentrations of formerly urban inmigrants. With few exceptions (E. Cape, 1984, 1987), Canadian researchers have not considered this factor. Its relevance, however, is apparent. In a study of patterns of adaptation to retirement, A. Martin Matthews and K. H. Brown (1981) found that of 150 "rural" retirees, 21 (14 percent) had, since retirement, moved from an urban setting of 5,000 or more population, and 11.3 percent had relocated from an urban area of 100,000 population. Similarly, only 11.4

percent of another sample of 236 rural elders were lifelong rural inhabitants. Of those who had moved into the rural environment, nearly 30 percent had relocated from an urban area (A. Martin Matthews et al., 1984). These urban "in-movers" to the rural area would not likely define themselves as rural. In fact, other research suggests some fundamental differences between those who relocate *into* rural areas in later life versus those who *stay* in the rural environment (A. Martin Matthews and A. Vanden Heuvel, 1986).

Failure to recognize earlier environmental history may influence many findings. The entire structure of the social support network and pattern of social integration into a community will potentially be affected. Environmental history therefore has distinct implications for the interpretation of findings on rural versus urban elders. Recognizing these research limitations, this chapter proceeds to examine four broad issues: health care utilization, social support networks, perceived quality of life, and transportation. Research and policy implications of these findings will then be discussed.

AGING IN RURAL CANADA: SOCIAL AND BEHAVIORAL CHARACTERISTICS

Health Status and Utilization of Health Care Delivery

"The extent to which rural-urban differences are relevant for the provision of care to elderly individuals is another continuing debate" (N. Chappell, et al., 1985). Overall, the data on the health status and health care utilization patterns show no significant differences in general health between rural and urban elders. Structural features of the environment, rather than characteristics of the elderly per se, account for rural-urban differences in utilization patterns.

In a recent Ontario study examination of seven health status variables did not reveal major urban-rural variations. Differences across communities were found in the use of the health care systems, with the rural elderly the least likely to see medical specialists and the least likely to be hospitalized (United Senior Citizens of Ontario, 1985).

A Manitoba health resource study reports considerable intraprovincial variation in the distribution of physicians and health care resources, with rural areas characterized by more hospital beds (7.6 versus 5.3 per 1,000 population) and higher occupancy rates (69 percent versus 82 percent) than urban areas (Shapiro and Roos, 1984). Since these variations persist when health status and other variables are taken into account, Shapiro and Roos posit three explanations for the comparatively high use of hospitals by the rural aged: (1) relative poverty may make home treatment less viable, leading to greater hospitalization by physicians; (2) winter travel and transportation problems may encourage in-hospital treatment that elsewhere might be provided on an ambulatory basis; and (3) the greater availability of hospital beds in rural as compared to urban Manitoba, which may encourage hospital admissions. They conclude that "although supply characteristics must be closely associated with variation in hospital use by the elderly, the differences between rural and urban bed supply are such as to have substantial implications for hospital usage"(Shapiro and Roos, 1984).

Data on utilization patterns of nonhospital health services in rural areas are more fragmentary. There is some evidence (based primarily on local agency surveys) that rural areas generally lack a broad spectrum of home support services to facilitate community living by the elderly (Ontario Advisory Council on Senior Citizens, 1982; B. D. McPherson, 1983).

Overall, rural Canada is generally well served in terms of institutional facilities. Nova Scotia had the largest proportion of such facilities in rural areas (24 percent), compared to 13 percent in Newfoundland and 3 percent in Manitoba. Perhaps recognizing the concentration of elders in areas with populations of 1,000 to 4,999, all the provinces except Prince Edward Island, Ontario, and British Columbia had the largest proportion of their institutional facilities located in areas of this size (Conference Planning Committee, 1985). Overall, it appears that in rural Canada, services are available for the elderly who are ill, but much less so for those who need assistance with daily living.

Social Support Networks

Comparison of social support patterns, especially informal exchanges among families of rural versus urban elderly, is fraught with conflicting findings. The debate involves whether rural as compared to urban elders are more or less integrated into a supportive family network. One Ontario study found that the rural elderly were less likely than urban elderly to rely on family members for assistance, and more likely to rely on neighbors and friends. This finding is particularly intriguing when one considers that the rural elderly had significantly larger family networks available to them than did the urban elderly. Almost one-half (45 percent, n = 76) of the rural elderly reported 13 or more family contacts; by contrast, 24 percent (n = 65) of the metropolitan sample reported contact with this many relatives. Rural elders did not, however, differ from the urban in their frequency of contacts by telephone or in person with family or friends (United Senior Citizens of Ontario, 1985).

A comparative study of the rural and urban elderly in Saskatchewan also identified patterns of family and social interaction. In general, rural elders were active participants in social networks involving family and friends. While urban elders were more likely to have a family member living close by, P. R. Grant and B. Rice conclude that "families in rural Saskatchewan live close to each other and are very much in contact" (1983). It is, however, noteworthy that 17 percent of the respondents lived more than 100 miles from their preferred family contact.

Research in Ontario similarly found few differences in patterns of family support. The rural aged were no more likely to share a household with other family members or to include, in descriptions of their family networks, different types of kin (children, nieces, cousins) than did the urban. A. Martin Matthews et al. (1984) did, however, find that the rural elderly had significantly higher levels of contact with brothers and sisters.

Another Ontario study focused on the informal support services available to elderly rural women. Only a fifth of the 168 women studied had children living in the same township; neighbors therefore provided most casual contacts, but planned social events primarily involved kinfolk, especially the children and their families (E. Cape, 1987). This study generally supports the finding that older rural women primarily depend on their age peers for friendship, and that friendship bonds are strengthened by duration of residential stability. But there were certain dysfunctions in the support system. Given the town and village clustering of the aged, there is a strong probability that their friends and neighbors are also elderly women living alone, thus limiting the amount of practical assistance to be offered by neighbors. Neighbors contributed the least amount of service, even with such traditional neighborly activities as cutting grass or shovelling driveways in winter. The likelihood of having a confidante also declined with age, with widowhood, and with community residence, in spite of the concentration of elderly widows in small settlements where access was not a problem and the women were no strangers to one another.

There was also evidence of a different "category of care-giver, one seldom marked in the literature, but a major source of assistance for these respondents: the paid employee" (Cape, 1987). Paid employees provided significantly more household assistance than did either relatives or neighbors, and the same overall amount as children. Over half the female elders had some kind of practical assistance, mainly with their household work. There was a strong association between age and the likelihood of having such help, indicating that the informal support network was working well for these rural women. However, a substantial proportion of this help came from paid employees, and the question does arise: Had this kind of assistance not been available, would their kinfolk be able and willing to make up the difference? In sum, the practical assistance offered to these elderly rural women by their offspring and kinfolk and by neighbors and friends epitomized the rural support network in general: long on emergencies and short on routine care (Cape, 1987).

A Quebec study found that rural elders see relatively few people if one considers their potential network of acquaintances, but that they develop more contacts with those that they do meet. Most members of the family network in rural areas were much physically closer than in the urban areas studied (E. Corin, 1984; E. Corin et al., 1984). A Manitoba study also examined the rural-urban differences in support networks of forty-four individuals entering an adult day care program. Many similarities and relatively few differences between the rural and urban participants were identified. The differences that exist are in terms of a wider social network for the rural elderly, specifically nonhousehold, nonkin individuals. There was also evidence that "the rural elderly are more likely than the urban elderly to receive support from local organizations" (L. Strain and N. L. Chappell, 1983).

On the basis of these varied and disparate studies, what are we able to conclude about the social supports of the rural aged? There are many conflicting findings. Given conceptual and measurement inconsistencies in rural-urban comparisons of informal support, it is currently impossible to ascertain whether observed differences are a function of methodology or whether they reflect local, or even regional, variations in patterns of informal social support to rural elders. There is some evidence that certain regions of the country (eastern Canada, and Newfoundland in particular) have strong familistic orientations which guarantee high levels of support to the aged (A. E. Martin, 1974; B. J. McCay, 1983). For the most part extant data indicate that the rural aged are as integrated as the urban into family and nonfamily support systems, and probably even more so. The reliability of these informal supports is, however, likely more precarious: children live farther away, the rural aged have fewer personal visits, they have older neighbors, and their access to formal supports is more limited. These factors likely explain their necessary reliance on the support of paid employees.

Perceived Quality of Life

Researchers have noted a striking disparity between objective and subjective indicators of the quality of life of the rural elderly. Faced with a lower quality of environment as measured by objective indicators, rural elders apparently do not perceive these factors to be barriers to their quality of life or life satisfaction. Rural households headed by the elderly are less likely to have such taken-for-granted amenities as private flush toilets and piped hot and cold water or the convenience of freezers, dishwashers, or automobiles than are urban households; rural elderly persons typically occupy older homes than do rural households without seniors, suggesting higher expenditures for maintenance and heating (Ontario Advisory Council on Senior Citizens, 1980). These objective factors appear, however, to be ignored or considered less important than the quality of social relationships and the meaning of the social milieu in subjective assessments of quality of life (McPherson, 1983).

In a study of 453 elderly residents of two rural and two urban communities, A. Martin Matthews et al. (1984) compared rural and urban elders on seventeen dimensions of perceived quality of life, including satisfaction with health, financial security, friendship, housing, self-esteem, spouse, transportation, family relations, life as a whole, their lives compared to what they wanted, deserved, and needed. There were only two significant differences in these assessments. Rural elders were more optimistic that their lives would stay essentially the same five years later and were substantially more likely to express dissatisfaction with public and private transportation.

These results corroborate previous research in finding few rural-urban differences in perceived quality of life. A 1977 national survey (Ontario Advisory Council on Senior Citizens, 1980) of over 3,000 adult Canadians—including 270 urban and 90 rural elders—reached similar conclusions. On assessments of satisfaction with life as a whole, general happiness, such aspects of life as finances, health, marriage, friendships and spare time, and the extent to which people feel they can run their own lives, there were no significant differences between the rural and urban elderly. Rural elders were, however, substantially less satisfied with shopping facilities and public transportation, and they were less likely than other groups to think that their lives were getting better. More rural elderly than any other group thought that the government doesn't care about people like them, and that they don't have any say in what the government does (Ontario Advisory Council on Senior Citizens, 1980). These findings indicate that the rural elderly are physically isolated people who feel somewhat ostracized from the mechanisms of government.

Other studies identify additional areas of rural-urban differences in subjective assessments of quality of life. In a study of 200 rural and 200 urban Newfoundland elders, A. Kozma and M. J. Stones (1983) found that health was the most important predictor of happiness for rural people, whereas housing satisfaction was most important for nonrural subjects. Overall, rural elders reported higher levels of happiness than did the urban elderly. M. L. Snell (1985) similarly found that among recently retired men and women, rural elders, and women in particular, expressed high levels of morale.

Overall, the findings confirm high levels of life satisfaction among the rural elderly. In comparison with other *rural* residents, the elderly report the highest overall levels of personal life satisfaction (Ontario Advisory Council on Senior Citizens, 1980). Caution must however be exercised in interpreting these findings. The rural elderly may report higher levels of satisfaction than others because they have lower aspirations or a more limited idea of what is possible for them to achieve. It may be the result of unwarranted resignation, or conversely, genuinely having more to be satisfied about.

Transportation

Transportation is the most investigated topic in Canadian rural gerontology. While the lack of access to adequate transportation has consistently been identified as a major concern of rural elders (Alberta Council on Aging, 1980; M. B. Armstrong and A. M. Fuller, 1979; B. J. Brennan, 1984; E. S. Darwin, 1978; P. R. Grant and B. Rice, 1983; G. Hodge, 1984; B. J. McCay, 1983; Ontario Advisory Council on Senior Citizens, 1982; Senior Citizens Research Committee, 1980), estimates of need level vary considerably both within and between provinces and according to the nature of the inquiry. Overall, there is no doubt that, compared to their urban counterparts, rural elders have less access to transportation, as many small towns and villages do not have public transit systems and some do not have private taxis.

In a comprehensive study of transportation issues in Saskatchewan, Grant and Rice (1983) report that although 51 percent of the rural elderly usually drive themselves, 18.5 percent have a serious problem with transportation to almost all destinations. Approximately one-fifth (18.6 percent) of rural elders had difficulty getting around in their local town at least once a week, and 24.1 percent had trouble getting to a larger center at least once a month. Those with the most serious transportation problems were typically "very old widowed women who lived alone on a low income and did not own a car. In addition, a significant minority were physically frail, saw their friends infrequently and never socialized outside their own home" (1983).

Various solutions to the problems of transportation for the rural elderly have been tested in Canada, the implementation of the "mobility club" concept in rural Ontario, and the Rural Transportation Assistance Program in Saskatchewan among them. However, under current circumstances, the lack of even a basic system of public transportation in rural areas restricts personal choice and structures the behavior of many rural elders.

A relevant finding from Cape's (1987) work, which foreshadows the plight of the widowed as transportation-disadvantaged as described by Grant and Rice (1983), is the fact of the vital contribution made by husbands to family transportation of the rural couple. Only about half of the women studied were drivers, and even fewer drove in the winter; widowhood was therefore likely to be attended by physical as well as social immobility. The disadvantage of this is particularly acute in the rural context, where, Cape observed, "Driving went beyond the strictly utilitarian to become something of an occupation and a regular source of companionship, especially for retired farm couples who appeared to spend a significant portion of weekday time on motor junkets, euphemistically known as 'going shopping' "(1987).

CONCLUSIONS AND POLICY IMPLICATIONS

This research overview identifies several features of the rural environment which are directly relevant to the process of policy development and service delivery. Primary among these is the demographic maturity of rural towns and villages, where the concentrations, if not absolute numbers, of elders ensures that the adequate provision of services will be dominant community concerns.

The examination of patterns of health care utilization, social support networks, perceived quality of life, and access to transportation indicates, overall, that structural features of the rural environment rather than characteristics of elders per se account for observed rural-urban differences. What also emerges is the perception that rural Canada responds relatively well to the needs of its elders at two extremes of the continuum from independence through to dependency. The well elderly—those with a spouse and the ability to drive—benefit from the emotionally supportive environment of the rural community, and express very high levels of life satisfaction. At the other end of the continuum, elders in need of acute hospital services or long-term institutional care typically will have these services available to them. For the very substantial group in the middle of the continuum, however, rural life is fraught with disadvantage. In terms of health care, community-based services for those seeking some assistance with daily living are quite limited in most parts of rural Canada. In terms of social support, children are often distant; and neighbors themselves are older, and may be unable to provide informal support, thus contributing to greater social isolation for some elders. Physical isolation is also perpetuated by a lack of public transportation and limited availability of private services.

It is not so much that support services are totally unavailable in rural areas, but rather that they are frequently inaccessible. A medical specialist may be available, but located forty miles away. A Meals-on-Wheels program may exist, but may serve only a specified area within a township. A day center program may be in place, but distantly located and therefore difficult to reach during winter months when it is most needed. The challenge of service provision to rural elders is to enhance the *accessibility* as well as *availability* of programs to those in need.

Recognition of two important factors must, however, govern the process of policy development with respect to rural elders. The first is the independent spirit found in the rural elderly, an attribute in which they take particular pride. For example, in suggesting solutions to lack of public transportation, one proposal is for a local transportation system run by the transportation-disadvantaged and other community volunteers (Grant and Rice, 1983). If government programs are to be successful in rural areas, they must not only acknowledge but also reinforce the independent spirit of its elders.

A second factor is the diversity of rural life. Life in northern areas of Canada is quite different from the south, simply because it is embedded in a rural rather than an urban context. Some characteristics of rural living are essentially peculiar to the north: the generally prosperous but limited economy; certain migration patterns; certain political expectations; and the presence of single industry towns. It is therefore quite inappropriate to assume that the needs of the rural elderly are similar in areas of clay-belt farming and in mine or rail towns. An adequate understanding of the lives and needs of the rural elderly will thus require attention to the inherent diversity of rural life.

While rural elders will benefit from the development of policies and programs that better reflect their unique environmental circumstances, greater attention to their concerns will also help to inform the policy development process for the future. Many small towns currently have the proportions of aged in their populations that the rest of the country is not expected to achieve until 2031. Knowledge of the impact of relatively high proportions of elders on required community resources and on community social structure and dynamics is thus vitally important to the process of policy development and program planning.

The author gratefully acknowedges the assistance of the staff of the Gerontology Research Centre, particularly Marlene Oatman and Amy Cousineau, in the preparation of this chapter. Data cited were collected as part of SSHRCC Grant # 492–79–0017 and University of Guelph Research Board Grant #5089.

REFERENCES

Alberta Council on Aging, Rural Transportation Committee (1980). *Rural Transportation Study: An Examination of Transportation Concerns as Expressed by Senior Citizens Clubs and Organizations in Rural Alberta*. Edmonton, Alta.: The Council.

Armstrong, M. B., and Fuller, A. M. (1979). Transportation in the Countryside: An Ontario Case Study. Paper presented at the annual meeting of the Canadian Association of Geographers. Victoria, B.C.

Brennan, B. J. (1984). The Elderly in Huron County: An Exploratory Analysis. Guelph, Ont.: University of Guelph, Department of Sociology and Anthropology.

Cape, E. (1984). The Distaff Side of Retiring to the Country. Paper presented at the Annual Meeting of the Canadian Sociology and Anthropology Association. Guelph, Ont.

Cape, E. (1987). Aging women in rural settings. In Victor W. Marshall, ed., *Aging in Canada: Social Perspectives* (2nd ed.). Toronto: Fitzhenry & Whiteside.

Chappell, N., Strain, L., and Blandford, A. (1985). *Aging and Health Care: A Social Perspective*. Toronto: Holt, Rinehart and Winston.

Conference Planning Committee, 4th Manitoba Conference on Aging (1985). *The Profincial Fact Book on Aging—Manitoba*. Winnipeg, Man.: Manitoba Council on Aging.

Corin, E., Tremklay, J. Sherif, T., and Bergeron, L., (1984) Strategies et tactiques: Les modalites d'affrontement des problemes chez des personnes agees de milieu urban et rural. *Sociologie et Societes*, 16(2): 89–104.

Corin, E. (1984). Manieres de vivre, manieres de dire: Reseau social et sociabilite quotidienne des personnes au Quebec. *Questions de Culture*, 6, 157–186.

Darwin, E. S. (1978). *The Unmet Mobility Needs of Rural Canadians: The Problems and the Responses.* M.Sc. thesis, Carleton University.

Government of Canada (1982). *Canadian Governmental Report on Aging.* Ottawa: Ministry of Supply and Services Canada.

Grant, P. R. (1983). Creating a Feasible Transportation System for Rural Areas: Reflections on a Symposium. *Canadian Journal on Aging,* 2 (March), 30–35.

Grant, P. R., and Rice, B. (1983). Transportation Problems of the Rural Elderly. *Canadian Journal on Aging,* 2(November), 107–124.

Health and Welfare Canada (1983). *Fact Book on Aging in Canada.* Ottawa: Ministry of Supply and Services.

Hodge, G. (1984). Time and the Environment of the Small Town Elderly. Paper presented at the Annual Scientific and Educational Meeting of the Canadian Association on Gerontology. Vancouver, B.C.

Hodge, G., and Qadeer, M. A. (1983). *Towns and Villages in Canada: The Importance of Being Unimportant.* Toronto: Butterworths.

Kozma, A., and Stones, M. J. (1983). Predictors of Happiness. *Journal of Gerontology, 38,* 626–28.

Lin, J., Neilson, P., and Purcell, C. (1972). *Older People in Kingsville, Ontario: A Study of their Living Arrangements, Health and Social Relations.* M.S.W. thesis, University of Windsor.

Lindsay, C. (1980). Population. In H. J. Adler and D. A. Brusegard, eds., *Perspectives Canada III.* Ottawa: Ministry of Supply and Services.

Marshall, V. W. (1980). *Aging in Canada: Social Perspectives.* Toronto: Fitzhenry and Whiteside.

Martin, A. E. (1974). *Up-along: Newfoundland Families in Hamilton.* Unpublished M.A. thesis, Department of Sociology, McMaster University, Hamilton, Ontario.

Martin Matthews, A., and Brown, K. H. (1981). Retirement and Change in Social Interaction: Objective and Subjective Assessments. Paper presented at the joint meeting of the Canadian Association on Gerontology and the Gerontological Society of America, Toronto.

Martin Matthews, A., Fuller, A. M., Guldner, C., Michalos, A. C., Norris, J. E., Tindale, J. A., Ujimoto, K. V., Wolfe, J. S., and Wood, L. A. (1984). Stability and Change in Assessments of Quality of Life of the Elderly. Guelph, Ont.: Research Board.

Martin Matthews, A., and Vanden Heuvel, A. (1986). Conceptual and Methodological Issues in Research on Aging in Rural Versus Urban Environments. *Canadian Journal on Aging,* 5(1), 49–60.

Matthews, R. (1983). *The Creation of Regional Dependency.* Toronto: University of Toronto Press.

McCay, B. J. (1983). *Old People and Social Relations in a Newfoundland Outport.* Unpublished manuscript, Rutgers State University, Department of Human Ecology, New Brunswick, N. J.

McGhee, J. L. (1983). Transportation Opportunity and the Rural Elderly: A Comparison of Objective and Subjective Indicators. *The Gerontologist,* 23(5): 505–511.

McPherson, B. D. (1983). *Aging as a Social Process*. Toronto: Butterworths.

National Council of Welfare (1985). *Poverty Profile*. Ottawa: Government of Canada.

Ontario Advisory Council on Senior Citizens (1980). *Towards an Understanding of the Rural Elderly*. Toronto: The Council.

Ontario Advisory Council on Senior Citizens (1982). *A Model for Delivery of Services to Remote and Northern Communities in Ontario*. Toronto: The Council.

Ontario Ministry of Municipal Affairs and Housing (1983). *Towards Community Planning for an Aging Society*. Toronto: Queen's Printer.

Ontario Ministry of Northern Affairs. Strategic Planning Secretariat (1982). *The Elderly in Northern Ontario: A Handbook of Useful Statistics*. Toronto: The Ministry.

Ryan, N. (compil.). (1985). *Rural Aging in Canada: An Annotated Bibliography*. University of Guelph: Gerontology Research Centre.

Santerre, R. (1982). Masculinité et vieillissement dans la Bas Saint-Laurent: Notes de recherche. *Anthropologie et Sociétiés*, 6(3), 115–128.

Saskatchewan Senior Citizens' Provincial Council (1983). *Profile '83: The Senior Population in Saskatchewan: I Demo-graphics*. Regina, Sask.: The Council.

Senior Citizens Research Committee (1980). Property Taxes and the Problems of the Elderly in Nova Scotia. Halifax, N.S.:Dalhousie University, Regional and Urban Studies Centre.

Shapiro, E., and Roos, L. L. (1984). Using Health Care: Rural/Urban Differences among the Manitoba Elderly. *The Gerontologist*, 24(June), 270–74.

Simmons, J., and Simmons, R. (1974). *Urban Canada* (2nd ed.). Toronto: Copp Clark Publishing.

Snell, M. L. (1985). *Qualitative and Quantitative Aspects of Social Interaction in a Sample of Retired Men and Women*. Unpublished M.Sc. thesis, Department of Family Studies, University of Guelph, Guelph, Ont.

Social Planning and Review Council of British Columbia (1976). *Health Needs of the Independent Elderly: A Report From Four Communities*. Vancouver, B.C.: Sparc.

Statistics Canada (1982a). *Population: Age, Sex and Marital Status, Canada, Provinces, Urban Size Groups, Rural Non-Farm and Rural Farm*. Cat. 92–901, Ottawa: Ministry of Supply and Services (September).

Statistics Canada (1982b). *Population: Geographic Distributions*. Cat. 93–901—93–912. Ottawa: Ministry of Supply and Services (June).

Statistics Canada (1984). *Urban Growth in Canada*. Cat. 99–942. Ottawa: Ministry of Supply and Services (May).

Strain, L., and Chappell, N. L. (1983). Rural-Urban Differences among Adult Day Care Participants in Manitoba. *Canadian Journal on Aging*, 2(December), 197–209.

Thompson, R. (1983). *Persistence and Change: The Social and Economic Development of Rural Newfoundland and Labrador, 1971 to 1981*. Government of Newfoundland and Labrador: Department of Rural, Agricultural and Northern Development.

United Senior Citizens of Ontario (1985). *Elderly Residents in Ontario: Rural-Urban Differences.* Ministry of Community and Social Services.

Wallace, J. (1977). *Transportation of the Elderly and Handicapped in Rural Areas— The Manitoba Experience.* Manitoba Department of Highways and Transportation.

CHAPTER 10

Aging in the Rural United States

Raymond T. Coward

Nearly one out of every four elders in the United States resides in a small town or a rural community—a total of almost 6.5 million elders according to the 1980 Census (W. B. Clifford et al., 1985). Despite the magnitude of these numbers, in the minds of many the life circumstances of rural elders remain shrouded in nostalgic images, misinformation, and myth. As a consequence, public policies for the aged frequently contain an inherent urban bias, and the distinctive needs of rural elders are seldom incorporated into service planning.

A recent surge in gerontological research concentrating on the rural elderly in the United States has greatly improved the empirical base from which policymakers and service providers can act (R. T. Coward and G. R. Lee, 1985; J. A. Krout, 1986). In the sections which follow, this research is briefly reviewed and highlighted. The chapter is organized around four sections that compare the rural-urban circumstances of elders in the United States. The first section relies heavily on census data to examine key demographic trends. The second attempts to compare the quality of life of rural elders with their urban counterparts on several important indicators, including income, health status, mental health, housing, family and kin relationships, and community participation. In the third section the availability and use of health and human services is examined, and in the final section the difficulty of developing public policies for the rural elderly will be discussed.

THE DEFINITION OF RURAL

Rural gerontology is plagued by definitional problems. The literature contains many different methods for defining rural. The two most widely used classification systems in the United States, those created by the U.S.

Bureau of the Census, are both population based, i.e., they are focused primarily on the number of people who reside in a particular location.

In the first schema *rural* is distinguished from *urban*. The urban population includes anyone living in an urbanized area *or* in a place of 2,500 or more people and the rural population as those living elsewhere. The second dichotomy distinguishes *metropolitan* from *nonmetropolitan*. In this classification metropolitan places (called Standard Metropolitan Statistical Areas or SMSAs) are counties that contain at least one city, or two adjacent cities, with a population of 50,000 or more. The SMSA includes all contiguous counties which are socially and economically integrated with, and dependent on, the metropolitan area. Nonmetropolitan residents are those living in counties that do not conform to these criteria.

Although these definitions are widely used, they both suffer from oversimplification. As Clifford et al. (1985) have commented, "American society is not sharply divided into two clearly differentiated parts; rather, considerable overlap and blurring exist" (p. 26). But our traditional focus on a dichotomy (rural/urban or metropolitan/nonmetropolitan)—as opposed to a continuum of residence—has resulted in an extended argument over the precise *boundary* between the categories and has sometimes served to deflect attention away from seeking a better understanding of the different ways in which the environment (both physical and social) can influence human behavior and interaction.

One further definitional clarification must be made. In the United States agriculture and farming are no longer synonymous with rural. Although the proportion of residents living in *rural* areas over the last quarter of a century has remained fairly stable, the percentage living on *farms* has declined sharply—from 15.6 million in 1960 to 5.6 million in 1982 (U.S. Department of Agriculture, 1984). In contemporary rural America farming is an important, but not the dominant, life-style.

Despite popular images to the contrary, contemporary rural America embodies important variations in ethnic background, employment patterns, family structure, and economic development. As a consequence, contemporary rural America embodies important variations in ethnic background, employment patterns, family structure and economic development (R. T. Coward, 1983). Each of these forms of diversity serves to destroy the simplistic image of a uniform rural America. Diversity is one of the basic threads of the rural fabric that serves to shape and mold the life circumstances of rural elders in the United States.

DEMOGRAPHIC PERSPECTIVES ON AGING IN THE RURAL UNITED STATES

This section of the chapter concentrates on comparisons of key demographic factors between the rural and urban elderly in the United States. The data underlying this discussion are drawn from the U.S. Bureau of the

Table 10.1
Total Population and Population Aged 65 Years and Over by Residence Areas for the United States, 1980

Residence Areas	All Ages	Number 65 and Over	Percent
Total	226,472 *	25,539	11.3
Urban	167,024	19,042	11.4
Inside urbanized areas	139,151	15,194	10.9
Central cities	67,029	8,014	12.0
urban fringe	72,122	7,180	10.0
Outside urbanized areas	27,873	3,848	13.8
Places of 10,000 or more	13,480	1,736	12.9
Places of 2,500 to 10,000	14,393	2,112	14.7
Rural	59,448	6,497	10.9
Places 1,000 to 2,500	7,035	1,085	15.4
Other rural	52,413	5,412	10.3

*Numbers in thousands
Source: W. B. Clifford, et al., "The Rural Elderly in Demographic Perspective," in R. T. Coward and G. R. Lee, eds., *The Elderly in Rural Society: Every Fourth Elder* (New York: Springer Publishing Company, 1985), Table 2.7, pp. 39–41.

Census and use the rural and urban definitions created by that agency. (See earlier discussion.)

The Magnitude of the Rural Elderly Population

Table 10.1 contains comparisons of the total population and the population aged 65 years and over by residence areas for the United States. Approximately equal percentages of the total population and the aged population live in rural communities (26.2 percent and 25.4 percent respectively). However, Clifford, et al. (1985) have noted that, in general, the 1980 Census data indicated that the proportion of elderly increased as the size of the place declined. (See Table 10.1.)

Personal Characteristics of the Rural Elderly

Although the greatest percentage of elders of all races live in urban areas, a slightly higher proportion of White elders live in rural areas—23.6 percent of all White elders live in rural areas and only 17.4 percent of Black elders and 17.3 percent of the elders in the "other races" category live in such places. However, if *pro rata* shares are compared (i.e., comparisons of the distribution of the total population of a particular race with the distribution of those over 65 years of age within that same racial category), a slightly different pattern is observed. Central cities, smaller cities, and villages had more than their pro rata share of the White aged. In contrast, the Black elderly tended to be concentrated in all places outside urbanized areas—especially in the "other rural" category. For the "other races," the elderly were most heavily concentrated in central cities and in rural areas.

Residential differences in marital status have also been reported. Using the 1980 census, Clifford et al. (1985) indicated that 57.3 percent of the nonmetropolitan population over the age of 65 years were married whereas 52.0 percent of metropolitan elders were married. When nonmetropolitan residents are divided into farm and nonfarm dwellers, the differences become even more striking. Nearly three out of every four (73.3 percent) elderly nonmetropolitan farm residents were married.

When the interaction of marital status and gender is examined, it becomes clear that these residential differences are most noticeable in females. The proportions of elderly males that are married in metropolitan, nonmetropolitan nonfarm, and nonmetropolitan farm are relatively similar; 74.8 percent, 79.1 percent, and 78.3 percent respectively. However, among feamles the differences are quite marked; 36.7 percent, 40.1 percent, and 67.0 percent respectively.

The Geographic Distribution of the Rural Elderly

Because the rural elderly are *not* evenly distributed across all parts of the United States, statements about aging must always take into account important regional variations. Comparing the four census regions of the United States, for example, illustrates the significant variations existing among different locales in the percentage of the overall population which are rural and elderly. Whereas 17.1 percent of the total population in the North Central states are elders living in all-rural, nonmetropolitan counties, only 10.6 percent of the population in the Western region are in a similar category. (See Table 10.2 for the proportions in the other regions.)

When even smaller geographical areas are compared, these differences become even more pronounced. For example, in subregional comparisons the range extends from 10.4 percent in the Pacific states of the Western

Table 10.2

Percent 65 Years and Over of the Total Population by Residence Areas for U.S. Census Regions and Divisions, 1980

Regions *	Total	Metropolitan Counties	Part-Urban Nonmetro Counties	All-Rural Nonmetro Counties
UNITED STATES	11.3	10.7	12.8	14.3
NORTHEAST	12.3	12.2	13.4	14.9
New England	12.3	12.1	12.6	15.1
Middle Atlantic	12.4	12.2	13.6	13.6
NORTH CENTRAL	11.4	10.2	13.7	17.1
East North Central	10.8	10.2	12.8	15.4
West North Central	12.8	10.5	14.8	17.9
SOUTH	11.3	10.4	12.8	13.2
South Atlantic	11.8	11.6	12.1	12.7
East South Central	11.3	10.2	12.3	12.8
West South Central	10.4	8.7	14.3	15.0
WEST	9.9	9.8	9.8	10.6
Moutain	9.3	8.9	10.0	10.9
Pacific	10.2	10.0	11.4	10.4

*The states contained in the regions and divisions are: NORTHEAST: *New England* (Connecticut, Massachusetts, Maine, New Hampshire, Rhode Island, and Vermont) and *Middle Atlantic* (New Jersey, New York, and Pennsylvania); NORTH CENTRAL: *East North Central* (Illinois, Indiana, Michigan, Ohio, and Wisconsin) and *West North Central* (Iowa, Kansas, Minnesota, Missouri, Nebraska, North Dakota, and South Dakota); SOUTH: *South Atlantic* (Delaware, District of Columbia, Florida, Georgia, Maryland, North Carolina, South Carolina, Virginia, and West Virginia); *East South Central* (Alabama, Kentucky, Mississippi, and Tennessee); and *West South Central* (Arkansas, Louisiana, Oklahoma, and Texas); WEST: *Mountain* (Arizona, Colorado, Idaho, Montana, Nevada, New Mexico, Utah, and Wyoming); and *Pacific* (Alaska, California, Hawaii, Oregon, and Washington).
Source: W. B. Clifford, et al., "The rural elderly in demographic perspective," in R. T. Coward and G. R. Lee, eds., *The Elderly in Rural Society: Every Fourth Elder* (New York: Springer Publishing Company, 1985), Table 2.7, pp. 39–41.

region to 17.9 percent in the West North Central states. And when individual states are compared, there is almost a fivefold difference found from a high of 19.7 percent in Kansas to a low of 4.1 percent in Alaska.

Moreover, over the past decade the growth of the segment of the population over 65 years of age who live in small towns and rural communities has shifted in opposite directions in different regions of the country. Between 1970 and 1980 the Southern and Western regions experienced an increase

in the percentage of elders living in all-rural, nonmetropolitan counties—
19.8 percent and 13.5 percent respectively. In contrast, both the Northeast
(−3.2 percent) and the North Central (−1.4 percent) regions reported declines in this segment of the population.

Inmigration Patterns of the Rural Elderly

The 1970 and 1980 censuses documented an important reversal in the
migration trends of the population in the United States. Prior to those dates,
more than a century of migration tracking had reported a continuous stream
of individuals moving from small towns and rural communities into the big
cities. These newer data, however, reflected a different pattern—hundreds
of rural counties across the country that had previously been declining in
population were unexpectedly indicating population gains via migration.
What surprises many Americans is the prominence of the elderly in this
movement. Previous migrational studies had indicated that those that move
tended to be primarily younger adults and their families. Yet G. V. Fuguitt
and S. J. Tordella (1980) were able to demonstrate that the elderly were
overrepresented in the early inmigrants of the so-called rural renaissance.
J. J. Zuiches and D. L. Brown (1978) reported data that indicated that
persons over the age of 65 years accounted for 18.4 percent of the net
metropolitan to nonmetropolitan migration between 1970 and 1975. Those
elders who have moved to rural communities are often significantly different
from the resident elderly they join—better educated and more affluent (N.
Glasgow, 1980), more apt to live in independent households (W. B. Clifford,
T. B. Heaton and G. V. Fuguitt, 1982), and more likely to have a living
spouse (W. B. Clifford et al., 1985). Rural communities with mild climates
and developed recreation sectors experienced the greatest gains in elderly
migrants (Heaton, Clifford, and Fuguitt, 1981).

There is some evidence that the inmigration of the elderly to rural communities, combined with the in-place aging of rural populations, has had
positive economic impacts on rural economies. Despite images of the elderly
being a drain on local economies (because of their lower incomes and higher
demands for certain services), G. F. Summers and T. A. Hirschl (1985) have
argued that improvements in retirement plans during the past quarter of a
century have resulted in retirees having increased discretionary spending
income and thus representing a significant source of dollars flowing into a
community.

QUALITY OF LIFE

In this section the quality of life of rural elders will be compared with
their urban counterparts on several important indicators. Examining the
evidence that is available, it is difficult to conclude that one group is uni-

formly advantaged over the other. That is, some comparisons indicate that the urban elderly, as a group, hold an advantage over their rural cohort (e.g., in average income levels); whereas in other comparisons the opposite seems to hold (e.g., the greater availability of spouses among the elderly living in rural communities). In still other areas there seems to be no appreciable difference (e.g., in kin relationships) and factors other than residence appear to more powerful in explaining the patterns which have been observed.

Sorting through this twisted maze of multiple and sometimes conflicting findings is a difficult and frustrating task. Perhaps the so-called bottom-line is that we *cannot* assume that the two segments of the population (rural and urban) share the same quality of life nor can the idyllic images of aging in a rural context, which are sometimes promoted in the popular media, be accepted unchallenged.

Income

As a group, rural residents have lower average incomes than their urban counterparts. This pattern is consistent across both occupations and gender (L. A. Bescher-Donnelly and L. W. Smith, 1981). Moreover, these residential differences persist in comparisons of the aged in the United States. W. J. Goudy and C. Dobson (1985) reported:

The rural elderly in general had lower incomes than the urban elderly, with the median income of older farm families being 71 percent and that of older nonfarm families being 65 percent of the median income of older urban families. Rural-urban differences were similar for unrelated individuals, although the median income levels were much lower (p. 65).

These income levels have meant that a greater proportion of the rural elderly, as contrasted with urban elders, live in poverty. In 1980, 12.0 percent of the metropolitan elderly had incomes below the poverty threshold, whereas 20.5 percent of the nonmetropolitan elderly had incomes at that level. Although the proportion of elders living in poverty declined dramatically during the decade of the 1970s (particularly in the first half of that decade) in both metropolitan and nonmetropolitan America, there remain significant differences between the two groups. (See Figure 10.1.)

Farmers have later-life work patterns that are quite different from other occupational groups (P. L. Rones, 1978). We must again remember, however, that in the United States most rural workers of any age are not involved in agriculture and its related industries. Among those who do farm, greater percentages stay in the labor force at later stages of their lives. In 1982 nearly a fifth of Black and a sixth of White males over the age of 70 years were farmworkers, compared with less than 4 percent of all males 25 years and over (U.S. Department of Commerce, 1983).

Figure 10.1
Percent of Persons 65 Years and Older in Poverty by Residence

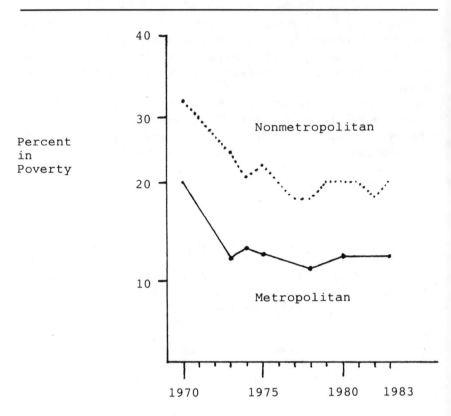

For older females the trend for participation in the labor force is quite different—being lower than male participation and remaining quite steady in the recent past. Estimating fully the participation of older females in *farm* work is very difficult. Although decades of research have documented the significant contribution that women often make to a farming operation, in many ways they remain "invisible" farmers because much of the research on agricultural production fails to enumerate the unpaid labor of farm wives. Examining farming operations where women were the principal operators (really just the tip of the iceberg when trying to estimate the work patterns of farm women since a much greater percentage of women would likely be an unnamed partner in the operations), J. Z. Kalbacher (1985) found that

15.5 percent of the female farm operators in her national sample were aged 65 years or older.

Health Status

Very different conclusions are reached when rural-urban comparisons are calculated for both mortality and morbidity rates. When mortality rates among the elderly are compared, there appear to be only minor variations between rural-urban or metropolitan-nonmetropolitan populations (W. R. Lassey and M. L. Lassey, 1985). In contrast, comparisons of morbidity rates have generally indicated critical differences. For example, in older males (aged 65 to 74 years), farm residents were found to have the greatest number of restricted activity days but the fewest number of disabilities requiring days in bed (L. Paringer et al., 1979).

Mental Health Status

R. J. Scheidt (1985), in an excellent comprehensive review of the literature, noted that some studies have reported higher prevalence rates among the rural elderly in alienation and low morale (A. K. Schooler, 1975), psychiatric disorders (J. Schwab, G. Warheit, and C. Holzer, 1974) and psychopathology (D. L. Phillips, 1966); whereas others have found no significant differences in prevalence rates for agitated depression or lonely dissatisfaction (Schooler, 1975) or a composite mental health index (R. J. Scheidt and P. G. Windley, 1982). Although the findings in this area are not clear-cut, they should put to rest the notion that elders living in rural areas have been somehow protected from the strains and stressors of modern living, or that the beautiful surroundings in which they live serve as some kind of buffer that reduces the likelihood of mental disorders.

Housing

Housing can influence the quality of life of elders either positively or negatively. As an aggregate, rural elders live in distinctly different housing than their urban counterparts. R. A. Bylund (1985) has suggested that nonmetropolitan elders are more likely to live in single, detached housing units and are more likely to own the home in which they are living. He reported that if mobile homes are included in detached units, 93.8 percent of the rural elderly in 1975 lived in such places in contrast to 57.4 percent of metropolitan elders. From that same housing survey, it was found that 82.9 percent of the rural nonmetropolitan elderly owned the home in which they lived as opposed to 65.0 percent of the metropolitan elderly.

A number of studies have reported that a greater proportion of the rural elderly live in substandard housing—defined as dilapidated or lacking in either hot running water, flush toilet for private use, or bathtub or shower for private use—than do urban elders (R. C. Atchley and S. J. Miller, 1975). Despite mental images of decaying urban neighborhoods and run-down boarding houses, it is the *rural* elderly, as a whole, that seem to be disadvantaged. Not only are the houses in which they live more apt to be in need of repair but the small towns and rural communities in which they reside are less likely to have alternative living options like congregate housing (Bylund, 1985).

Transportation

The ability of elders to be mobile and to move freely throughout their community is a major factor that contributes to their sense of independence and well-being. For the rural elderly a declining ability to transport themselves may interact with certain distinctive features of rural environments to create circumstances where individuals are particularly at risk of becoming socially isolated or unable to access needed goods and services.

For example, consider the declining ability of elders to transport themselves as it might interact with the following characteristics of rural transportation systems as outlined by I. Kaye (1983): (1) the percentage of households without access to an automobile is much higher in rural than urban areas; (2) intercity bus lines serve only 40 percent of towns between 2,500 and 10,000 population and only 15 percent of towns and places under 2,500; (3) rural roads and bridges are often not properly constructed or maintained; and (4) the cost of both public and private transportation in rural areas tends to be greater because of the distances involved, economies of scale, and public policies of deregulation. These factors, in combination with such things as the weather, produce a set of circumstances that increases the probability that a rural elder will become isolated. Rural providers of services to the elderly continually identify transportation as a major factor that impedes their ability to meet the needs of persons in their communities and increases their costs.

Family and Kin Relationships

Rural elders have been portrayed as immersed in a social and familial network that is eager and able to come to their aid in times of need. Yet there is little empirical evidence to support such notions. Indeed, after an exhaustive review of the literature, G. R. Lee and M. L. Cassidy (1985) concluded that with "respect to the family patterns of the elderly, residential location has very little explanatory utility" (p. 165). It is *not* that rural elders don't have family and friends with whom they interact and social networks that provide aid and support with the tasks of daily living; rather, it is that they are *not particularly advantaged* when they are compared to their urban counterparts. It would seem that variables other than residence are much more powerful predictors of the interpersonal interaction patterns that are observed in families.

Community Participation

A number of researchers have documented the importance of participation in community activities and social networks for the general well-being of older adults. V. R. Kivett (1985) divided nonkin community relationships into two types: "(1) associations through *formal organizations* such as voluntary participation in clubs, civic and social groups, or the church; and (2) immersion in *informal networks* that occur through interactions with neighbors and friends" (p. 171).

In each of these dimensions, rural-urban differences have been noted. For example, some have reported that older rural persons are less likely than urban elders to attend meetings, hold memberships, or remain highly involved with community organizations (Schooler, 1975). Moreover, when rural elders do participate in such formal activities there is evidence to suggest that the organizations with which they affiliate are quite different from those attended by urban elders (Kivett, 1985).

There is also some evidence to suggest that rural elders have more frequent contact with friends and neighbors and that they are more likely to perceive themselves as situated conveniently to friends (Schooler, 1975). W. C. McKain (1967) has also reported several significant differences among a rural-urban sample from Kentucky: rural elders were (1) more likely to know people within the community; (2) engage in more informal visiting; and (3) identify a larger number of persons as close friends.

THE AVAILABILITY AND USE OF HEALTH AND HUMAN SERVICES

There is firm evidence that there are fewer health and human services for elders in rural America and that those that do exist are in a narrower range (R. T. Coward and E. Rathbone-McCuan, 1985). For example, examining the number of services provided by Area Agencies on Aging, G. Nelson (1980) found that nearly 40 percent of the urban agencies offered more than eight services, whereas among rural agencies just half that percentage (23 percent) reported that they offered that number of services. Similarly, P. Taietz and S. Milton (1979) compared the availability of 25 specific services in a sample of rural and urban counties in upstate New York in 1967 and again in 1976. Although the number of services in both contexts had increased dramatically by 1976, rural counties still lagged behind their urban counterparts in the average number of services available. (See Table 10.3.) Indeed, V. L. Greene (1984) has argued that the absence (or defi-

Table 10.3
Percentage Comparisons of the Availability of Services in Rural and
Urban Counties in 1967 and 1976

Service	1967		1976		Percent Increase	
	Urban (n=16)	Rural (n=37)	Urban (n=16)	Rural (n=36)	Urban	Rural
Visiting nurse	63	8	100	97	59	1113
Information and referral	44	17	100	97	127	471
Homemaker service	69	56	100	92	45	64
Reduced Taxes	63	36	94	95	49	164
Home health aides	50	14	100	92	100	551
Meals-on-Wheels	19	3	94	86	395	2767
Discount on general purchases	6	3	88	86	1367	2767
Escort Service	6	8	100	78	1567	875
Discount on medicines	25	0	94	75	276	0
Special library program	63	39	94	75	49	92
Home repair service	6	6	88	75	1367	1150
Discount on public events	63	11	88	69	40	527
Public housing for elderly	56	17	94	58	68	241
Shopping assistance	6	8	81	64	1250	700
Friendly visitor service	50	28	88	53	76	89
Special adult education courses	50	17	100	47	100	176
Job training & placement	44	3	75	44	70	1367
Sheltered workshop	19	3	75	44	295	1367
Senior center	56	17	94	31	68	82
Discount on transportation	0	3	75	39	0	1200
Special media features	19	11	69	33	263	200
Special outlet for sale of products	19	6	31	44	63	633
Vacation planning service	38	6	50	28	32	367
Preretirement courses	13	3	56	22	331	633
Foster home service for elderly	0	6	38	17	0	185

Source: P. Taietz and S. Miller, "Rural-Urban-Differences in the Structure of Services for the Elderly in Upstate New York Counties," *Journal of Gerontology 34* (3) (1979): 429–37.

ciencies) of the community based services network of rural communities (such services as home health care, homemaker aides, escort services, adult day care services, or respite care) has led to the premature institutionalization of some rural elders—in his sample of nursing home patients in Arizona, he found that those from rural communities were younger and less disabled than their urban counterparts.

These deficits in the rural long-term care system extend as well to the institutional end of the continuum of care and include differences in the availability of hospital and nursing home beds (H. Richardson and A. R. Kovner, 1985). More important, in hospital services at least, these discrepancies seem to be expanding, rather than declining, as a result of the severe financial strains which have caused many rural hospitals to close their doors. For the elderly, who are high consumers of hospital-based services, such losses may represent particular difficulties.

Paralleling insufficiencies in facilities and services are shortages in personnel. Most rural agencies face significant difficulties in recruiting and retaining professional staffs. As a consequence, personnel maldistributions have been reported in a number of health and human service professions essential to the development of a comprehensive system of gerontological services.

Service Utilization

The rural elderly in the United States are generally portrayed as being more resistant than their urban counterparts to the receipt of formal services. The empirical base for this generalization, however, is weak. Studies of whether or not the attitude of self-reliance is more prevalent or stronger among the rural elderly have been equivocal in their findings and have suffered from severe methodological problems.

The untangling of the possible influence of *rurality* on attitudes of self-reliance among the aged is further confounded by the migration patterns which have occurred in the United States and which have seldom been accounted for in such studies. For example, there are a large number of elders presently residing in urban areas who were raised in a rural environment as well as a significant number of elders who have retired to non-metropolitan areas but who spent their entire adult lives in an urban context. Only research which is conceived more rigorously will permit the isolation of the effect of residence on the service utilization patterns of elders. At this time it is simply unclear what those effects are.

DEVELOPING SOCIAL POLICY DIRECTIONS

A number of reviews of current programs for the aged in the United States have identified an urban bias to domestic social welfare policy. Differences in funding levels, reimbursement rates, or special targeted programs for specific geographic areas, all seem to have a disproportionately urban flavor.

There is not a calculated conspiracy to deny rural areas their just due; rather, there appears to be a benign neglect or indifference to uniquely rural needs within the larger United States population. Many state and federal policymakers seem convinced of the "good life" for rural elders and of the isolation of rural communities from the evils of modern-day society. Such images are in contrast with portrayals of urban elders isolated from neighbors, abandoned by families, and left to the wills and whims of the concrete jungle. As a consequence, the distinctive features of creating and delivering gerontological services in a rural context are seldom acknowledged as public policy is developed.

What is clear is that *rural* public policy, to date, has consisted of a mishmash of disjointed initiatives (R. T. Coward and G. R. Lee, 1985). There is no overall *rural* policy in the United States—and perhaps nowhere is this more evident than within the social welfare arena. There is no systematic *plan* to address the distinctive needs of *rural* elders and, as a consequence, there is tremendous variation across the nation in the degree to which the distinctive features of rural environments are taken into account when developing public policy and regulations.

United States public policymakers are also unclear as to how to achieve a goal of providing equal services to both rural and urban elders. Does equal mean *the same* service (delivered in the same quantity and by the same type of provider) or some notion of *the equivalent* service?

CONCLUSION

When the United States reaches a level of awareness in its social welfare planning where the distinctive features of rural environments are acknowledged and incorporated into policy, then we will be poised, as a nation, in a position to provide for the needs of the rural elderly. To achieve that stance will require discarding nostalgic images of life in rural America and forging a new, more contemporary, understanding of the aging process as it occurs in rural society.

Although the recent focus of Americans on the so-called farm crisis has served to reorient our nation to the importance, both psychologically and economically, of the rural segment of our society, the crisis has failed to acknowledge and take into account the life circumstances of rural families who are not engaged in farming. As a consequence, *rural* policy in the United States has once again operationally become *agricultural* policy. Thus there is little reason to believe that the solutions that will emerge from this context will address the needs of the majority of rural residents.

The empirical base of knowledge which now exists provides firm evidence that the place of residence is an important factor in understanding the life circumstances of elders. The precise nature of the influence of residence on different aspects of the lives of elders, however, is still poorly understood. As a consequence, researchers, service providers, and policymakers, building on the scientific base reviewed in the previous sections, must continue to search for a clearer understanding of the multiple ways in which aging in a rural environment differs from the same process in a more urban setting.

REFERENCES

Atchley, R.C. and Miller, S.J. (1975). Housing and Households of the Rural Aged. In T.O. Byerts, S.C. Howell, and L.A. Pastalan, eds., *Environmental Context of Aging: Life-Styles, Environmental Quality, and Living Arrangements*. New York: Garland STPM Press, 62–79.

Bescher-Donnelly, L. A., and Smith, L. W. (1981). The Changing Roles and Status of Rural Women. In R. T. Coward and W. M. Smith, Jr., eds., *The Family in Rural Society*. Boulder, Col.: Westview Press, 167–185.

Bylund, R. A. (1985). Rural Housing: Perspectives for the Aged. In R. T. Coward and G. R. Lee, eds., *The Elderly in Rural Society: Every Fourth Elder*. New York: Springer Publishing Company, 129–150.

Clifford, W. B., Heaton, T. B., and Fuguitt, G. V. (1982). Residential Mobility and Living Arrangements among the Elderly: Changing Patterns in Metropolitan and Nonmetropolitan Areas. *International Journal of Aging and Human Development*, 14, 139–156.

Clifford, W. B., Heaton, T. B., Voss, P. R., and Fuguitt, G. V. (1985). The Rural Elderly in Demographic Perspective. In R. T. Coward and G. R. Lee, eds., *The Elderly in Rural Society: Every Fourth Elder*. New York: Springer Publishing Company, 25–56.

Coward, R. T. (1983). Family Life in Small Towns and Rural Communities: Persistence, Change and Diversity. In R. Craycroft and M. Fazio, eds., *Change and Tradition in the American Small Town*. Jackson, Miss.: University Press of Mississippi, 73–86.

Coward, R. T., and Lee, G. R. (1985). An Introduction to Aging in Rural America, In R. T. Coward & G. R. Lee, eds., *The Elderly in Rural Society: Every Fourth Elder*. New York: Springer Publishing Company, 3–16.

Coward, R. T., and Rathbone-McCuan, E. (1985). Delivering Health and Human Services to the Elderly in Rural Society. In R. T. Coward and G. R. Lee, eds., *The Elderly in Rural Society: Every Fourth Elder*. New York: Springer Publishing Company, 197–222.

Fuguitt, G. V., and Tordella, S. J. Elderly Net Migration: The New Trend of Nonmetropolitan Population Change. *Research on Aging*, 2, 191–204.

Glasgow, N. (1980). The Older Metropolitan Origin Migrant as a Factor in Rural Population Growth. In A. J. Sofranko and J. D. Williams, eds., *Rebirth of Rural America: Rural Migration in the Midwest*. Ames, Iowa: North Central Regional Center for Rural Development, Iowa State University.

Goudy, W. J., and Dobson, C. (1985). Work, Retirement, and Financial Situations of the Rural Elderly. In R. T. Coward and G. R. Lee, eds., *The Elderly in Rural Society: Every Fourth Elder*. New York: Springer Publishing Company, 57–78.

Greene, V. L. (1984). Premature Institutionalization among the Rural Elderly. In R. T. Coward and S. M. Cordes, eds., *Emerging Issues in the Delivery of Rural Health Services*. Washington: U.S. Senate, Committee on Agriculture, Nutrition and Forestry, 23–30.

Heaton, T. B., Clifford, W. B., and Fuguitt, G. V. (1981). Temporal Shifts in the Determinants of Young and Elderly Migration in Nonmetropolitan Areas. *Social Forces*, 60, 41–60.

Kalbacher, J. Z. (1985). A Profile of Female Farmers in America. Washington: U.S. Department of Agriculture, Economic Research Service, Rural Development Research Report No. 45.

Kaye, I. (1983). Transportation. In D. A. Dillman and D. J. Hobbs, eds., *Rural Society in the U.S.: Issues for the 1980s*. Boulder,Col.: Westview Press, 156–63.

Kivett, V. R. (1985). Aging in Rural Society: Non-Kin Community Relations and Participation. In R. T. Coward and G. R. Lee, eds., *The Elderly in Rural Society: Every Fourth Elder*. New York: Springer Publishing Company, 171–92.

Krout, J.A. (1986) *The Aged in Rural America*. Westport, Conn.: Greenwood Press.

Lassey, W. R., and Lassey, M. L. (1985). The Physical Health Status of the Rural Elderly. In R. T. Cowarad and G. R. Lee, eds., *The Elderly in Rural Society: Every Fourth Elder*. New York: Springer Publishing Company, 83–104.

Lee, G. R., and Cassidy, M. L. (1985). Family and Kin Relations of the Rural Elderly. In R. T. Coward and G. R. Lee, eds., *The Elderly in Rural Society: Every Fourth Elder*. New York: Springer Publishing Company, 151–70.

McKain, W. C. (1967). Community Roles and Activities of Older Rural Persons. In E. G. Youmans, ed., *Older Rural Americans*. Lexington, Ky.: University of Kentucky Press, 75–96.

Nelson, G. (1980). Social Services to the Urban and Rural Aged: The Experience of Area Agencies on Aging. *Gerontologist*, 20, (2), 200–207.

Paringer, L., Bluck, J., Feder, J., and Holahan, J. (1979). *Health Status and Use of Medical Services*. Washington: Urban Institute.

Philips, D.L. (1966). The "True" Prevalence of Mental Health in a New England State. *Community Mental Health Journal*, 2, 35–40.

Richardson, H., and Kovner, A. R. (1985). Implementing Swing-Bed Serves in Small Rural Hospitals. *Journal of Rural Health*, 2 (1), 46–60.

Rones, P. L. (1978). Older Men—The Choice between Work and Retirement. *Monthly Labor Review*, 101(11), 3–10

Scheidt, R. J. (1985). The Mental Health of the Aged in Rural Environments. In R. T. Coward and G. R. Lee, eds., *The Elderly in Rural Society: Every Fourth Elder*. New York: Springer Publishing Company, 105–128.

Scheidt, R.J. and Windley, P. G. (1982). Well-being Profiles of Small-Town Elderly in Differing Rural Contexts. *Community Mental Health Journal*, 18, 257–67.

Schooler, K. K. (1975). A Comparison of Rural and Non-rural Elderly on Selected Variables. In R. C. Atchley and T. O. Byerts, eds., *Rural Environments and Aging*. Washington: Gerontological Society of America, 27–42.

Schwab, J., Warheit, G., and Holzer, C. (1974). Mental Health: Rural-Urban Comparison. *Mental Health and Society*, 1, 265–74.

Summers, G. F., and Hirschl, T. A. (1985). Retirees as a Growth Industry. *Rural Development Perspectives*, 1(2), 13–16.

Taietz, P., and Milton, S. (1979). Rural-Urban Differences in the Structure of Services for the Elderly in Upstate New York Counties. *Journal of Gerontology*, 34(3), 429–37.

U.S. Department of Agriculture (1984). *Chartbook of Nonmetro-Metro Trends.*

Washington: U.S. Department of Agriculture, Economic Research Service, Rural Development Research Report No. 43.

U.S. Department of Commerce (1983). *America in Transition: An Aging Society.* Washington: Current Population Reports, Special Studies, Series P–23, No. 128.

Zuiches, J. J., and Brown, D. L. (1978). The changing character of the nonmetro population: 1950–75. In T. R. Ford, ed., *Rural USA: Persistence and Change.* Ames, Iowa: Iowa State University Press, 55–72.

SUMMARY

Life in rural regions of both countries is undergoing significant change. Drastic transformations in farming patterns and the economic bankruptcy of rural trade centers have shifted daily life and residential composition. With those shifts come many problems for the rural elderly and their informal networks as well as greater demands for new service delivery programs. A. Martin Matthews pointed to the policy questions related to transportation needs that have captured the attention of many researchers. A consistent, if somewhat implicit, implication of different studies is the need to devise models of transportation for the impaired aged—models that are acceptable in design to local rural areas.

Designing access strategies and assuring the availability of formal supports to enhance informal resources are issues that continue to dominate rural gerontology. According to the authors' evaluation, neither country has found an acceptable solution. The shifting demography of each country and the resulting configurations of population aging must be accurately projected and applied if policies and programs are to have long-term relevance to the rural aged.

The United States federal government has given special attention to the rural elderly on a sporadic basis. Special federal grant initiatives targeted for rural areas have been instrumental in funding some assessments of need and problem identification projects, but fewer funds have been available for permanent program development. The state-by-state impact of cyclical grants has been uneven, at best. Some states have been effective in building permanent programs originally started on a special federal grant. Many more states have had to drop innovative demonstration programs because no state funding was available to replace federal funds and to continue such programs.

Provincial governments face the responsibility of designing policies and programs that can accommodate great rural diversity. While many provinces have successfully balanced distribution of hospital and special facility beds in the rural areas, they have been less successful in distributing other resources. Reimbursement for assistance in daily life activity is very uneven within and between provinces. However, service solutions must be found to sustain informal community resources for frail elderly individuals.

Some similar policy development issues face both countries regarding policy decisions about how to best serve very high risk rural subgroups. There is a need to anticipate accurately the future pattern of retirement relocation from urban to a rural residency. Preretirement preparation, under whatever sponsorship, should address the many potential changes and contingency conditions involved in the change of retirement residency. Rural practitioners in Canada and the United States are serving greater numbers of elderly who "go to the village" only to find the village an unsuccessful retirement option once they become ill or frail. At present, many Canadian practitioners are dealing with large caseloads of elderly men who outnumber older women in their areas. Other small towns are filled with inmigrated elderly widows. Agencies are having to provide formal supports to substitute for nonexistent informal networks. Research on the impact of environmental change and on the continuity of environmental history should be noted as immediate research priorities for Canadian and United States rural gerontologists.

Increasingly, rural areas in the United States are bringing the "free market" strategy into play as a resolution for underserved rural areas. That strategy is also being applied for long-term care options, both institutional and community-based. Profit-based strategies will find little acceptance in Canada as compared to the United States, given the different health and welfare systems. On the other hand, Canada faces a need to find cost-efficient methods to meet rural elderly service needs. A commitment among all providers to share innovative approaches to serve the rural elderly is overdue. A solution might be for each province to identify its most creative models and then subject them to assessment and outcome evaluations that would answer questions about transferability to other rural sectors throughout the country. Interstate sharing is equally important in the United States. Greater effort should be made in both countries to exchange information about successful cost-effective rural service models.

VI
AGING VETERANS

The historically differential involvement of Canada and the United States in the arena of international conflict has set the stage for differing veteran cohorts in the two countries. In both countries commitments to providing financial stability and health care to those who have served in the military is a nonnegotiable value. This commitment is expressed differently on the basis both of the broader social history of each country and the variations in veteran cohorts. Specifically, World War I veterans are still of major concern in Canada as they constitute over one-third of the population of Canadian males over the age of 84. Veterans of the Korean conflict and the post-Korean era are a very small group as Canada was not involved in the Vietnam War. Therefore, the age structure of veterans in the United States parallels the age structure of the total population much more closely than is the case in Canada.

Another major difference exists because of the universal publicly insured health care system in Canada. In other words, Canadian veterans and nonveterans who receive care in the medical and institutional portions of the health care system receive the same services and, in most instances, at little or no expense to the individual. The noninstitutional care system varies across Canada, but is equally accessible to veterans and nonveterans. By contrast, in the United States nonveterans are financially responsible for all health care not covered by Medicare or Medicaid or their private insurance policies. In the latter milieu U.S. veterans have a great financial advantage and distinctly better access to care as compared to their nonveteran peers.

The chapter by Margery Boyce and Ellen M. Gee as well as the one by Philip G. Weiler set the stage by developing the organizational history of services and care to veterans within the social context of each country. This is further developed by discussions of the organizational structures in the U.S. Veterans Administration (VA) and the Canadian Department of Veterans Affairs (DVA). These authors address the special nature of the aging veteran population in the discussions contained in the demographic sections of their chapters.

Boyce and Gee note that virtually all Canadian veterans are currently over the age of 49. This has led DVA to being concerned essentially about older males. By contrast, Weiler points out that almost 40% of U.S. veterans are under the age of 45, precluding the concentration of concern by the VA with the older veteran, let alone older males.

An ironic outcome of this disproportionate age structure of veterans in Canada has been to augment provincial health care and national pension programs with a broad range of services for aging veterans; but to ignore research about aging, aging males and more particularly aging veterans. Boyce and Gee are able to draw on more examples of service utilization by aging veterans and to discuss more services within the Departmental mandate and services of Veteran Non-governmental Organizations than is Weiler. On the other hand, Weiler is able to discuss more research, education and clinical examples with a geriatric/gerontological focus that are internal to the Administration and funded by the Administration than is possible for the Canadian authors. Even though the services may not be as comprehensive in the United States, the services that exist have been more thoroughly evaluated than have Canadian services.

The research commitment in the U.S. is driven, at least in part, by a desire to be better prepared for future older veteran cohorts, specifically the aging of veterans of the post-Korean era, including those who served in Vietnam. It is also implicitly assumed that the United States may be involved in future international armed conflicts and that a state of readiness must be maintained. Canada implicitly assumes that its participation in armed conflict will be more limited and sees less specific advantage to preparing for future cohorts of aging veterans. The tragedy of this perspective is of two kinds: first, the programs specifically developed by DVA are being inadequately evaluated so neither DVA nor others (including the VA) can benefit from DVA's experience; and second, a unique opportunity to study older Canadian males and their aging is being lost.

Both the VA in the United States and DVA in Canada have had much more experience in dealing with males and little attention has been paid to the needs of female veterans, spouses of veterans, and widows of veterans. Certainly in Canada, concern about these women must become a major priority as suggested by Boyce and Gee. Over the next several decades the number of veterans will decrease very rapidly but the number of widows will actually increase. In the United States this relationship is not as dramatic until after the turn of the century, but Weiler notes that the VA needs to know more about veterans' spouses. He identifies spouses as the women who are and will have to continue providing most of the informal support and care to aging veterans.

CHAPTER 11

Aging Veterans in Canada

A. Margery Boyce and Ellen M. Gee

INTRODUCTION

Before 1918, legislation relating to veterans was of an ad hoc nature, although the years spanning World War I saw significant activity in the implementation of policies and services designed to aid veterans, particularly in the health area. By the end of 1918, a package of rehabilitative assistance to veterans of World War I had been developed, marking the beginning of an integrated program in Canada. While improvements were made during the interwar years (particularly in pension legislation and in policies concerning health and rehabilitation), 1944 and 1945 were benchmark years. In 1944 a department solely concerned with veterans (the Department of Veterans Affairs or DVA) was created . Initially, the administrative activities of DVA were divided between two branches, Treatment Services and Welfare Services, while pensions were the responsibility of a separate agency, the Pension Commission. In 1945 the Veterans Rehabilitation Act was passed, embodying a number of core principles regarding aid to veterans; it became widely known as the Veterans Charter (Veterans Affairs, 1947).

Since the end of World War II, a number of important changes have occurred: bureaucratic reorganization, including the merger of Treatment Services and Welfare Services under one jurisdiction—Veterans Services; the development of five regional offices designed to eliminate, as much as possible, bureaucratic work at the local level; and the relocation of the head office from Ottawa, Ontario, to Charlottetown, Prince Edward Island; improvements in the structure of financial benefits; and the gradual transfer of departmental hospitals to the provinces. Despite this last change, DVA has played an important role in fostering geriatric care in Canada.

Table 11.1
Eligible Groups of Clients, December 1984

Eligible Groups of Clients, December 1984	
Eligibility Groups	Number of Clients
War Veterans Allowance (WVA)	50,356
Civilian War Allowance (CWA)	3,982
Canadian Pension Commission (CPC)	99,684
Spouses and Widows of WVA/CWA recipients	36,327
Spouses and Widows of CPC recipients	41,771
Orphans, Siblings, Parents (CPC)	1,038
Near-recipients	23,611

Source: Veterans Affairs Canada.

Description of Veterans Affairs Canada

At present DVA consists of four branches and one division: the Pensions, Health, and Social Programs Branch; the Veterans Land Administration Branch; the Finance, Personnel, and Administration Branch; the Field Operations Branch; and the Audit and Evaluation Division. DVA is a component of the Veterans Affairs Portfolio, along with the Veterans Appeal Board and the Bureau of Pensions Advocates.

Seven major eligibility groups of clients are served by DVA. See Table 11.1 for the populations receiving major income-related benefits.

Veterans in receipt of a disability pension (CPC) receive compensation for disability or aggravation of a preenlistment disability incurred during, or attributable to, wartime military service. Pensions are also awarded under the same conditions for military service in peacetime. Civilians may receive pensions from the commission for service during World War II, e.g., Canadian merchant seamen, Royal Canadian Mounted Police, overseas welfare workers, etc. Compensation for prisoners of war is also covered.

Veterans receiving a War Veterans Allowance (WVA) are persons, or their dependents, who meet service-eligibility requirements and who, because of age or incapacity, are unable to work and have insufficient income as determined by a modified income test. An allowance may be awarded to a male veteran at 60 and a female veteran at age 55. The same benefits apply for persons receiving Civilian War Allowances (CWA), subject to certain conditions of length and area of service.

Spouses and widows (CPC) may be awarded pensions if the injury or disease which caused the disability or death of the veteran was attributable to, or incurred during, wartime service. Spouses and widows (WVA/CWA) may be awarded an allowance, provided the deceased veteran was eligible.

Widows qualify at age 55 whereas widowers qualify at age 60. Also, orphans, siblings, and parents may receive a pension (CPC) if they were dependent upon the deceased veteran.

Health-related benefits and services are also available. Institutional care
is available for recipients of CPC, WVA, and near-recipients in departmental
and nondepartmental facilities; CWA recipients are eligible for nondepartmental institutional care only. Veterans with theater of war service are
eligible for departmental institutions. Health care team assessments are
available to all veterans (and their spouses) who qualify for other benefits.
The Veterans' Independence Program (discussed in a later section), which
was established in 1981, provides services for clients whose self-sufficiency
is at risk. This program currently is available to CPC pensioners whose
health care needs are related to their pensionable disabilities, to war disa-
bililty pensioners 65 years of age and older who also receive WVA, and to
WVA recipients 75 years of age and over. Other health-related benefits are
available, including Programs-of-Choice (doctors, dentists, pharmacists, po-
diatrists, etc.), transportation related to health care needs, special equipment,
and home adaptations.

DEMOGRAPHICS

This section describes the demographic characteristics of the Canadian
veteran population. This population is a heterogeneous one, with a large
percentage not eligible for, or in need of, assistance from Veterans Affairs.
For the purposes of this chapter, we are treating the veteran population as
totally male. This assumption creates slightly inflated values in the estimation of veterans as a percentage of the total male population.

Population and Age Composition of Veterans

In 1985 there were approximately 675,700 veterans in Canada. While
this figure represents less than 3 percent of the total Canadian population,
it accounts for nearly one-quarter of the Canadian male population aged
50 and over. Virtually all Canadian veterans are 50 years of age and over,
as the Korean conflict was the last war in which Canada participated. The
average age of all Canadian veterans is 65, with average ages varying depending upon war involvement: the average age of World War I veterans
is 88; of World War II veterans, 65; and of Korean War veterans, 56
(Veterans Affairs Canada, 1985c).

Approximately 24 percent of the total male population aged 50 and over
consists of veterans. However, the percentage within various age groupings
differs significantly. (See Table 11.2.) Veterans comprise substantial portions
of the population aged 60–64 and 65–69 (over 44 percent in both cases)

Table 11.2
Veteran Population by Five-Year Age Groupings and Percent of Male Population, Canada, 1985

Veteran Population by 5-Year Age Groupings and Percent of Male Population, Canada, 1985		
Age	Number of Veterans	Percent of Male Population
-50	1,691	-
50-54	22,959	3.7
55-59	87,459	14.7
60-64	234,356	44.3
65-69	179,294	44.2
70-74	85,188	26.2
75-79	30,987	14.9
80-84	13,602	12.0
85-89	14,799	33.0
90+	5,306	26.4
Total	675,641	23.6

Source: Veterans Affairs Canada and Demography Division, Statistics Canada.

and of the population aged 85–89 (33 percent). In contrast, veterans form a small portion of the male population aged 75–79 (14.9 percent) and 80–84 (12.0 percent). There are basically two population groups of veterans. This uneven age distribution reflects the relationship between the timing of Canadian war involvement and individual ages, i.e., men who are now aged 75–84 were generally too young to participate in World War I and too old for World War II.

Barring Canadian participation in another war, the size of the veteran population will decrease from 675,641 in 1985 to 150,288 in 2006, a reduction of approximately 78 percent. Accompanying this reduction in size will be a significant aging of the veteran population. (See Table 11.3.) These Veterans Affairs Canada projections are based on the following assumptions: (a) no outmigration, and (b) 1971 age-specific mortality rates will apply over the period. It is our opinion that the mortality assumption overestimates the decline in the veteran population.

Less than one-half of veterans are aged 65 and over, with only 5 percent aged 80 and over. By 1991 the percentage of the veteran population aged 65 and over will increase dramatically to approximately 88 percent, reflecting the movement of large numbers of World War II veterans into socially defined old age. By 2001 all Canadian veterans will be aged 65 and over. The percentage of veterans that are *very old*, defined as 80 and over, will increase steadily after 1991 so that by 2006, a full 77 percent will be in this category.

Geographical Distribution of Veterans

Nearly 42 percent of veterans reside in Ontario, Canada's most populous province. The remainder are fairly evenly distributed across Canada, al-

Table 11.3
Veteran Population by Five-Year Age Groupings and Veteran Population as a Percentage of Total Male Population by five-Year Age Groupings, 1985–2006

Veteran Population by 5-Year Age Groupings, and Veteran Population as a Percentage of Total Male Population by 5-Year Age Groupings, 1985–2006

Age	Number of Veterans					Percentage of Total Male Population				
	1985	1991	1996	2001	2006	1985	1991	1996	2001	2006
50-54	22,959	0	0	0	0	3.7	0	0	0	0
55-59	87,459	17,798	0	0	0	14.7	3.0	0	0	0
60-64	234,356	47,594	16,203	0	0	44.3	8.4	2.8	0	0
65-69	179,274	193,282	40,986	14,005	0	44.2	39.2	7.8	2.6	0
70-74	85,188	156,578	156,243	32,719	11,238	26.2	42.8	36.1	7.0	2.4
75-79	30,987	71,459	114,862	113,766	23,387	14.9	27.2	39.1	32.6	6.2
80-84	13,602	21,842	45,149	72,274	70,792	12.0	15.1	25.2	35.6	29.4
85-89	14,799	6,835	10,923	22,624	36,006	33.0	11.9	14.9	24.7	34.5
90+	5,306	5,305	3,290	4,422	8,865	26.4	27.5	14.3	15.1	24.2
Total	673,950	520,693	387,656	259,810	150,288	23.6	16.5	11.0	6.5	3.4
%65+	48.7	87.4	95.8	100.0	100.0	29.5	33.9	24.3	12.1	8.4
%80+	5.0	6.5	15.3	38.2	77.0	18.8	15.4	21.5	30.6	30.3

Source: Veterans Affairs Canada and Statistics Canada, Demography Division.

though the western regions contain proportionately more veterans than do the eastern regions. (See Table 11.4.) It is noteworthy that the geographic distribution of veterans does not correspond closely with the geographic and age distribution of the total male population. Veterans are somewhat overrepresented in all regions except Quebec, where they are greatly underrepresented. Only 12 percent of veterans live in Quebec, a province containing 25 percent of the male population aged 50 and over. Migration flows may account for some of the lack of geographical correspondence between the veteran population and the total male population. But the most significant factor was French Canadian hesitation to participate in World War II, as many French Canadians opposed the principle of conscription. When compulsory legislation was enacted late in the war, their involvement became more significant. Resistance to involvement in World War II was not limited to French Canadians. Some other ethnic groups were hesitant, but our data do not identify these groups, which are less geographically concentrated than the French Canadians.

The veteran population is expected to shift steadily westward from 1985 to 2006. Substantial losses will be experienced by Quebec (from 12.4 percent to 8.4 percent) while large gains will occur in the Pacific region (from 16.7 percent to 23.5 percent). This westward shift is based on the assumption that there will be a continuation of past trends whereby some portion of veterans move west, as they age, particularly to the Pacific region.

Population and Age Composition of Widows

In 1985 there were approximately 282,800 widows of veterans. A small portion of surviving spouses are widowers, but our focus is on widows only. The number of widows is expected to increase steadily to 1996, when it will approach 329,000, and then decline to approximately 323,000 in 2001. (See Table 11.5.) Overall, from 1985 to 2001 the widow population will increase by about 14 percent. This increase reflects both the death of veterans and the longer life expectancy of women. These Veterans Affairs Canada projections are based on the following assumptions: a) no outmigration, b) 1971 age-specific mortality rates for males and females will apply over the period, and c) widows are, on average, three years younger than their spouses. A correction factor for nonmarried veterans is applied. It is our opinion that the mortality assumptions underestimate the increase in the widow population.

The widow population will also age over the period. Nearly 40 percent of widows are under the age of 65. By 2001 virtually all widows will be over 65 years.

Table 11.4
Geographical Distribution of Veteran Population, 1985–2006

Geographical Distribution of Veteran Population, 1985–2006

Region	Number of Veterans (1985)	Percent of Veterans				
		1985	1991	1996	2001	2006
Atlantic	66,100	9.8	9.8	9.8	9.3	8.3
Quebec	83,650	12.4	11.5	10.7	9.7	8.4
Ontario	281,900	41.7	41.6	41.3	39.6	37.3
Prairies	131,100	19.4	19.9	20.3	21.4	22.6
Pacific	112,700	16.7	17.2	17.8	20.0	23.5
Total	675,700[a]	100.0	100.0	99.9	100.0	100.0

Source: Calculated from data supplied by Veterans Affairs, Canada, and from data in Veterans Affairs Canada (1985, p. 2) and Statistics Canada (1985, p. 200).
*Numbers are rounded to nearest hundred.

Table 11.5
Widows of Veterans Population by Five-Year Age Groupings, and Widows of Veterans Population as a Percentage of Total Female Population by five-Year Age Groupings, 1985–2001

Widows of Veterans Population by 5-Year Age Groupings, and Widows of Veterans Population as a Percentage of Total Female Population by 5-Year Age Groupings, 1985–2001

Age	Numbers of Widows of Veterans				Percent of Total Female Population			
	1985	1991	1996	2001	1985	1991	1996	2001
-55	8,951	1,125	0	0	–	–	–	–
55-64	96,981	51,124	8,901	2,389	8.0	4.2	7.1	0.2
65-69	46,762	84,872	62,006	9,714	9.8	14.8	10.7	1.7
70-74	29,811	73,093	107,060	77,200	7.3	16.0	20.2	14.3
75-79	21,631	43,414	81,909	119,160	7.3	11.9	20.4	25.4
80-84	37,953	22,121	40,122	76,109	20.0	9.1	13.7	23.3
85+	40,802	37,245	28,798	38,893	26.8	19.1	11.8	12.8
Total	282,828	312,994	328,796	323,465	10.0	10.2	10.0	8.9
%65+	62.6	83.3	97.3	99.3	11.6	14.2	15.6	14.5

Source: Calculated from data supplied by Veterans Canada and in Statistics Canada (1985).

Table 11.6
Veteran Population and Widows of Veterans Population, by Age, 1985–2001

Age	Number of Veterans			Number of Widows		
	1985	2001	% Change	1985	2001	% Change
55–64	321,815	0	−100.0	96,981	2,389	− 97.5
65–69	179,294	14,005	− 92.2	46,762	9,714	− 79.2
70–74	85,188	32,719	− 61.6	29,811	77,200	+159.0
75–79	30,987	113,766	+267.1	21,631	119,160	+450.9
80–84	13,602	72,274	+431.3	37,953	76,109	+100.5
85+	20,105	27,046	+ 34.5	40,802	38,893	− 4.7
Total	650,991	259,810	− 60.1	273,940	323,465	+ 18.1

Source: Calculated from data supplied by Veterans Affairs Canada.

Population and Age Composition of Widows and Veterans Compared to Total Female Population Aged 55 and Over

Widows of veterans comprise 10 percent of the total female population aged 55 and over. This percentage is expected to decline slightly to approximately 9 percent by 2001. The growth in the population of widows of veterans will nearly match the growth in the comparably aged total female Canadian population over the rest of this century.

Comparative Demographic Trends: Veterans and Widows of Veterans, 1985–2001

The most striking differences concern projected trends in population size. Whereas the veteran population aged 55 and over is expected to decrease by 60.1 percent between 1985 and 2001, the widows of veterans population is expected to increase by 18.1 percent over the same period. (See Table 11.6.) This difference is a reflection of the fact that as married veterans die, they leave behind widows who have a longer life expectancy because of their younger age and the lower mortality levels of women.

The two groups share trends regarding age composition. The age distribution of both the veteran population and the widow population will become older. For both groups there will be a substantial reduction of numbers in age categories under 70 and a large increase in the population aged 75–84.

Table 11.7
Veteran In-Patients at Departmental and Nondepartmental Institutions, by Diagnostic Category, 1985

Veteran In-patients at Departmental and non-Departmental Institutions, by Diagnostic Category, 1985

Primary Diagnostic Category	Number of in-patients	Percent
Cardiovascular Disease	918	23
Respiratory Diseases	798	20
Cerebrovascular Disease	718	18
Diseases of the Digestive System	519	13
Psychiatric Disorders	200	5
Other Diseases/Miscellaneous	838	21
Total	3991	100

Source: Data are estimates supplied by W. J. Holloway, director of Health Care Facilities.

Health Characteristics

The March 1985 patient census undertaken by Veterans Affairs Canada indicated that 3,991 veterans were institutionalized. Only three departmental institutions are in existence at the present time—Ste. Anne's Hospital (Quebec), Rideau Veterans Home (Ontario), and Saskatoon Veterans Home (Saskatchewan). In total, they house 1,160 veterans, with the majority (953) at Ste. Anne's Hospital. In addition, there are approximately 2,830 patients residing in nondepartmental institutions (both contract and hospital-of-choice facilities) (Veterans Affairs Canada, 1985b).

A diagnostic breakdown of the veteran patient population in both departmental and nondepartmental institutions is provided in Table 11.7. These data should be taken as rough estimates only. According to Dr. J. A. McDonell (1985), there has been a trend away from collecting diagnostic information since so many patients have multiple conditions. As would be expected with an older male patient population, diseases of the heart and vascular system comprise the largest category. Also, the 5 percent figure for psychiatric disorders conforms to the national average. However, it has been noted (W. J. Holloway, 1985) that a secondary or tertiary diagnosis of alcohol-related problems is very prevalent among the veteran patient population. Similarly, the incidence of respiratory disease is substantial, related to high rates of cigarette smoking among the veteran population (Holloway, 1985). Thus the particular configuration of health problems among many veteran in-patients reflects a life-style in which smoking and drinking played a prominent role.

Unfortunately, no health-related data are available on other categories of veterans, e.g., those utilizing community health services and those requiring no special medical attention. In referring to inpatients, we do not mean to imply that all or even most veterans choose life-styles having deleterious health consequences.

Economic Characteristics

The eligible veteran population may receive income benefits from DVA (WVA/CWA) and/or the CPC, as well as benefits available to the general population. (See Chapter 3 of this book.) Additional pension-related benefits may be paid to those who are totally disabled or have an exceptional incapacity. Also, special compensation is payable to those who were prisoners of war.

At the end of 1984, 84,256 persons received WVA: 50, 356 veterans; 33,345 widow(er)s; and 55 orphans. Persons in receipt of CWA totalled 4,469: 2,982 civilians; 1,477 widow(er)s; and 10 orphans. Effective April 1, 1985 maximum monthly benefits were $660.99 for a single or widowed person, with higher amounts available depending on marital status and number of dependents. A total of 142,193 persons received a disability pension (CPC). As of April 1, 1985, the monthly rate for a single person varied from $1,146.82 to $57.34, depending upon the severity of disability. Rates are adjusted upward depending upon the marital status and number of dependents (Veterans Affairs Canada, 1985b, Section 1–15).Disability pensions are tax-free and no additional income data are required in order to qualify.

Because of the lack of data, especially for disability pensioners (CPC), no information exists on the income levels of eligible veterans. The only group for whom income data are available is the approximately 85,000 persons in receipt of WVA/CWA, who are, by definition, poor. As can be seen in Table 11.8 the average monthly income is low.

CURRENT POLICY AND PROGRAMS

Health Programs

Acute care. Eligible veterans were assured priority access in hospital transfer agreements. The Hospital-of-Choice Program made provision for acute and rehabilitative care in facilities convenient to the veteran. In 1984–85, a total of 106,353 patient-days were purchased.

Long-term care. As veterans age, a shift to long-term care is evident. In 1984–85 518,922 patient days were purchased for chronic medical care and 67,878 patient days for chronic psychiatric care in hospital facilities. For veterans unable to function independently in the community, a total of

Table 11.8
Average Monthly Income and Sources of Income, Clients Receiving War Veterans Allowance/Civilian War Allowance, 1985

Type of Client	Average Monthly Income ($)	Sources of Income (%)				
		WVA/CWA	CPC	CPP/QPP[a]	OAS/GIS[b]	Other
Veteran	883	59.5	3.8	6.0	21.8	8.9
Widow(er) of Veteran	688	38.2	1.4	9.9	45.8	4.6
Civilian	927	50.8	0.1	5.4	38.7	5.0
Widow(er) of Civilian	700	41.7	–	7.3	48.6	2.3

Source: Calculated from data supplied by Veterans Affairs Canada.
[a]Canada Pension Plan/Quebec Pension Plan
[b]Old Age Security/Guaranteed Income Supplement

425,331 patient days were purchased for extended nursing and supervised residential care. Establishing Veterans Care Units is gradually being superseded by the use of local nursing homes and homes for the aged.

Other long-term care programs. The first Canadian geriatric day hospital began at Deer Lodge Hospital with support from Health and Welfare Canada, Veterans Affairs Canada, and the Royal Canadian Legion. The success in maintaining long-term care patients in the day hospital program and its extension to home care services provided the model upon which the Veterans' Independence Program was based.

No data are available concerning the number of eligible veterans currently participating in day hospital programs, since most veterans are served through nondepartmental facilities.

Recreational programs, established in the convalescent centers after WWII, were important for rehabilitation and in activating older persons. As a result, DVA augmented recreational activities in two contract hospitals and funded Canadian Red Cross Arts and Crafts Programs in twelve others at a cost in excess of 2 million dollars in 1985–86.

Pastoral care service, provided on a contractual basis, has been maintained by DVA. This service has fostered interest in palliative care and a holistic approach to health care that recognizes spiritual needs.

Other health care programs. While Canadian veterans benefit from Canada's universal Medicare Program, a substantial number of health-related benefits are in place to ensure access for eligible veterans to specialist care and other services not fully covered by provincial health plans. Artificial limbs and other devices to ensure maintenance of functional capacity were provided through the Prosthetic/Orthotist-of-Choice Program at a cost of

6 million dollars for some 5,000 services in 1984–85. Dental care is available through 16 Departmental Clinics and a Dentist-of-Choice Program. War disability pensioners (CPC) receive dental services related to their pensioned condition while persons in other eligibility groups may also receive dental services through the same sources. In 1984–85, 28,710 visits were made to departmental clinics and 25,726 claims were made under the Dentist-of-Choice Program at a total cost of 7 million dollars.

Through the Pharmacist-of-Choice Program pharmacists bill DVA directly for prescribed drugs, other medications, and supplies required by disability pensioners and low-income veteran clients. In 1984–85, 1.3 million prescriptions were dispensed at a cost of 21 million dollars. The Special Equipment and Home Adaptation Program provides a broad range of devices to facilitate independent living or to compensate for the effects of aging by adapting the home environment. This program cost 3 million dollars in 1984–85. Treatment, transportation, and related allowances cover the cost of out-of-pocket expenses related to medical examination or treatment while the veteran is in hospital, is an out-patient, or attends a health care appointment. This program cost 7 million dollars in 1984–85.

All veterans and their dependents may receive counseling for problems related to changing social and economic conditions. Information about and assistance in accessing Veterans Affairs programs and other community resources are provided. This service generally is provided by Departmental Counselors based in the District Offices. In 1984–85 they made approximately 45,000 home visits at a cost in salaries of 7 million dollars.

Veterans' Independence Program

With the aging of the veteran population and the trend away from institutional care, the DVA in 1981 established the Veterans' Independence Program. The primary purpose of the program is to provide long-term care in the community, preferably in the veterans' home. It is aimed at encouraging and assisting eligible veterans to maintain independent living. The pilot phase limited eligibility to pensioners where need was related to their pensionable disability. The elements of the program were ambulatory health care services, which included user fees, meals, transportation to community specialist services, e.g., day hospitals (to a maximum of $500 per year per recipient); home care, including direct patient care, nursing care, housekeeping and groundskeeping (maximum $4,300 per year); adult residential care, including personal and supervisory care, assistance with the activities of daily living, and room and board (maximum $60.20 per day less a patient contribution of $8.00 per day); and nursing home intermediate care providing direct nursing care by qualified staff (with the same limits as adult residential care).

Phased-in expansions of the program were to serve veterans perceived as "most in need." In late 1984 war disability pensioners aged 65 and over who also receive WVA (i.e., older, disabled, and poor veterans), and WVA recipients 75 years of age and over (i.e., the poor and old) were included. A new element was added, i.e., transportation for the social activities of daily living (maximum $600 per year).

In the fiscal year 1984–85 approximately 5,500 persons received benefits under the Veterans' Independence Program at a cost of about 6 million dollars. By March 31, 1986, 9,515 veterans or 10 percent of the eligible population was receiving benefits.

Other Health and Social Services

Assistance Fund. In 1949 the Assistance Fund was initiated to prevent WVA recipients from experiencing inadequacies in such basic commodities as housing, food, clothing, etc. Since 1980 this fund has provided single cash grants of up to $500 per year to WVA/CWA recipients for emergencies which cannot be met from other sources. In 1984–85, 6,250 grants were given, with a total expenditure in excess of 1.5 million dollars.

Veteran Insurance and Estates Program. The Veteran Insurance Program was enacted to assist veterans who would not qualify for regular life insurance coverage because of war-related health conditions. The Estates Program administrates the estates of those veterans who die while receiving hospital treatment through the department. The role of the department has been to assist dependents and widows to bring estates to a satisfactory and inexpensive conclusion.

Benevolent Funds. Funds have been raised by organizations created to assist veterans and their dependents whose financial and social needs could not be adequately met through departmental programs. The Army Benevolent Fund is made up of profits derived from army canteens and clubs operating during the Second World War. It provides financial assistance to veterans of World War II or their dependents for unexpected needs arising from sickness, accident, etc. This fund also operates the Canadian Army Welfare Fund providing similar assistance to servicemen and their dependents who served in the Canadian Army from October 1, 1946 to February 1, 1968. Ex-service personnel from other branches may receive similar help through the Royal Canadian Navy Benevolent Fund and the Royal Canadian Air Force Benevolent Fund.

The Last Post Fund provides for burial for all ex-service personnel who otherwise would be the responsibility of the public welfare system. First organized and supported by voluntary contributions, it has received an annual federal grant since 1922. The Department of Veterans Affairs administers the fund.

Services Provided by Veterans Nongovernmental Organizations

The role of veterans organizations in influencing the development of Canadian public policy cannot be underestimated. When the DVA was created in 1944, it gave substance to the view expressed by organizations representing ex-service personnel that all veteran legislation should be the responsibility of one ministry. The Veterans Charter (Veterans affairs, 1947) was a cooperative venture with veterans organizations playing a prominent part in its development.

The Royal Canadian Legion is the largest veterans organization in Canada. While its broad accomplishments are too numerous to list, those which have influenced developments in aging are highlighted.

Advocacy in the areas of pension reform and welfare assistance has influenced improvements in income support and assisted in broadening eligibility. By pointing out difficulties experienced by veterans and their dependents in accessing benefits, it has aided in creating more efficient methods of processing claims for pensions and allowances. Employment of older veterans has been encouraged. The Legion has assisted widows and veterans not eligible for veteran's benefits to find suitable employment.

Housing has been an area in which the Royal Canadian Legion has shown leadership. Veterans ineligible for benefits were assisted in locating suitable foster home accommodation and in obtaining placement. Starting in 1956, the legion developed more than 3,000 units of low-cost housing for older veterans and their widows. These housing projects began to be phased out in the 1970s as the provinces built more modern facilities of a similar type.

Education and training in geriatrics have been encouraged by the establishment of legion grants for postgraduate study in geriatric medicine and nursing. Geriatric Assessment Units have been developed in contract institutions with ongoing legion support. At the community level a number of legion branches operate Meals-on-Wheels programs, and provide transportation services and recreational activities for veterans.

The War Amputations of Canada represents veterans whose war injuries resulted in amputation of limbs. Financed mainly through the sale of automobile key tags throughout Canada, its main objectives are member education and advocacy on their behalf. Its staff assists veterans in preparing and defending pension claims.

Numerous other veterans organizations exist, bringing together persons who share unique experiences, e.g., the Sir Arthur Pearson Association of War Blinded, the Hong Kong Veterans Association, associations representing former prisoners of war, and those who received reconstructive surgery.

All these organizations advocate governmental support through pensions, allowances, and improved health care, and they serve as models for self-help groups. With the exception of the legion, they comprise a national coalition, the National Council of Veterans Organizations.

Initiatives Within Veterans Affairs Canada

While the needs of the rapidly increasing numbers of older veterans and their spouses and widows were raised by both veterans organizations and staff of Veterans Affairs Canada, the potential for DVA leadership in the field of aging was not widely recognized. In fact, the department's unique role in serving veterans was seen as limited, given the advancing age of its clientele. With the move of the department's head office, a hiatus in planning for gerontological services resulted. Two scenarios are possible: (1) services to veterans will continue to be integrated with those for all Canadians; or (2) Veterans Affairs Canada will assume a leadership role in the development of services to an aging population client base.

Revising Policy to Meet the Needs of Aging Veterans

Recognizing that the aging of its clients made it more difficult to access required services, DVA moved to reduce administration at the local level and to improve availability and accessibility of services. DVA transferred administrative responsibilities to the newly created regions and merged Treatment and Welfare Services into a new branch, Veterans Services. In 1986 that branch was merged with the Canada Pension Commission to form the Pension, Health, and Social Programs Branch. Colocation of services was brought about with district offices established where they would be most accessible, e.g., in shopping centers.

Line workers, called *counselors*, were provided in-house training to become familiar with multi-disciplinary assessment. The department adopted the principle of supporting the aging veteran to maintain independent living outside institutions. All counselors were encouraged to participate in gerontology training programs with the department assuming responsibility for costs of tuition, travel, and accommodation.

Planning in Concert with Provincial Governments

The terms of hospital transfer agreements with provincial governments varied from province to province. In effect, DVA accepted provincial standards for long-term care.

With the development of the Veterans' Independence Program, a somewhat different principle was established. While most provinces had developed home care and home support services, comprehensiveness varied across and within provinces. Further, most provincial home care services, initially developed to reduce demands on acute care hospital services, were often limited to providing short-term support. DVA wanted to ensure that its clients would be served equitably wherever they lived and was aware that most would require services over a long period of time. While avoiding duplication, the Veterans' Independence Program was designed to be comprehensive with services provided by the department if they did not exist elsewhere.

Close cooperation was developed with provincial and municipal health and social service personnel to publicize and coordinate the services available to eligible veterans. However, a recognition that a number of veterans might "fall between the cracks" led the department to explore methods to improve its delivery system.

A Comprehensive Service Delivery System

The health and social services system within Canada is a complex interaction of institutions, programs, and services developed and provided under various auspices—governmental, nongovernmental, nonprofit and profit-making. A knowledge of the boundaries of each segment of the system is necessary to ensure that clients are well served. Contacts, linkages, and knowledge of regional differences and points of access are all crucial to avoid unnecessary delays, duplication, and communication problems.

DVA counselors are entering a new era. Within the past five years a plan has been developed to introduce case management, to increase the effectiveness of counseling interventions, and to improve interagency and intergovernmental cooperation.

Community health nurses have been employed in all regional and district offices and physician services have been increased. The services of occupational and physiotherapists, and other health care professionals, have been increased to ensure that multidisciplinary assessment is comprehensive.

Further interdepartmental training initiatives are planned to improve the skills of counselors. The department no longer provides a complete continuum of services, but integrates its services with those of other providers to facilitate access for clients.

ISSUES FOR THE FUTURE

Harmonizing Benefits within Governments

Since low-income Canadians receive the Guaranteed Income Supplement (GIS) to augment the basic Old Age Security at age 65, a number of clients who receive benefits under WVA and CWA cease to receive DVA support at that time. In 1984 approval was given for a harmonization of WVA/CWA with GIS, providing a common definition of income, one income test for clients, and simplified administration. Since WVA and CWA serve as access points to health care programs, the new system guarantees that these benefits are retained.

Transfer of Hospital Facilities

While transfer of the remaining departmental facilities is an ongoing objective, the need to modernize and adapt them and other contract institutions is recognized. Plans have been made to contribute substantial funds to the building of new facilities in cooperation with provincial governments across Canada. Redevelopment plans have been completed for St. Anne's Hospital, Rideau Veterans Home, and Saskatoon Veterans Home. Meanwhile, alternative contractual arrangements are being explored to allow veterans requiring institutional care to be treated in their home communities, closer to families and friends.

Options for Independent Living

Housing. While the original mandate of the Veterans Land Administration has been met, veterans who benefitted are now entering older age categories and the housing stock has grown old and is often difficult to maintain. Preliminary discussions have been held with government departments whose primary responsibilities are in housing to explore cooperative strategies. Group homes, congregate housing, "granny flats," and home sharing are some of the possibilities being explored.

Health promotion and self-care. While the habits acquired over a lifetime may be difficult to change, the opportunity to develop a health promotion strategy for veterans and their spouses is being explored with Health and Welfare Canada. A small pilot project in one DVA district showed potential for dispelling some of the myths and stereotypes about aging, and for motivating older veterans and their spouses to improve dietary and exercise habits (Veterans Affairs, 1983).

The effects of stress on care givers are a concern of DVA since many women have provided continuing care to their veteran spouses over the years. Cooperation with voluntary agencies and government departments will be sought in developing strategies in this regard.

Increasing Emphasis on Widow Needs

As discussed earlier, the number of widows is expected to increase substantially in the coming years, and their age composition will shift upward. These demographic changes pose new challenges for DVA, which has historically served a male client base. Increasingly, DVA will be dealing with an aged, female clientele. As S. Tubb (1985) put it to us, "DVA's last customer will be a woman."

The needs of aged widows differ significantly from the needs of the traditional male veteran population. These women will not have a spouse for physical and emotional support in their later years; the financial situation of older women is worse than that of their male counterparts; and their health is such that they suffer a greater number of chronic conditions than men, although their health problems are of a less life-threatening nature. Thus, in the areas of social support, finances, and health, the department may be required to change its focus to women's issues, or at least ensure that women's needs receive attention from other levels of government.

CONCLUSION

In our opinion the role of Veterans Affairs Canada must take three directions—in the areas of health, in the development of community services, and in research.

The aging of the veteran population means that health care needs will be altered in the future. In the immediate future gaps in home care programs need to be addressed to ensure that unnecessary institutionalization is avoided. These measures include increased housing options and the further expansion of the Veterans' Independence Program.

Dr. Jack McDonell (1985) has pointed to deteriorating mental health as the major health care problem of veterans in the future. Specifically, the incidence of organic brain syndrome, in general, and Alzheimer's disease, in particular, is expected to increase at a greater rate than in the general male population of comparable ages in Canada. McDonell attributes this anticipated trend to the association between organic brain dysfunction and other conditions such as arteriosclerosis and alcohol-related pathologies more prevalent in the institutionalized male veteran population. He also points to an increased need for palliative care as the veteran population ages. In addition, the health needs of women will become an increasing concern for DVA.

Community services of a supportive nature are provided under various auspices in Canada. They are more widely available in urban areas than in rural ones. The goal of maintaining independent living requires that a broad range of services, particularly transportation, meal services, household maintenance, and adult day care will be required in all parts of the country.

It has been our experience while preparing for and writing this chapter that a large gap exists in data and knowledge about the life conditions and needs of veterans. It was impossible to determine how many veterans are in receipt of health benefits from all sources. This results in little appreciation for the role of research in providing a base of information that would be of direct use to clients and critical for departmental planning.

If DVA is to assume a leadership role in the field of aging, then research, and the necessary data, must be a top priority. The department has taken some preliminary steps and is seeking cooperation with other governmental departments to develop a research strategy. Given the present climate of restraint, the department must actively pursue this endeavor. If not, an important reservoir of research information will be untapped, with deleterious consequences for veterans and the society at large.

This research was funded, in part, by Veterans Affairs Canada. However, the opinions and interpretations are those of the authors alone. We would like to thank the following individuals for the help in the preparation of this chapter: W. J. Holloway (director of Health Care Facilities, DVA) and Amanda McDonald (chief, Management Information Systems, DVA) for help with data compilation; S. Tubb (retired senior advisor, Veterans Serives) and Dr. J. A. McDonell (retired medical director, Deer Lodge Hospital, Winnipeg) for providing insights based on their long experience with DVA; Amanda McDonald, G. I. Hurley (former director general, Health and Social Services Division, DVA), and W. D. Mogan (senior director, Health Services Program Directorate, DVA) for providing comments on an earlier draft of this chapter, our co-editors, Betty Havens and Eloise Rathbone-McCuan for their helpful comments and editorial direction, and Donna Popovic (Gerontology Research Centre, Simon Fraser University) for typing this manuscript.

REFERENCES

Holloway, W. J. (1985). Personal communication.

McDonell, J. A. (1985). Personal communication.

Statistics Canada (1985). *Population Projections for Canada, Provinces and Territories, 1984–2006*. Ottawa: Statistics Canada. Catalogue #91–520.

Tubb, S. (1985). Personal communication.

Veterans Affairs (1947). *The Veterans Charter: Acts of the Canadian Parliament to Assist Canadian Veterans*. Ottawa: King's Printer.

Veterans Affairs (1983). *An Evaluation of Health Care for Veterans*. Charlottetown, PEI: St. John's Ambulance Program, Department of Veterans Affairs.

Veterans Affairs (1985a). *Annual Report, 1984–1985*. Veterans Affairs. Charlottetown, P.E.I.:

Veterans Affairs (1985b). *Briefing Book: Minister of Veterans Affairs*. Charlottetown, P.E.I.: Public Affairs Division, Veterans Affairs.

Veterans Affairs (1985b). *Veterans Services: Program Activity and Trends 1984–85*. Charlottetown, P.E.I.: Management Information Systems, Branch Planning and Coordination, Veterans Affairs.

CHAPTER 12

Aging Veterans in the United States

Philip G. Weiler

INTRODUCTION

Established by executive order in July 1930, the Veterans Administration (VA) is the primary agency within the federal government in charge of all veterans affairs. Following World War II the nation's veteran population swelled and Congress extended VA care to poor, nonwar-injured veterans. The Department of Medicine and Surgery was created within the VA in 1946, and the program of affiliating VA hospitals with medical schools was begun. The Veterans Administration, the principal advocate for America's veterans, is now facing a unique challenge in planning and developing services for the increasing number of elder veterans. This profound demographic impact on the VA health care system will be changing its makeup and complexion over the next decades. Realizing that the demographic imperative is affecting the VA system sooner than the general population of the United States, the Veterans Administration has begun to organize to meet the changing needs of the elderly veterans.

Organizational Structure of the Veterans Administration System

The VA's main operating departments are the Department of Veterans Benefits, the Department of Medicine and Surgery, and the Department of Memorial Affairs. The responsibility for caring for the older veteran is primarily in the VA's Department of Medicine and Surgery, which operates the nation's largest integrated health service delivery system. It carries out a congressional mandate to provide high-quality health care to eligible veterans in an efficient and effective manner. In addition to this, the department has responsibilities for research into the causes and treatment of diseases and a significant role in the health care professional education system.

The Department of Medicine and Surgery (U.S. Veterans Administration, 1984) operates 172 hospitals, 99 nursing homes, 16 domiciliaries, and 226 out-patient clinics. To staff these, the department employs over 200,000 persons or 2.2 employees per occupied hospital bed compared to 3.8 in the non-VA sector and had a budget of 9.1 billion dollars for fiscal year 1985. Furthermore, veterans are provided contract care in non-VA hospitals that includes support for care in 45 state veterans' homes and 3 annexes in 33 states. Contract care is care provided in non-VA-owned facilities under contract with the VA for certain services provided to veterans. There are also nearly 1,000 health care professional programs and university health centers affiliated with the VA Health Care System.

The VA Department of Medicine and Surgery consists of three significant administrative units:

1. Office of Academic Affairs: This unit administers the largest national coordinated health professional education training program involving 132 VA health care facilities and 40 outpatient clinics affiliated with over 100 medical and 59 dental schools. In 1981 96,858 health professionals were trained in VA health care facilities, including 25,036 medical health staff and 20,106 medical students.

2. Office of Geriatrics and Extended Care: This office oversees a variety of programs, including the VA Nursing Home Care, Community Nursing Home Care, Domicilary Care, State Home Care (Nursing Home, Domicilary and Hospital), Hospital-based Home Care, Adult Health Care, Residential Care, and the Geriatric Research Educational Clinical Centers (GRECC) program. In addition, pilot hospice programs and geriatric evaluation units are being developed.

3. Office of Professional Services: Training programs are offered which support the ongoing need for professional education and staff development in geriatrics and patient family health education. Programs include geriatric physician fellowships, dentist geriatric fellowships, and other health professional scholarship programs. An Interdisciplinary Team Training in Geriatrics (ITTG) program was established to develop a team of health practitioners with knowledge, skills, and competencies required to provide interdisciplinary team care and leadership in the area of geriatrics. In 1972 Congress established geographically dispersed regional medical education centers to provide continuing education for career personnel in the Department of Medicine and Surgery.

Two other major service departments of the Veterans Administration are the Department of Veterans Benefits and the Department of Memorial Affairs.

1. Department of Veterans Benefits: Congress enacted legislation during World War II to provide benefits to veterans. The Department of Veterans Benefits was established in 1953 to administer the Veterans Benefits Program and assume responsibility for the VA's large compensation and pension program. The purposes of the Department of Veterans Benefits are to assist veterans in readjusting

to civilian life; to administer compensation to veterans and dependents for disabilities or deaths resulting from military service; and to promote other VA benefits and services authorized by Congress. Another program provided by the Department of Veterans Benefits is the Aid and Attendance Program. For eligible veterans additional income is provided to secure regular aid and attendance for the VA patient in a nursing home or home-bound. There are also compensation, pension and other assistance programs.

2. Department of Memorial Affairs: The Department oversees eighty-two national cemeteries and twenty-one VA cemeteries to insure burial space for all veterans, active-duty military personnel, and eligible dependents and to maintain graves in perpetuity. The department operates the National Cemetery System and provides state grants to improve state-operated veterans cemeteries.

Eligibility for Medical Services

The priority of eligibility for medical services is based on several criteria. The first priority consists of veterans with illnesses or injuries incurred or aggravated in service. Second priority is given to veterans with service-connected disabilities who need treatment for ailments not associated with a service-connected condition. Third priority are veterans with nonservice connected conditions who are unable to pay for hospitalization elsewhere. The inability to pay requirement is waived for veterans who are 65 plus or receiving pensions or eligible for Medicaid; former POWs; or requesting medical services for exposure to Agent Orange or nuclear radiation. Of the 28,304,000 veterans alive in 1983, it was estimated that only 10 percent actually used VA facilities. The eligibility of veterans of all ages with non-service-connected conditions was changed with the passage of the Consolidated Omnibus Reconciliation Act of 1985. These veterans must now meet specific income requirements before being eligible for care, as will be discussed later in this chapter.

DEMOGRAPHICS

Demographic and epidemiologic conditions of the aging are affecting the health care system. The aging trend is accelerated in the veteran population (U.S. Veterans Administration, 1984). In 1980 there were 3 million veterans over the age of 65 or 10.5 percent of the veteran population. By 1990 there will be 7.2 million veterans 65 years of age and over or 26.6 percent of the veteran population. In 2020 over 44 percent of the veteran population (7.8 million) will be 65 or older. The number of veterans over 65 will peak in the year 2000 at 9 million while their proportion of the total veteran population will not peak until 2020. As shown in Figure 12.1, the veteran population aggregates in age groups related to service during the major conflicts. There is a steady influx of veterans in peacetime, which is small compared to the number of veterans who served during the major conflicts.

Figure 12.1
Age Distribution of Veteran Population by Period of Service, Millions of Veterans—1983

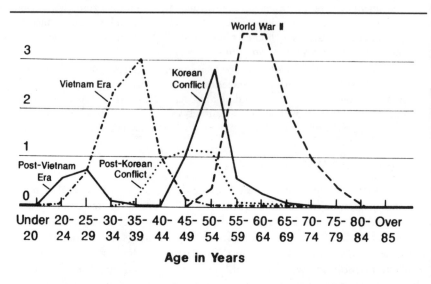

Source: Veterans Population—Office of Reports and Statistics, Research Division, Veterans Administration, December, 1982.

Post–World War II and the Korean conflict veterans are moving into the older age groups. Because of the large number of veterans in the World War II and Korean conflict cohorts, they influence the average age of the entire veteran population as well as the ranks of veterans 65 years and older.

The first wave of veterans served in World War II. Although many World War II veterans are already over the age of 65, 66 percent of this cohort is between 55 and 64. Within the next 10 years the remaining veterans in this cohort will reach age 65. There are 5.3 million veterans in the Korean conflict cohort who are slightly younger. Of the veterans who served only in the Korean conflict, 92 percent are between age 45 and 54 and will reach age 65 around the turn of the century. Other waves of veterans exist after the Korean and Vietnam conflicts. For the most part these veterans are relatively young with about 79 percent falling between the ages of 30 and 44. It will be around 2010 before most of the Vietnam-era veterans reach age 65.

Another observation is depicted in Figure 12.2. As a result of the size of the veteran cohort in the Korean conflict and World War II, veterans over 65 will represent a growing proportion of all males over 65 during the next two decades. In 1980 about 27 percent of all American males over 65 were veterans. By the year 2000 this percentage will have peaked at about 62 percent of the entire male population. This means that almost two out of

Figure 12.2
Male Veteran Population as a Percentage of Total Male Population, 1980–2020

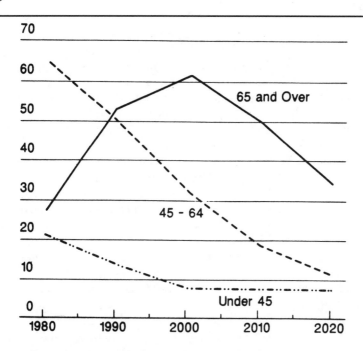

Source: VA Office of Reports and Statistics (March 1983)

every three elderly males will be eligible for VA medical care if they elect to use it.

There is another difference between veterans and the general population, that is, composition by sex. In the general population services for the elderly will be predominantly for the female population, while in the veteran system males will predominate. By the year 2000 the number of elderly female veterans will reach 396,000, nearly twice the 1980 level. Over the next 40 years the female veteran population will increase by 18 percent. With the greater longevity of females, female veterans as a proportion of all older veterans will increase steadily, reaching a high of 8 percent by the year 2030. Caring for female veterans and the female spouses of veterans needs to become part of the planning of VA services.

The number of frail "old-old" veterans, those over age 85, will grow at a substantial rate over the next forty years. In 1980 7.2 percent of the aging veteran population was over age 85. By the year 2020, 17.6 percent will be over age 85. By 2010 veterans over age 75 will account for 47.8 percent of all aged veterans and 21 percent of the total veteran population.

CURRENT POLICY AND PROGRAMS

Veterans Administration Programs

The centerpiece of the VA geriatric program is the Geriatric Research Educational Clinical Centers (GRECC), which were set up as centers of excellence designed for the advancement and integration of geriatric and biomedical research, education and clinical care in the VA system. The GRECCs were established to develop new knowledge in aging, coordinate existing knowledge, and develop state-of-the-art alternatives for geriatric care, education, and training for health professionals. The first GRECCs were established in 1975. There are currently ten GRECCs at Bedford, Mass.; Brockton-West Roxbury, Mass.; Durham, N.C.; Gainesville, Fla.; Little Rock, Ark.; Minneapolis, Minn.; Palo Alto, Calif.; St. Louis, Mo.; Seattle-American Lake, Wash.; Sepulveda, Calif.; and West Los Angeles,Calif.

The VA operates four institutional extended care programs. First, the VA Nursing Home Care Units were established in 1965. In 1965 the average daily census was 150 in the VA nursing home component; by 1983 the average daily census had grown to 8,849. The VA Nursing Home Program requires that nonservice-connected veterans under age 65 not receiving pensions and not entitled to a State Medicaid Program demonstrate their inability to afford the cost of care elsewhere. Physicians must request the nursing home placement and show evidence of medical need for a veteran to be placed in a VA Nursing Home Care Unit. An interdisciplinary team will assess the patient's need for admission and establish the treatment plan. In 1985 there were ninety-nine VA Nursing Home Care Units with an average bed occupancy rate of 94 percent.

The VA also operates a Community Nursing Home Care Program to assist veterans and their families in the transition from the hospital to the community. The program consists of VA-approved homes that meet VA standards which are reimbursed for services provided under a contractual agreement with the medical center. In addition to the standards required by Medicare and Medicaid programs, the VA requires twenty-four-hour coverage by licensed nursing at intermediate care facilities. These homes are individually evaluated by a VA team of a social worker and nurse. The Community Nursing Home Care Program in 1983 supported an average daily census of 10,212 veterans and treated 34,092 veteran patients during the year.

The third institutional program available for veterans is through the State Veterans Home Programs. This is funded in part by the VA through two individual grant programs. The first is a per diem reimbursement to assist states in providing domiciliary care and nursing home care in hospitals to eligible veterans. The second grant program makes assistance available to states in the construction of new domiciliary and nursing home facilities.

The fourth institutional extended care program is the VA Domiciliary Program, which provides care with backup services for chronically ill veterans who do not require acute hospitalization or nursing home placement. In 1983 there were 16 domiciliaries with an average daily census of 6,852. The Domiciliary Program has undergone considerable change and is more therapeutically oriented than in the past. The primary program goals are active rehabilitation to enable veterans to attain a better level of functioning and continuing treatment. The domiciliary patients consist of three groups: the socially disaffiliated; i.e., chronic alcoholic and psychiatric patients; second, patients with medical and surgical diagnoses who are older and require a sheltered environment on an indefinite basis; and third, patients with much potential for rehabilitation but not needing more intensive care.

In addition to the institutional system of care, the VA also offers a number of noninstitutional extended care programs. This includes community residential care provided at the veteran's own expense in private homes inspected by the VA but chosen by the veteran. The veterans receive monthly follow-up from VA health care professionals. The program provides room and board, unlimited personal care, and supervision for veterans who do not require more intensive levels of care, but are not able to live independently. In 1983 an average daily census in the residential care program was 11,195 in approximately 3,045 private homes.

Another major noninstitutionalized care program is the Hospital-Based Home Care Program. This program, which must meet JCAH standards, enables early hospital discharge of veterans with chronic illnesses to their own homes and reduces readmission to the hospital. The program delivers interdisciplinary care and relies on informal support systems such as the family to provide personal care when health professionals are not present. The Hospital-Based Home Care Program was established as a pilot program in 1970. Over fifty programs were in operation in 1986 with thirty more being planned by the year 1990. In 1983, 7,423 patients were treated.

Another noninstitutional extended care program is Adult Day Health Care. This is a therapeutically oriented, ambulatory program that provides health maintenance and rehabilitative services to frail individuals in a congregate setting during daytime hours. One purpose of the program is to prevent unnecessary institutionalization. The programs provides assistance in attaining or maintaining adequate health for community living; follow-up care of individuals discharged from hospitals or institutions; prevention of physical and mental deterioration; case management; tracking of participants' health status; and relief to persons caring for veterans at home. In 1986 over fifteen VA medical centers had initiated Adult Day Health Care programs, and the VA planned approximately ten more programs. A thorough cost-effectiveness evaluation of these Adult Day Health Care programs is planned for 1987.

Approximately fifteen VA medical centers have hospice programs. The number of in-patients served by the hospice programs in 1983 was 108 and of out-patients 138.

Respite care enables elderly individuals to be institutionalized periodically, providing a period of relief for the care-giving spouse or relative. There are currently twelve respite programs in the VA system, but no formal respite programs are sponsored by the VA central office.

Another extended care program developing within the VA is the teaching nursing home. The concept of the teaching nursing home program is to bring skilled nursing facilities into the mainstream of health care services by providing them with the type of stimulation and affiliation that teaching hospitals have developed since World War II. One VAMC has a teaching nursing home grant from the Robert Wood Johnson Foundation program, and the VA central office is developing program guidelines to further stimulate teaching nursing homes or academically affiliated nursing homes. This program will build on the strength of the Interdisciplinary Team Training Program in Geriatrics and the geriatric fellowship programs.

The congregate housing programs and respite programs in senior centers are additional programs being proposed for development within the VA system to provide a more enriched continuum of care for the elderly VA patient. The VA is becoming more involved in looking for alternatives to institutionalization. If the current trend continues, the need for nursing home beds would become enormous by the turn of the century. To address this need, the VA has become increasingly interested in long-term care alternatives, e.g., case management, community-based programs, adult day health care, hospice, respite care, homemaker services, and special nutrition services.

Though the data supporting these programs as alternatives to institutionalization are still preliminary, it seems that two of the alternatives, hospital-based home care and adult day health care, are evolving as true alternatives to nursing home placement (R. J. Vogel et al., 1982). However, many investigators (W. G. Weissert, 1978); J. J. Callahan, 1981; P. E. Raber, 1983) feel more data are needed before a final decision can be made on the cost effectiveness of these programs.

Health Care Utilization

Most studies (W. F. Page, 1982; L. A. Seitz, 1981; NAS, 1977) have shown that the VA has been an attractive source of health care to the lower-income groups. Findings indicate that 48 percent of all veterans who use the VA as their only source of hospital care had incomes of less than $5,000. Another 47 percent of these veterans had incomes between $5,000 and $15,000, and only 5 percent who relied entirely on VA for their hospital care had an income of more than $15,000.

Research (NCHSR, 1982; Page, 1982) also indicates that the use of health care services is related to age. Aged veterans constitute a much larger user group than their representation in the veteran population as a whole. Over 39 percent of all VA in-patient care was consumed by veterans age 65 or older and 16 percent by those aged 75 or older in 1983. This corresponded to a disproportionate number of aged veterans in almost all in-patient treatment categories. However, a smaller proportion of frail veterans appears to use out-patient care. About 16 percent of all in-patients are 65 + while only 6 percent of VA out-patients are 65 +.

One study (W. R. Lawson, 1980) reviewed insurance coverage held by veterans with the following findings: 39 percent of all veterans are covered by Medicare but about 90 percent of those 65 + are covered. Many veterans 65 +, with incomes of less than $10,000 have only hospital insurance, Medicare Part A, and are vulnerable to medical expenses. About 6 percent of all male veterans 55 + are covered by Medicaid, which declines with increasing income. Medicaid coverage is highly correlated with age. Only 2 percent of veterans 55 to 59 are covered by Medicaid—a statistic that increases to 17 percent for those 75 +. About 80 percent of the 55 + age group are covered through group or private health insurance plans. Private coverage is related to income and the quality of private coverage is more closely related to income than age.

Marital status is also related to the utilization of health services. Marital status is particularly important in determining an aged person's need for health-related services. The Survey of Aging Veterans (1982) found that the proportion of married male veterans is higher than all married males, 82 percent and 67 percent, respectively. A much lower percentage of male veterans has never been married than the nonveteran population. This has important implications for the informal support systems that take care of elderly veterans in the community and prevent institutionalization. Information from the annual patient census confirms that marital status affects the need for VA services. In 1983 only 38 percent of veterans treated in any in-patient setting were married. The highest percentage of married veterans, 44 percent, used hospital care. A relatively high percentage also received care in nursing homes, 36 percent. The majority of VA institutional users, 62 percent, are not married. Every nonmarried category is disproportionately represented in the user population.

Health Status

Figure 12.3 shows an increasing frequency of age-related discharges from VA hospitals for heart disease, cancer, diabetes, respiratory disease, and arthritis. There is rapid increase in chronic diseases with age, with the exception of cancer. All are serious conditions requiring continuing care. The most frequent surgical procedures in the VA hospitals are also age-related, including cataracts, hyperplasia of the prostate, and fracture of the

Figure 12.3
Common Disease Classes—Discharges from Veterans Hospitals per 10,000 Veterans, by Age

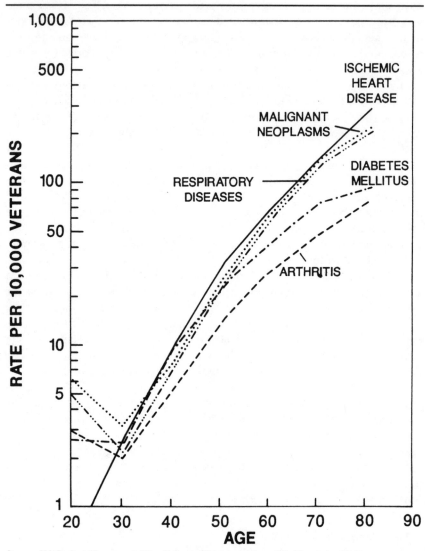

Source: VA Patient Treatment File: Patients Discharged from VA Hospitals, 1975.

neck of the femur. Surgery for hip fractures, cataracts, and prostatic obstruction accounts for about 50 percent of all surgery in patients 65 years. VA discharge rates for schizophrenia, alcoholism, and drug abuse decrease with advancing age. For alcoholism, it remains about constant between ages

40 and 70 and subsequently declines rapidly. The subsequent decline may be due to either selective mortality or a reluctance in making a diagnosis in older patients. One psychiatric problem most common in the elderly is dementia, and it is increasing in frequency. This will create placement problems. Accumulative incidence of senile dementia in males should reach over 500 per 10,000 in the 8th and 9th decades. These geometric increases in age-related conditions create a tremendous demand for both short- and long-term VA health services.

R. W. Besdine et al. (1984) point out that it is essential to understand the aged veteran's health and illness behavior to anticipate future health care needs. Presentation of disease is different in the elderly, and aging veterans may represent a unique subset in these disease categories. Diseases or disorders such as giant cell arteritis, dementia, basal cell carcinoma, Parkinson's, urinary incontinence, and autoimmune disease may become more prevalent problems to the VA in the future with the aging of new cohorts.

ISSUES FOR THE FUTURE

It is difficult to take these demographic and epidemiological characteristics of veterans and project the need for health care services to be supplied by the VA system. A conceptional framework was developed to assist in analyzing demand which explicitly includes eligible veterans who do not become system users. Using this approach, the primary concern is for eligible veterans who are users actively demanding care. The second subpopulation is eligible veterans who are sick and would use VA care if they were aware of it and had access to it. The third category of eligible veterans includes those who are well or are not interested in VA care. The fourth group is veterans who are not eligible for care.

Using various predictive methods the VA has projected the possible range of need for health services among aging veterans. (U.S. Veterans Administration, 1984). These methods produce both high and low estimates from 1992 to 2020. The projections for hospital discharges vary from 1.0 million to 2.8 million a year. Projections show a steady increase in the ambulatory care services needed through the year 2010 before a slow decline begins in 2020. Projected out-patient visits in the year 2000 range from 26 to 33 million visits compared to the 19 million visits. For institutional extended care the expected increase in average daily census ranges from a peak in 2010 of approximately 110,000 to 140,000 to a range of 98,000 to 126,000 in 2020. This compares to an average daily census in 1985 of 40,000. Noninstitutional extended care is also expected to increase, but data available within the system are insufficient for accurate projections. For fiscal year 1985 15,000 veterans were receiving care in noninstitutional extended care programs; by the year 2000 this is expected to peak at 760,000 veterans receiving service. These projections vary because of the unknown impact that changes in public policy might have on VA eligilibity or the Medicare or Medicaid programs, which would greatly influence the number of veterans seeking and qualifying for VA care.

In the report *Caring for the Older Veteran* (U.S. Veterans Administration, 1984) several policies are specified to serve the increasing number of aging veterans. Strategies were developed which cover hospital, ambulatory, and extended care. It also includes a national community coordination strategy and a research and education strategy. The report points out that to meet the real needs of veterans in the year 2000 will require a 68 percent increase in in-patient beds; development of Geriatric Evaluation Units; increased satellite clinics, as part of ambulatory surgery programs; and a combination of domicilary and nursing homes. The need for extended care will require a bed capacity for at least 53,000 veterans in 1990 and 97,000 in 2000. It is anticipated that the Hospital-Based Home Care and Adult Day Health Care Programs could reduce the need for additional extended care beds.

The VA is taking national leadership in developing community coordinative models. This model is to take advantage of non-VA capacities and to enhance the amount of service available to aging veterans. A Community Collaboration Officer (CCO) would be established in each VAMC. The CCO will serve several functions to promote development of community services; to liaise with community resources which share VA's interest in aging; to serve as information and referral coordinator; and to maintain data bases on availability of community resources and usage by VA patients.

To meet its aims and provide the services needed in these areas, including research and education, four types of resources are needed: authority, funds, staff, and physical facility. The VA has most of the legislative authority to carry out its mandate. But in selected areas critical to the success of these efforts, additional authority seems required. These include authority to establish seed money grants so the VA can participate more fully in developing community health strategies for the aging; expansion in the number of GRECCs; expansion, through contracts, of the Hospital-Based Home Care Program; and development of more Adult Day Health Care Programs.

Despite an apparent annual increase in expenditures of the Department of Medicine and Surgery, in constant dollars virtually level spending has occurred in each of the last eight fiscal years. This has had a critical negative impact on programs within the VA, causing uncertainty and cuts in existing medical services as well as forgoing the implementation of essential mandated programs, such as the Adult Day Health Care Program and the expansion of the GRECCs.

The cost experience of the Department of Medicine and Surgery has been better than that of the private sector (U.S. Veterans Administration, 1981). For example, the non-VA cost per patient treated has increased by 4 percent a year above general inflation or 50 percent in a decade. VA experience shows that costs per service, adjusted for general inflation, will remain constant. The fiscal projections to meet needs in the year 2000 vary between a high projection of about 24 billion dollars to a low of slightly over 15 billion dollars. These estimates assume no major shift in health insurance coverage among veterans over 65. Changes within Medicare, such as increased deductibles, copayments and more restrictive Medicaid coverage, could be expected to increase utilization and projected costs in the VA system.

To meet increased service needs, additional VA personnel will be needed. Employment per hospital discharge has increased by 2.7 percent annually in the non-VA sector in the past decade. In contrast, VA has achieved a small decrease in employment per discharge. In the same period the VA standards were 2.2 employees per occupied hospital bed compared to 3.8 in the non-VA sector. Estimates of personnel in the year 2000 vary from a high of 550,000 employees to a low of 350,000 employees. These figures do not take into consideration shifts in the mix of employee specialties to meet the needs of older patients in new settings.

The additional physical facilities projected to be needed by 2000 include hospital beds (ranging from 108,000 to 188,000); nursing home beds (from 30,000 to 32,000); and domiciliary beds (11,000).

CONCLUSIONS

The VA has a vast medical care system established in a protective environment by legislation to serve the nation's military veterans. It is currently under considerable stress because of changes in public spending policy; a more conservative administration; and an aging veteran population with new demands. The private sector also is undergoing considerable change and is increasingly competing in a price-competitive market (Inglehurst, 1985a, 1985b). The VA has helped set standards for geriatric care. If the VA is to continue providing national leadership and meeting the needs of aging veterans, national policy on aging health care must be developed which spans the VA and non-VA sectors. Budgetary cuts and the political climate are compromising the VA's ability to meet its mandate for the aging veteran.

Worries about the VA's ability to meet the future health care needs of aging veterans led to significant changes in eligibility in 1986. An attempt was made to target VA services more specifically to the frail and poor veterans and to shift the cost of care to Medicare, Medicaid, and the private sector.

An additional problem complicating the challenge to serve older veterans is the budget control imposed by the Balanced Budget and Emergency Control Act of 1985, popularly known as the Gramm-Rudman-Hollings legislation, which was enacted in September, 1985. This law requires cutbacks to achieve a balanced budget by 1991. As a result, health care cost containment within VA and non-VA programs has been greatly increased.

President Reagan's budget for the fiscal year 1987 called for spending cuts of 2 percent in veterans' health care benefits, by reducing the number of people treated, by requiring insurance companies to help pay the cost, and by making many more veterans show financial need to receive care in the VA system. There is no new money for nursing home construction. The budget contains a new long-term care policy emphasizing the use of community nursing homes and state institutions rather than VA federal facilities. The VA budget calls for a productivity increase of 1 percent a year for the next five years and reduces the number of lower priority veterans that can be treated. This will result in reducing the number of patients admitted to veterans hospitals by 62,000 in 1987.

The administration is proposing to collect from private insurance companies the reasonable cost of care provided to veterans with disabilities unrelated to their military service. Insurers would be legally obliged to pay for care to the same extent as if the patient were in a private hospital.

Under the current law, at age 65 a veteran is automatically eligible for medical care on a space-available basis without regard to financial need. With the change, the VA only has to provide hospital care to veterans with disabilities unrelated to military service if they have incomes less than $15,000 a year for single veterans and $18,000 a year for veterans with one dependent. On the basis of available resources, the VA may decide to care for people with higher incomes. Veterans without service-connected disabilities would have to pay for part of their care; e.g., $492.00 for the first 90 days if their income exceeds $20,000 a year for a single person, or $25,000 per married couple. Veterans with family incomes of more than $15,000 would have to pay substantially more before qualifying for VA health care. The impact of these changes has not been evaluated since they were not implemented until July 1986.

In one VA report (U.S. Veterans Administration, 1984), several strategies were developed to meet the growing needs of aging veterans. These strategies present dilemmas for policymakers and the options for action need to be further defined. In a report by E. Roybal (1986) of the Select Committee on Aging of the House of Representatives, several options were discussed. These include:

1. Expansion of the present system according to the projected need developed by the CBO (1984) and VA projections (U.S. Veterans Administration, 1981); given the current budgetary restrictions, this seems unlikely.

2. Under the current "no growth policy," another option is to change the target population by restricting eligibility or limiting benefits. This has been partially implemented and there are attempts to limit the VA health care budget by even more restrictive eligibility requirements. The first means-tested program was put

into effect in July 1986, but was not as restrictive as originally proposed. It could become more restrictive in the future. Another cost-saving proposal was the authorization to collect payment from private health insurance.

3. Another option for policymakers, is to adapt the present VA system to better meet the needs of the aging veteran in a more cost effective way. This could be done by increasing the noninstitutional extended care programs within the VA and increasing such programs as GRECCs and Geriatric Evaluation Units. Targeting resources through a gate-keeping case management system has been given serious consideration. The Veterans Administration Special Medical Advisory Group report (1983) suggested targeting based on age with highest priority for those age 75 and over, or service-connected disability, or receipt of VA pension.

4. Another frequently discussed option is to convert acute beds to extended care beds and make increasing use of community resources through development of collaborative community models. Specific proposals on how this can be done have been well described by Wetle and Rowe (1984).

If current trends are predictive, the VA will meet its challenge by developing creative relationships with community resources to expand its service potential and develop innovative new programs such as Geriatric Evaluation Units and Teaching Nursing Homes. The objective for VA geriatric care will become more oriented to improved social and health functioning and more targeted to serving the frail elderly. Close coordination of services with community resources and a greater continuum of available services will evolve. The system that will develop in the coming decades will depend on the public voice and political will.

REFERENCES

Besdine, R. W., Lewkoff, S., and Wetle, T. (1984). Health and Illness Behavior in Elder Veterans. In T. Wetle and J. Rowe, eds., *Older Veterans: Linking Veterans Administration and Community Resources*. Boston: Cambridge University Press.

Callahan, J. J. (1981). Delivery of Services to Persons with Long-Term Care Needs. In Meilty et al., eds., *Policy Options in Long Term-Care Needs*. Chicago: University of Chicago Press.

Congressional Budget Office (CBO) (1984). *Veterans Administrations Health Care: Planning for Future Years*. Washington: Government Printing Office.

Inglehurst, J. K. (1985a). The Veterans Administration Medical Care System and the Private Sector. *New England Journal of Medicine*, 313, 1552–56.

Inglehurst, J. K. (1985b). The Veterans Administration Medical Care System Faces an Uncertain Future. *New England Journal of Medicine*, 313, 1168–72.

Lawson, W. R. (1980). *Health Insurance Coverage of Veterans*. Washington: National Center for Health Services Research Expenditures Study, Data Preview and Department of Health and Human Services.

National Academy of Sciences (NAS) (1977). *Study of Health Care for American Veterans* (1977). Washington: National Academy of Sciences.

National Center for Health Services Research (1982). *Use of Health Care Services by Veterans*. Washington: National Center for Health Services Research.

Page, W. F. (1982). Why Veterans Choose Veterans Administration Hospitalization: A Multivariate Model. *Medical Care*, 20, 308–20.

Raber, P. E. (1983). Health Care Alternatives for Aging Veterans. *Geriatrics*, 38(3), 39, 43–44.

Roybal, E. (1986). *Aging Veterans in an Aging Society: Public Policy at a Cross Roads*. Report of Select Committee on Aging, House of Representatives. Washington: Government Printing Office.

Seitz, L. A. (1981). *The Aged Veteran: Part 1. The Impact upon the VA Health Care Delivery System of Older Veterans: The Hospital Inpatient System*. Washington: Health Systems Information Service, Office of Planning and Program Development, Department of Medicine and Surgery, VA HSI Report 81–88.

Special Medical Advisory Group (SMAG) (1983). *Task Force on the VA Geriatric Plan, Caring for the Older Veteran*. Washington: Government Printing Office.

Survey of Aging Veterans (SAV) (1982). *VA Study of the Needs, Resources, and Expectations of Veterans 55 and Over*. Washington: Veterans Administration, Office of Reports and Statistics.

U.S. Veterans Administration (1981). *Annual Report*. Washington: Government Printing Office.

U.S. Veterans Administration (1984). *Caring for the Older Veteran*. Washington: Government Printing Office.

Vogel, R. J., et al. (1982). *Long-Term Care: Perspectives from Research and Demonstrations*. Washington: Health Care Financing Administration, Department of Health and Human Services.

Weissert, W. G. (1978). *Long-Term Care: An Overview*. Washington: Department of Health and Human Services.

Wetle, T., and Rowe, J., eds. (1984). *Older Veterans: Linking Veterans Administration and Community Resources*. Boston: Cambridge University Press.

SUMMARY

Veterans can provide gerontologists with unique opportunities to study the special effects of stress, of conflict resolution and leadership styles, of peer support networks (which are especially unique among older males), and of long-term results of injury and disability as these factors relate to the process of aging. Veterans can also provide a potential pool of aging male research subjects for gerontological research. Finally, with the organization of services to veterans, both the VA and DVA can provide opportunities for demonstrating services; clinical training sites or field placements; and the evaluation of service programs that are or could be more diverse and accessible to study than most other sources of service.

A cross-national research project that can only be undertaken within North America should be mounted to study the characteristics of military volunteers (all Canadian and some United States veterans) versus those who were conscripted (the remaining United States veterans) for military services. The second aspect of this research should look for differential aging by volunteers as opposed to nonvolunteers. Further research should be undertaken to study the impact of geographic (Canadian) versus random (United States) military call-up systems. This impact should be investigated as it relates to marital patterns; occupational and retirement patterns; peer networks; mobility patterns; geographic concentrations of service delivery; differential requirements for care; availability of informal support networks; and patterns of aging. Both of these project areas should include the study of differential incidences and prevalences of disease, the experience of morbidity, and the analysis of mortality rates and patterns.

VII
NATIVE ELDERS

Minority group aging is of special concern to Canadian and United States gerontologists for multiple reasons: there are special risks associated with the health and
poverty status of minorities in earlier life that interrelate with the aging process and
old age; different minority groups have special needs that differ among the various
groups and from the larger white majority aged; and both countries have proclaimed
an increasing commitment to multiculturalism. Social welfare and economic advocacy for the needs of minority groups is promoted increasingly by the emerging
political leadership representing the different minority groups.

Indians were selected as the focal minority group because of the important historic
and current relationships between tribes and nations in both countries. Tribes moved
freely between the countries before there was an international border, and for native
people this border has special significance. This unit includes two chapters that
characterize the alternative research approaches most often applied to explore native
elder issues.

Both chapters address social change but from varying perspectives. R. M. Vanderburgh discussed the phenomenon of revitalization from the perspective of elders
of the Anicinabe tribe. Her description accounts for the disconnection with tribal
customs and traditions. This is an issue that is common to the elders of many
Canadian tribes. Major portions of the chapter recount how the Anicinabe are
rediscovering and reengaging the special characteristics of elderhood that were historically vital to intergenerational community life. Paul Stuart and Eloise Rathbone-
McCuan attend to issues of health and social service delivery as they are at present
distributed throughout the reservation networks in areas where there are high concentrations of elderly Indians.

The reader moves from the very specific tribal experiences of the Anicinabe in
148nada to the political debates of the United States Congress over motivations for
neglecting the special concerns of native elders and the native leaders' demand to
improve the required services. The issues of bringing the native elders back into the
center of renewed Canadian tribal culture and maintaining the Native American
elders within the tribal domain through residency on the reservations represent
important, but different questions for gerontologists and social service planners.

CHAPTER 13

The Impact of Government Support for Indian Culture on Canada's Aged Indians

Rosamond M. Vanderburgh

INTRODUCTION

In 1980 there were 320,000 registered Indians in Canada, constituting 1.2 percent of the total population (J. S. Frideres, 1983). Registered Indians fall under the legal and administrative responsibility of the Government of Canada, as defined in the Indian Act (1951). They are with a few exceptions attached to a specific band and listed on the roll of that band. *Band* is a term with both administrative and social-structural implications, and band designations are in the hands of the Minister of Indian Affairs. Frideres (1983: 138) notes that a band "is a group of Indians who share a common interest in land and money and whose historical connection is defined by the federal government". Individuals of Indian descent who identify themselves as Indians may not be registered because their forebears either failed to make an agreement with the Crown, or gave up Indian status voluntarily or involuntarily. The Indian Act ensures that an Indian woman who marries a non-Indian gives up her own and her children's Indian status. Indian men who marry non-Indians retain Indian status and extend it to their children. Political lobbying has recently resulted in changes to the discriminatory sections of the act, and many women are reclaiming Indian status. Individuals of Indian ancestry who are not registered may number 1,000,000 but because of unstandardized data and changing legal definitions adequate demographic data on the Native population in Canada is not available (Frideres, 1983).

While population trends show a decided aging of the overall Canadian population (F. T. Denton and B. G. Spencer, 1980; N. Shulman, 1980), the trend for the Native Indian population is in the opposite direction. According to Frideres (1983), in 1976 almost half of the registered Indians were younger than 15 years of age, in distinct contrast to the one-third of the total population in the same age category. In the 45- to 65-year-old category were less than 10 percent of registered Indians as opposed to nearly 20 percent of the total population, and in the category of 65 years of age or older, there were 5 percent of registered Indians in contrast with 8 percent of the total population.

The image of Canada as a modern multicultural nation is strongly supported by public funding at the federal, provincial, and municipal levels of government. Canadian policy emphasizes a continuing "mosaic" of ethnic and minority components rather than the "melting pot" of assimilation. The development of this policy of multiculturalism is linked to the growth during the 1960s and 1970s of awareness of minority rights in both Canada and the United States (P. Amoss, 1981b). Canada's Native peoples have also jumped onto the national bandwagon of multiculturalism, and clearly the federal government has viewed the fostering of pride in Native identity as one dimension in the solution of Canada's "Indian problem." Government funding for Indian culture has various implications for Indians of all ages, both on and off the reserves, but this chapter is concerned with its impact upon the aged and only secondarily, through the activities of the aged, with its impact upon younger members of the Native Indian community.

The provision of social, educational, and health services to registered Indians varies considerably from province to province. The federal government takes the view that its responsibility for these services ends when registered Indians live off-reserve; off-reserve Indians are seen as a provincial responsibility. Thus the provision of services is a matter for constant negotiation between federal and provincial jurisdictions. In general, "the federal government...has accepted responsibility for on-reserve services in more program areas than for off-reserve services" (Frideres, 1983: 222). Thus social and health services for aged Indians vary according to residence pattern and provincial jurisdiction.

Age structure of the Indian population, together with the support and funding of multiculturalism, are important factors in the revival of a degree of cultural significance for the Indian aged. Such a revival has been especially well documented for the Salish Indians of British Columbia (and the State of Washington) by Amoss (1981a, 1981b) and W. G. Jilek (1974). The data presented in this paper are drawn from ongoing research among the Anicinabe of southern Ontario, and show that the revival of a status of cultural significance for the aged is taking place in Ontario as well as in British Columbia. It remains for future research to document whether such a revival is occurring across Canada among other Native peoples.

THE ANICINABE OF SOUTHERN ONTARIO

Historical Background

The Anicinabe of southern Ontario are a mixed population of Ojibwe, Odawa (Ottawa), and Potawatomi origins, who refer to themselves as *Anicinabe* or "original people." They share a linguistic and cultural heritage and were historically linked in the nineteenth-century migrations, removals, and resettlements of Native peoples in the Great Lakes area. Southern Ontario acted as a refuge area for Anicinabe of American origin during the last part of the eighteenth and the early nineteenth centuries when military conflicts and white settlement pushed them from their various homelands.

The settlement of the Anicinabe onto reserves in southern Ontario took place recently enough (1820s–60s) that a significant number of elderly Indians interviewed in the mid–1970s had close childhood contacts with grandparents who had experienced free access to the resources on which their lives were based before white hegemony was established by treaty over the southern area of the province. The following review of traditional elderhood refers to the patterns of those prereserve days; our understanding is drawn mainly from informants who were exposed in their childhood to elders who remembered the days "when there were no reserves." The accounts of these informants are supplemented by standard ethnographic and ethnohistorical sources (F. Densmore, 1929; R. W. Dunning, 1959; A. I. Hallowell, 1964; D. Jenness, 1935, etc.)

The Institution of Traditional Elderhood and Its Erosion

The meaning of elder status is difficult to reconstruct, but was apparently not linked to chronological age. The concept of elderhood held a number of meanings within the framework of the life cycle statuses; the individual who was a grandparent, or who belonged to the grandparental generation, tended to be perceived as an elder. Individual contributions to the family group were related to life-cycle status. Parents assumed subsistence functions, leaving child rearing and socialization functions to the elders, usually the grandparents. Although the grandparent/grandchild relationship was notably warm and fraternal in contrast to the authoritarian aspects of the parent/child relationship, elders expected, and generally received, deference and respect. Grandchildren, on the other hand, expected, and generally received, emotional and pragmatic support in growing up within their cultural tradition. The pragmatic support that "grandparents" provided during the socialization process consisted primarily of information about the techniques of managing social relationships. Success in the field of social relationships was a critical survival factor in traditional Anicinabe times, as the management of both natural and human resources was framed within the concept of kinship.

The powerful spirits that in Native ontology controlled the natural resources upon which the Anicinabe depended were incorporated within the circle of kinship and called by the same terms for grandparents that children learned to apply to human elders (Hallowell, 1964). The skills necessary to maintain good relationships with these "other-than-human" grandparents were passed on by the human grandparents, who taught primarily through the use of oral narratives, and secondarily by example. Elders used two forms of narrative in passing on their skills/wisdom to the younger generation; the Ojibwe language (one of the three glossed as *Anicinabe*) distinguishes the myth/legend or sacred tale (*atiso'kanak*) from the anecdotal narrative (*tabatcamowin*), which Hallowell calls *news or tidings* (ibid.: 56).

The transmission of traditional ritual and sacred information is a key function of the aged in many nonliterate societies. Frequently the aged also tell stories about their own life experiences. However, the linguistic evidence for an institutionalized dual structuring of oral narratives among the Anicinabe is particularly significant in understanding the full breadth of the Anicinabe elder's role. Elderhood was an institution charged with responsibility for cultural maintenance through the transmission of the core cultural values (the myths/legends) and with teaching adaptation to culture change (in the anecdotal narratives). Elders were passing on both received cultural information and new information about how to cope with new situations that they experienced. Traditional elderhood thus embodied tremendous adaptive potential.

Anicinabe elders had things other than tales to pass on. Attainment of personal successs depended upon the incremental building-up of supernaturally derived power during the life course through the maintenance of proper relationships with spirit powers. Survival to old age validated the existence of an elder's personal power, which was often shared with children through such institutions as the naming ceremony. Powerful elders might also teach children specific skills in the manipulation of the supernatural.

It is not possible to ascertain from this distance in time whether *all* older Anicinabe in the grandparental generation functioned as elders. However, the old people interviewed in the 1970s stated unequivocally that they had admired, respected, and loved their elders, and this seems to strongly support the view that in traditional times elders served as important role models for the younger generation. In sum, the transmission of survival wisdom and power was entirely in their hands. The young person who roused an elder's wrath risked loss of access to that wisdom and power, and the possibility that the power might be turned against him or her. The force and vitality of traditional elderhood cannot be emphasized too strongly.

When the Anicinabe settled onto reserves, they became more accessible to the efforts of missionaries and educators, and the context of survival changed rapidly and radically. No longer was vital survival information controlled and transmitted by Indian elders, but by missionaries and school-teachers who mocked the knowledge and power of elders as "superstition." The children were taught in school and church to view the elders' knowledge and skills as dangerous to their health and spiritual well-being. These children, in their turn, grew old urging their own descendants to acquire in school the survival skills demonstrably effective in the larger society. Christian values, literacy and mathematics, farming skills, manual training, and domestic science came to be defined as paramount. White role models were found and the force of the elders' experiential narratives dwindled as their prestige disappeared. The Anicinabe aged were no longer *elders* in traditional terms; their status now approximated that of the aged in the larger society, and in the marginal economy of the reserves they became liabilities.

Anicinabe Revitalization

The spread of pan-Indianism and political consciousness-raising in the Canadian Native community during the 1960s and early 1970s fostered a rebirth of traditional culture not equally welcomed by all Anicinabe. In southern Ontario this rebirth includes diverse expressions of linked local *revitalization movements*. As defined by A. Wallace (1956), such movements, phrased in either religious or secular terms, constitute group reaction to stress that is unresolvable within the known cultural system. They grow through a uniform process, deliberately and consciously instituted, and have occurred worldwide as a Native reaction to colonialism. Relatively few are successful in long-term stress resolution.

Stresses felt by modern Anicinabe are related to their generally low socioeconomic position and marginal political status. While no formal research has been initiated to determine the limits of resolvable stress, specific Anicinabe communities have experienced crises such as high rates of attempted and/or completed suicide among the young. The roots of Anicinabe revitalization lie in a combination of pan-Indianism, national policy confrontation, government funding of Indian culture, and the developments of Native Studies Programs in several Ontario universities.

Several recent historical events reflecting the rise of pan-Indianism have influenced revitalization. In the early 1960s Christian churches in Canada and the United States began to reconsider relationships with Indian people. Within this context was established an annual Indian Ecumenical Conference, stimulated by cooperation among Indian academics, Native spiritual leaders, and Christian church leaders. This conference, which has gradually drawn attendance from most southern Ontario Anicinabe reserves, has been designated by J. A. Price (1978) as a new religious revitalization movement.

Policy confrontations begun in 1969 between Indians and the federal government have also stimulated Anicinabe revitalization. The Department of Indian Affairs and Northern Development (DIAND) has been the key agency involved in this process. It administers the Indian Act, assuming responsibility for social services to registered Indians (including the aged) on reserves, and maintaining various arrangements with the provinces that accommodate off-reserve registered Indians. In 1969 DIAND announced a virtual termination policy aimed at forced integration of Indians into the larger society. Nationwide, Native leaders organized political resistance to this policy that was successful in forcing a change in the DIAND position. This new DIAND position, combined with the increase in federal funding for multiculturalism, resulted in the early 1970s in the initiation of DIAND's Cultural/Educational Centers Program. This produced funding for sixty centers, five of them in Ontario and one on Manitoulin Island, spiritual heartland of the southern Anicinabe. Program policies were legislatively formalized in 1977. The statement of program philosophy clearly sanctions Indian tradition and emphasizes ideological manipulation rather than legislated equality and confirmation of Native rights:

Indian... people who have a firm base in their own culture, and who are given the opportunity to acquire a solid understanding of the traditions and values of their culture, will be able to participate with pride and dignity in their own community life and that of the larger society.... The ultimate goal of the Centers' Program is to stimulate a greater sense of self-awareness, self-worth and self-reliance among [Native] people (Government of Canada, 1977).

Details of the program objectives articulate the interdependence of Native heritage, language, and culture, and centers operating under the program have the mandate to develop specific local programs to facilitate the retrieval and maintenance of Native language and culture. Over the past fifteen years a network of communication among centers has developed that expands the expression of pan-Indianism in Canada.

In Native Studies Programs at Trent University and the University of Sudbury (Laurentian University), the staff members are predominantly Natives. They have developed in-depth courses covering traditions, culture, language, arts, and education. The staff of the Sudbury Native Studies Program, with a particular interest in the revival of Anicinabe religious institutions, have reestablished almost forgotten links with the Midewiwin, the Grand Medicine Society of the Ojibwe (W. J. Hoffman, 1891; R. Landes, 1968; J. Redsky, 1972) that once had followers in some of the local reserve communities. A community of modern mide people has been established under the guidance of Sudbury faculty, with members on a number of local reserves. Exchange visits with American Midewiwin groups have established yet another type of pan-Indian network.

Revival of Cultural Significance for the Aged Anicinabe:
A Case Study

In 1973 on Manitoulin Island a group of Native women trained as teachers and teachers' assistants formed the Manitoulin Indian Studies Committee to investigate ways to stop further erosion of Native language and culture. With funding from the Cultural/Educational Centers Program, the committee set up the Ojibwe Cultural Foundation (OCF) on the West Bay Reserve and undertook to discover resources upon which to develop its linguistic/cultural maintenance and retrieval programs.

A review of the OCF's first year of operation reveals that, in addition to language, the following activities already established on Island reserves were defined as significantly "Indian," and thus worthy of support and promotion: local pow-wows, a local Indian drum group, crafts people, and the Indian Art Club at the Island's high school. The OCF's language concerns were addressed through the organization of a conference on Indian education for local chiefs, band councils, the school committees of those councils, and Indian teachers. Native people involved in Indian education were brought in from across Canada, and part of the dialogue at the conference was carried on in the local Native language.

During its first year of operation the OCF had virtually no involvement with the local elderly. The earliest programmed utilization of the elderly as resource people was in 1975, when both local and imported resource people were involved in the teaching of ritual and legends to the young people who attended the Summer Art Program. Local elderly were involved primarily in the more mundane areas of caretaking and cooking, but medicine men from western Canada and the United States, elders in the old institutional sense of the term, were invited to introduce authentic Indian rituals, as there were no known local ritual experts.

This first recognition and utilization of elders set the scene for the development of the foundation's emphasis on the revival of traditional spiritual values and ritual, an emphasis subsequently developed into the focal aspect of the OCF's programming and operation. That development has involved not only imported elders but increasing numbers of elderly Anicinabe from Manitoulin Island and vicinity. By 1978 elderhood in the traditional sense had been revived by a few of these aged Anicinabe, although the context in which they were operating was a very different one from the former familial context. In 1978 the OCF sought funding for an *Elders' Program*, which continued to bring in functioning elders, not only from American Anicinabe communities but also from Sioux (South Dakota) and Cree (Saskatchewan) communities. These outside elders were located in part through the foundation's networks with the Department of Native Studies in Sudbury, other Cultural/Educational Centers across the country, and its delegates to the Indian Ecumenical Conference in Morley, Alberta.

Although approximately three-quarters of the funding for the OCF's programs is derived from DIAND's Cultural/Educational Centers Program, support for the foundation's *Elders' Program* in 1978 was sought and obtained from various ministries of government of the Province of Ontario. By this date the OCF had more or less consolidated its position and gained acceptance among the communities it served, although in interviews some of the local aged were still expressing anxiety about the foundation's emphasis on the revival of Native religious traditions.

Staff of the foundation, under the leadership of the director of the Elders' Program, began to work slowly, with no intent to change spiritual beliefs, toward the involvement of more local elderly. The timing was good; national Indian leaders were beginning to pay lip service to the elderly as elders. Local Catholic missionaries had begun to implement an ecumenical policy, attending the Native ceremonies presented by the foundation and inviting Native spiritual leaders to attend Catholic ceremonies. The Elders' Program opened with intensive work with the few surviving local healers. The link between pragmatic and spiritual healing techniques in the traditional culture meant that these elderly medicine people invariably possessed both spiritual and herbal knowledge. The Elders' Program emphasized a mentoring relationship between healers and staff, modelled upon the traditional elders-as-transmitters-of-cultural-information role. This patterned relationship assured the cooperation of the elderly healers, who were now perceived by those they instructed as acting in traditional elder fashion.

Full realization of the strength of local elder resources made an enormous impact on the island. New understanding of the vital part that story telling had played in the transmission of Anicinabe core values encouraged mid-life adults to recall and reevaluate tales their grandparents had told. Local elders passed on tales heard in their youth, a number of which dealt with places of spiritual power, thus giving a new impetus to the reviving ceremonialism. When the foundation declared in its 1978 Annual Report to DIAND that "these elders *are* the culture and with their involvement in all future projects, success is inevitable", the director and staff were affirming a commitment that has guided the OCF ever since.

Elders began to be invited to the foundation's board meetings, and since 1978 have become involved in all of the foundation's programs. Their language skills are utilized in local schools, and they have been active in the Summer Art Programs, passing on Anicinabe traditions to the young artists. They attend the craft training workshops, where they pass on specific skills and delight in acquiring new ones. They have participated in such varied foundation activities as a Medicine Man's seminar, a meeting with Ontario's Lieutenant Governor, and the 1984 Canadian Indian Bilingual Conference. They have acted as expert resources in the preparation of land claims, and for the Native Studies Department at the University of Sudbury. Elder delegates regularly attend the Indian Ecumenical Conference, and in

1983 they attended the World Assembly of First Nations in western Canada. Groups of elders have traveled to Ottawa to take training in methods of genealogical research, and to Harbor Springs, Michigan, to investigate the historical links between Michigan and Manitoulin Anicinabe. In 1983 the OCF established the Elders' Advisory Council to the foundation's board of directors, and one of the first activities of this council was to meet with Iroquoian elders from Akwesasne (St. Regis Reserve) to arrange a formal covenant of peace and friendship between these two historically hostile Native nations.

At the more immediate level of coping with the kinds of crisis situations that triggered the move toward revitalization, women elders have worked with the foundation and local schools to arrange informal counseling of suicidal teenage girls. These elders have sought to involve the girls in activities such as quilting and cooking for public occasions, where the ladies chat and tell stories as they work. It must be emphasized that although these Manitoulin elders are beginning to again receive cultural attention, they are now operating in the entirely new context of a voluntary association, the OCF. Yet the adaptive potential of Anicinabe elderhood is becoming more evident, and it is nowhere more visible than in the OCF's annual Elders' Conferences, begun in 1979. The next section summarizes the 1984 conference and clarifies the contemporary relevance of the elders' traditional and experiential wisdom.

The Elders' Conference, July 30 to August 3, 1984

The conference agenda reflected such issues as the loss of Indian status by women who marry non-Indians, the problems of raising children to function in both the Native and Canadian cultural contexts, the provision of child-welfare services, and drug and alcohol abuse. The audience included young adults and teenagers as well as some local political leaders and elders from across Canada, with a few from the United States.

Each session was organized around relevant elderly individuals, and the appreciation of their messages by the younger generations was very evident. Elders actually played all the public organizational and leadership roles. In the center of the meeting place was the conference fire, tended around the clock by young boys who were learning responsibility through keeping this fire continually burning. All those in attendance took ashes from this fire back to their own comunities.

Regular morning and evening rituals were conducted by the various spiritual leaders present, symbolizing the spiritual sanctioning of all conference proceedings. The various masters/mistresses of ceremony were flexible in encouraging visiting elders to speak on an impromptu basis. This is significant as it underlines one of the important sources of an elder's mandate to speak with authority; sincerity and the intuition of when to reveal what is in one's heart.

It is worthwhile to review the bases of the elders' mandate to speak with authority for the light shed upon the institution of elderhood. One important basis of the elders' mandate to speak is clearly their experience in living. Each elder, in validating his or her right to speak publicly, reviewed personal origins and significant life events. Especially prominent in these reviews were mistakes that had been overcome, such as alcohol addiction, the abandonment of "the old ways," and refusing to listen to the elders. Willingness to use these life experiences to help "your community" by teaching from experience was a second basis of the elders' mandate, and clearly relates to the use of the anecdotal narrative, as these elders told story after story to illustrate their meanings.

The elders' mandate is also located in the deep conviction that leads one to speak "from the heart," which seems to be linked to the intuition that the moment to speak has arrived. Yet another base of the elders' mandate is found in dreams, which offered lessons for both speaking and acting. Elders related not only their own dreams but those of their mentors. Women elders located a significant part of their mandate in motherhood and grandmotherhood, underlining their attempt to validate their right, and the right of their children, to retain legal Indian status in marriages to non-Indian men.

A final mandate for the elders' authority was expressed frequently in terms of *survival*. This was distinguished from life experiences; survival through situations of tragic deprivation was cited by a significant number of elders. One woman, still middle-aged, was implicitly granted elder status on the basis of her survival story.

The issues reflected on the conference agenda are those of paramount concern in all Canadian Indian reserve communities today. One session covered "child-rearing, discipline, alcohol and drug abuse from the elders' perspective, and the role of child welfare agencies." The difficulties of parenting in what was referred to as a bicultural environment were emphasized as well as the continuing importance of teaching by setting a good example. The ecumenical approach to expressing the Christian life in Native terms formed an important theme expressed when Native spiritual elders and Jesuit priests joined in the performance of a mass, and an unscheduled faith healing took place. A well-organized session revolving around the concerns of women emphasized the building of self-respect through pride in Native traditions. Self-respect was presented as the basis of tolerance, and tolerance was perceived as a critical factor in the working of the multicultural (a frequently used word) Canadian society.

Another important issue emerged in both introductory and concluding remarks when reference was made to the role of the elders in passing on traditional wisdom about social control, customary law, and leadership.

This particular category of wisdom is viewed as critical today in the current quest for Native self-government. Federal support for Native self-government is found in the report of the Parliamentary Special Committee on Indian Self-Government (1983), which has recommended that each Indian group should work out its own governmental system reflecting traditional forms of government. The oral narratives of the elders are seen as necessary supplements to historical records on these matters.

CONCLUSION

The situation for elderly Anicinabe has considerably improved in the last decade. Many of them are rediscovering a pattern encompassed in the institution of traditional elderhood, making it possible for them selectively to function in a more culturally significant fashion. Not all Anicinabe elderly are interested in this kind of participation, but those who are so functioning are worthy of the status of *elder*, as it has been traditionally understood in this culture. This distinction between the elderly and the elders is not, however, made by all Anicinabe. Many of the younger generation tend to view *all* elderly individuals as *elders*. The elderly themselves are generally aware of the distinction, and will articulate it if pressed. For elderly Anicinabe chronological age still is not a criterion of elderhood; rather it is the set of behaviors discussed above, and the exercise of the mandate to speak with authority that determine elder status.

Some Anicinabe elders and elderly are not involved in the revival of traditional spiritual beliefs. Many are deeply concerned with the formulation and practice of an ecumenical life way. The revitalization picture in southern Ontario is a complex one, and the movements that fall into this category of behavior are taking many forms. Significant here is the fact that most of these movements are supported to some extent through funding from various levels of government—funding that has been designated as support for Indian culture; a renewed interest in the traditional elders' role is everywhere emphasized.

The specific context of change for Canadian Indians is marked by the large proportion of their young population, by government support for multiculturalism extending to the support of Indian culture, and by the resulting emphasis upon the maintenance of Indian identity. In this context the elderly have come to be perceived as making a major contribution to the maintenance of Indian identity; they help to formulate that identity and they are its validators, insofar as they have themselves had validating youthful experiences with traditional elderhood.

Whether the institution of elderhood in its contemporary expression will survive the loss of today's elders with these validating experiences and the inevitable aging of the Native population that must accompany the progress through the life of today's young population, is problematic. If elderhood can bridge the gap between tradition and change in a model similar to the dual patterning of the Anicinabe elders' narratives, it may remain a vital institution. Certainly more and more elderly Indians are having significant and valuable experiences in modernizing situations involving the move to urban life and coping with alcohol and drug addiction, as well as with the welfare, health, and educational systems (Vanderburgh, 1977; 1982). Some Anicinabe elders are already using such experiences as the basis of their anecdotal narratives. As long as the information that elders transmit remains vital to the context of survival, elderhood should endure as a viable institution.

The research upon which this paper is based was supported by the Canada Council (Grant S74–0105, 1974–75) and the Social Sciences and Humanities Research Council of Canada, Population Aging Programme (Grant 492–82–0010, 1982–83). Erindale College, University of Toronto, has provided ongoing support in the form of travel grants. In addition, I am indebted to Gelya Frank for certain insights into the bases of the elders' mandate to speak with authority.

REFERENCES

Amoss, P. (1981a). Coast Salish Elders. In P. Amoss and S. Harrell, eds., *Other Ways of Growing Old: Anthropological Perspectives*. Stanford, Calif.: Stanford University Press.

Amoss, P. (1981b). Cultural Centrality and Prestige for the Elderly: The Coast Salish Case. In C. Fry, ed., *Dimensions: Aging, Culture and Health*. New York: Praeger.

Canada, Government of (1977). Treasury Board Minute 753033 (December 1).

Canada, House of Commons (1983). Indian Self-Government in Canada. Report of the Special Committee on Indian Self-Government. Ottawa: Queen's Printer.

Densmore, F. (1929). *Chippewa Customs*. Smithsonian Institution, Bureau of American Ethnology, *Bulletin 86*. Washington.

Denton, F. T., and Spencer, B. G. (1980). Canada's Population and Labour Force: Past, Present and Future. In V. W. Marshall, ed., *Aging in Canada*. Don Mills, Ont.: Fitzhenry and Whiteside.

Dunning, R. W. (1959). *Social and Economic Change among the Northern Ojibwa*. Toronto: University of Toronto Press.

Frideres, J. S. (1983). *Native People in Canada: Contemporary Conflicts*. Scarborough, Ont.: Prentice-Hall Canada.

Hallowell, A. I. (1964). Ojibwa Ontology, Behavior, and World View. In S. Diamond, ed., *Primitive Views of the World*. New York: Columbia University Press.

Hoffman, W. J. (1891). *The Midewiwin or "Grand Medicine Society" of the Ojibwa*. Smithsonian Institution, Bureau of American Ethnology, *7th Annual Report*. Washington, D.C.

Jenness, D. (1935). *The Ojibwa Indians of Parry Sound: Their Social and Religious Life*. National Museum of Canada Bulletin 78, Anthropological Series 17.

Jilek, W. G. (1974). *Salish Indian Mental Health and Culture Change.* Toronto: Holt, Rinehart and Winston of Canada.

Landes, R. (1968). *Ojibwa Religion and the Midewiwin.* Madison, Wis.: University of Wisconsin Press.

Price, J. A. (1978). *Native Studies: American and Canadian Indians.* Toronto: McGraw-Hill Ryerson.

Redsky, J. (1972). *Great Leader of the Ojibwa: Mis-quona-queb.* Toronto: McClelland and Stewart.

Shulman, N. (1980). The Aging of Urban Canada. In V. W. Marshall, ed., *Aging in Canada.* Don Mills, Ont.: Fitzhenry and Whiteside.

Vanderburgh, R. M. (1977). *I Am Nokomis, too: The Biography of Verna Patronella Johnston.* Don Mills, Ont.: General Publishing.

Vanderburgh, R. M. (1982). When Legends Fall Silent Our Ways Are Lost: Some Dimensions of the Study of Aging among Native Canadians. *Culture,* 2, 21– 28.

Wallace, A. (1956). Revitalization Movements. *American Anthropologist, 58,* 264– 81.

CHAPTER 14

Indian Elderly in the United States

Paul Stuart and Eloise Rathbone-McCuan

This chapter reviews the demography of the American Indian elderly, the social and health characteristics of Indian elderly in the 1980s, United States policy toward the Indian elderly, key federal government agencies engaged in providing services to the Indian elderly, and issues involved in the long-term care of elderly Indian persons.

DEMOGRAPHY OF THE AMERICAN INDIAN ELDERLY

American Indians are a relatively youthful people; the median age was 19.6 years in 1930 and had increased only to 22.8 by 1980. (The term *American Indian*, as used in this paper, includes the aboriginal peoples of the United States, including American Indians and three groups of Alaska Natives, American Indians, Eskimos, and Aleuts.) The proportion of Indians who are elderly has remained relatively constant. Five percent of the Indian population was 65 years and older in 1930; 50 years later that proportion was 5.3 percent. Stability in the proportion of American Indian elderly was largely a result of two factors, a high birth rate and low life expectancy. Thirty-seven percent of American Indian deaths occur before age 45, compared to 12 percent in the general population. High death rates result in part from causes most likely to affect young adults, such as accidents, suicides, and homicides.

While the *proportion* of Indian elderly has not increased, the *number* of elderly American Indians has increased substantially. In part, the increase results from changes in the procedures for enumerating individual Indians. Since 1960 the census has increasingly relied on self-reporting of racial and ethnic status as the basis for various minority group enumerations. This coincided with an increase in ethnic pride and, it is thought, an increased willingness of respondents to identify themselves as American Indians (I. S.

Table 14.1
American Indians 65 Years and Older, 1910–1980

Year	Number 65 Years and Over	Percent of Total American Indian Population	Percent Female
1910	12,986	4.9%	53%
1930	16,357	5.0%	49%
1960	25,587	4.7%	49%
1970	43,802	5.7%	53%
1980	74,919	5.3%	56%

Source: Bureau of the Census, *Indians in the United States and Alaska: 1930* (Washington: U.S. Government Printing Office, 1937), p. 87; Bureau of the Census, *Census of Population: 1960. General Population Characteristics, U.S. Summary* (Washington: U.S. Government Printing Office, 1964): Bureau of the Census, *1970 Census of Population. General Population Characteristics, U.S. Summary* (Washington: U.S. Government Printing Office, 1973: Bureau of the Census, *1980 Census of Population. General Population Characteristics, U.S. Summary* (Washington: U.S. Government Printing Office, 1983), pp. 27–36.

Lowry, 1982). In 1930, the American Indian population 65 years of age and over was 16,357; the 1980 census set the number of American Indians 65 and over at 74,919, a fourfold increase. An increasing proportion of elderly American Indian people are women, as is true of the overall aging population.

American Indians have the lowest median age and the second smallest proportion of persons 65 years of age and over among American minority groups, reflecting their relatively disadvantaged position in society. However, the four major minority groups enumerated by the United States census share the characteristics of low median age and low percentage of persons 65 years of age and over relative to whites and to the general population. The reasons are similar, involving the relative poverty and shorter life expectancy of these groups when compared to whites. In addition, for some groups, such as Asians and Pacific Islanders and certain groups of persons of Spanish origin, immigration is less likely to involve the elderly.

The national data obscure significant local and regional variations in the

Table 14.2
Elderly Persons in the United States

	Number of Persons 65 and over	Percent Elderly in Population	Median Age	Males per 100 Females 65 and over
	(% of Total Elderly)			
Whites	22,948,193 (89.8%)	12.2	31.3	67.2
Total U.S.	25,549,427 (100%)	11.3	30.0	67.6
Blacks	2,086,858 (8.2%)	7.9	24.9	68.3
Persons of Spanish Origin	708,880 (2.8%)	4.9	23.2	75.6
Asians and Pacific Islanders	211,736 (0.8%)	6.0	28.7	96.4
American Indians, Eskimos, and Aleuts	74,919 (0.3%)	5.3	22.8	78.6

Source: U.S. Bureau of the Census, *1980 Census of Population, Vol. 1, Characteristics of the Population, General Population Characteristics, U.S. Summary* (Washington: Government Printing Office, 1983), pp. 27–36.

American Indian elderly population. For example, the population of American Indians living in "identified Indian areas" (reservations, historic Indian areas in Oklahoma, and Alaska Native villages) differs from the population living in urban areas and nonreservation rural areas. At the 1980 Census, for example, only 339,987 American Indians and Alaska natives of all ages, less than one-fourth of the total, lived on reservations. An additional 30,274 lived on off-reservation tribal trust lands, while 116,426 lived in the historic Indian areas of Oklahoma (excluding urbanized areas), and 39,301 lived in Alaska Native villages.

These *identified areas* contain a little over a third of the Indian and Alaska Native population. All are traditional homes for American Indians and Alaska Natives, but they differ in history, status, and characteristics (Bureau of the Census, 1984, 1985). There are 278 reservations. These are officially

Table 14.3
American Indians and Alaska Natives in 1980 by Place of Residence

	Total	American Indians	Eskimos	Alents
United States	1,423,043 (100.0)	1,366,676 (100.0)	42,162 (100.0)	14,205 (100.0)
In Identified Indian and Alaska Native Areas	525,988 (37.0)	494,483 (36.2)	26,718 (63.4)	4,787 (33.7)
On Reservations	339,987 (23.9)	339,836 (24.9)	95 (0.2)	56 (0.4)
On Tribal Trust Lands	30,274 (2.1)	30,265 (2.2)	4 -	5 -
In Historic Indian Areas of Oklahoma (excluding urbanized areas)	116,426 (8.2)	116,359 (8.5)	45 (0.1)	22 (0.2)
In Alaska Native Villages	39,301 (2.8)	8,023 (0.6)	26,574 (63.0)	4,704 (33.1)
Not in Identified Areas	897,055 (63.0)	872,193 (63.8)	15,444 (36.6)	9,418 (66.3)

Note: Corrected count.
Source: U.S. Bureau of the Census, *1980 Census of Population. American Indian Areas and Alaska Native Villages: 1980. Supplementary Report* PC80–S1–13 (Washington: Government Printing Office, 1984), p. 2.

recognized areas with boundaries established by treaty, statute, executive order, or court order within the various states. Reservation lands are held in trust for tribes or individual Indians by the United States government or, in the case of a small number of state reservations in some of the eastern states, by state governments. On reservations, tribal governments possess some of the attributes of sovereignty, including local civil and criminal jurisdiction in most states, the power to regulate marriage and divorce, and the power to define the qualifications for membership in the tribe.

There are other land units important to American Indians. Tribal trust lands are parcels of land, not within reservations, which are held in trust by the United States for individual Indians or tribes. Some parcels were public domain allotments which could be claimed by eligible Indians, and

Table 14.4
Indian Population 65 Years of Age and Over—National, Reservation,
Oklahoma Historic Areas, 1980

	United States	Reservations	Oklahoma Historic Areas
Elderly Indians (%)	74,919 (100%)	18,093 (24%)	10,796 (14%)
% of Indian Population in Area	5.3%	5.0%	9.5%
Median Age All Indians in Area	22.8	19.7	23.5

Source: U.S. Bureau of the Census, *American Indians, Eskimos, and Aleuts on Identified Reservations and in the Historic Areas of Oklahoma (Excluding Urbanized Areas)* (Washington: Government Printing Office, 1985).

others are lands to which the Indian title was never extinguished. The historic Indian areas of Oklahoma are sections of the state which were legally established reservations prior to Oklahoma statehood in 1907. While technically nonreservation areas, they remain areas with large Indian populations and are traditional homelands for the Oklahoma tribes. The 209 Alaska Native villages are the traditional homes of the Eskimos, Aleuts, and American Indians who were living in Alaska when the United States purchased the territory from Russia in 1867.

While there were only 18,093 Indians 65 years of age or older living on reservations in 1980 (or about 5 percent of the total Indian reservation population), nearly 10 percent of the Indian population of the historic Indian areas of Oklahoma, 10,796 persons, were 65 years of age or older. The median age of American Indians is higher in the Oklahoma Historic Areas than on reservations or in the general Indian population. (See Table 14.4.)

Other significant variations are tribal. The 278 Indian reservations and 209 Alaskan Native communities in the United States include 64 reservations and three Eskimo communities in Alaska with populations of 1,000 or more.

The Navajo reservation of Arizona, New Mexico, and Utah is the largest in the United States, with a population of 104,517 and nearly 5,000 elderly. (Many other Navajos live off the reservation, in nearby urban centers like Albuquerque and Gallup, New Mexico, and Phoenix, Arizona, and in such major metropolitan areas as Los Angeles, Dallas–Fort Worth, Denver, and Chicago.) With the urbanization of the American Indian population, many reservations have become the homes of the very young and the very old, as Indians in early adulthood have left reservations in search of economic opportunity. However, there are relatively small populations of elderly Indians on most reservations. Table 14.5 presents data from the 1980 census on the population of elderly Indians at a variety of reservations and Oklahoma historic Indian area locations.

Efforts to generate detailed statistical estimates of the needs of the American Indian elderly are complicated by population dispersion and varying definitions of who is an Indian. In preparation for the 1981 White House Conference on Aging, several major American Indian organizations devoted to elderly concerns compiled data on the Indian elderly and initiated special studies of their condition. The National Indian Council on Aging (1981a) prepared a general profile of need.

Major health problems of the American Indian elderly included obesity, diabetes, poor nutrition, hypertension, cancer, pneumonia, and vision and dental problems. When reservation Indians were surveyed for level of physical impairment, Indians aged 55 and above had levels of impairment comparable to those found in persons aged 65 and above in a survey of non-Indian urban dwellers. Major barriers to the provisioon of health care to elderly American Indians included lack of a national strategy for the delivery of preventive care; lack of coordination and linkages among the aging network and the Indian Health Service, the federal agency responsible for Indian health; lack of transportation to medical facilities; lack of information about health care; and lack of culture-sensitive medical care. The profile also discussed problems of the Indian elderly in the areas of economic status, family and community support, education and employment, housing, and long-term care. (See Table 14.6.)

American Indians have been identified as a *priority group* for services from the Administration on Aging (AoA), United States Department of Health and Human Services, because of multiple social, economic, and health problems. This designation formally acknowledges the special at-risk status of the American Indian elderly. Technically priority groups have special funding priority at the federal and state levels. However, actual expenditures do not always follow federal guidelines. Research and service demonstration funds are especially needed to identify and meet culture-specific needs among minority elderly.

Gaps in information about the American Indian elderly are large. Most research has been conducted on reservation samples despite the fact that

Table 14.5
Elderly American Indian Population—Selected Reservations and Historic Indian Areas, 1980

Reservation	Indian Population 65 and over	Percent of Total Indian Population	Percent Female	Median Age
Blackfeet (Montana)	324	5.9%	52.5%	20.7
Cherokee Nation* (Oklahoma)	3,982	10.4%	58.8%	24.2
Cheyenne-Arapahoe* (Oklahoma)	130	5.6%	62.3%	19.9%
Choctaw Nation* (Oklahoma)	1,538	11.3%	58.8%	23.8
Eastern Cherokee (North Carolina)	332	6.9%	51.2%	22.6
Hopi (Arizona)	526	8.0%	52.9%	21.8
Laguna Pueblo (New Mexico)	288	8.1%	59.3%	23.1
Menominee (Wisconsin)	136	5.7%	46.3%	20.3
Navajo (Arizona, New Mexico, and Utah)	4,974	4.8%	52.9%	18.7
Pine Ridge Sioux (South Dakota)	567	4.8%	51.5%	18.2
San Carlos Apache (Arizona)	248	4.3%	48.8%	19.5
Yakimi (Washington)	258	5.2%	60.1%	20.5

Note: *Indicates Historic Indian Area in Oklahoma.
Source: U.S. Bureau of the Census, *American Indians, Eskimos, and Aleuts on Identified Reservations and in the Historic Areas of Oklahoma (Excluding Urbanized Areas)* (Washington: U.S. Government Printing Office, 1985).

Table 14.6
Profile of the American Indian Elderly, 1981

Of the American Indian Elderly:

Economic Well-Being	65%	have incomes below the poverty level
	33%	receive Supplementary Security Income (SSI) as their sole source of income
	60%	support other family members
Family and Community Support	26%	care for at least one grandchild
	58%	live in households with two or more persons
	67%	live within five miles of relatives
Education and Employment	25%	have less than a fifth grade education
	65%	were semi-skilled, unskilled, or farm workers
Housing	26%	live in housing constructed before 1939
	25%	of all Indian households are without plumbing
Long-Term Care	5%	are in long-term care, but only 8 long-care facilities (410 beds) are located on reservations

Source: National Indian Council on Aging, *American Indian Elderly: A National Profile* (Albuquerque, N.M.: National Indian Council on Aging, 1981).

less than one-fourth of the Indian elderly live on reservations. Nearly half live in urban areas. The continuing increase of the elderly population has been repeatedly verified. The Indian Health Service (IHS) estimates that the Indian population in IHS service areas in 1990 will be 1,103,918 (up from 828,609 in 1980), based on an estimated average annual growth of 2.91 percent per year during the 1980s (Indian Health Service [IHS], 1986). The IHS service area includes reservations and nearby areas, as well as traditional Indian areas in the states of Alaska and Oklahoma.

UNITED STATES INDIAN POLICY

American Indians and Alaska Natives have a unique political status. Chief Justice John Marshall's description of the Indian tribes as *domestic dependent nations* provides the legal doctrine describing the unique political status of Indians in the United States (V. Deloria, Jr. and C. Lytle, 1984). Before the arrival of European people in North America, Indian communities were self-governing, sovereign nations. After white settlement Indian communities, as a result of conflict or voluntary agreement, became subordinated to external authority, either a European colonial power or, after independence, the United States. However, Indian tribes did not surrender all their sovereignty. It is this remaining sovereignty which provides the basis for a separate political existence for American Indian tribes today. (S. L. Pevar, 1983).

The United States Constitution gives the federal government exclusive and plenary (or absolute) power in Indian affairs. The *commerce clause* (Article I, Section 8) provides:

The Congress shall have Power...to regulate Commerce with foreign Nations, among the several states, and with the Indian Tribes....

In Article II, Section 2, the president is given the power to make treaties "by and with the Advice and Consent of the Senate...provided two-thirds of the Senators present concur." These two clauses provide the basis of federal powers in Indian affairs (Deloria and Lytle, 1983).

Indian tribal governments have been recognized as unique governmental entities. They retain certain attributes of sovereignty, consisting of those powers of government which have not been explicitly surrendered by the tribes or removed by Congress (Pevar, 1983). At times Congress has explicitly recognized one or another attribute of sovereignty, as when the Indian Child Welfare Act of 1978 provided tribal governments with certain powers related to child custody cases involving tribal members. Absence of explicit congressional recognition of a power does not mean that the tribe does not possess the power. Nor does a tribe's failure to exercise a power of self-government necessarily mean that it has relinquished the power. The test is whether the tribe has explicitly surrendered the power or it has been removed by the Congress.

The unique political–legal status of American Indians has significant implications for the treatment of the Indian elderly. The primary responsibility for providing social and health services to elderly Indians on reservations belongs to the federal government, not the states, except as Congress has explicitly transferred that responsibility to the states. At times the question of which level of government, the state or the federal, has primary responsibility for providing services is ambiguous.

The United States dealt with tribes by treaty until 1871, when the Congress, exercising its plenary power, ended the practice. The legislation which ended treaty making with Indian tribes explicitly provided that those treaties which Congress had ratified would remain in force (Indian Appropriations Act of 1871). After 1871 Congress made *agreements* with the tribes. The pattern for agreement making was similar to treaty making. The agreement was presented to the Congress for ratification as legislation. An agreement requires the assent of both houses of Congress, while a treaty requires the assent only of the Senate. The United States Supreme Court has held that agreements with Indian tribes have the same force as treaties (Deloria, 1971).

Many of the treaties ratified prior to 1871 provided that the federal government would provide health and other services to the tribes. Often such services were provided as partial compensation for lands ceded by the tribe to the United States or for other services rendered by the Indians. On the basis of these provisions, the Bureau of Indian Affairs (BIA) provided physicians at most reservations in the late nineteenth century. Educational services, food, clothing and shelter were also provided to Indian groups under the provisions of various treaties.

During the late nineteenth century assimilation of Indians into American society became a major goal of federal Indian policy. The General Allotment Act of 1887 provided a mechanism for accomplishing this, by dividing reservations into individually held tracts of land, title to which would be held in trust by the United States for twenty-five years. Following the expiration of the trust period, full title to the allotment would pass to the Indian owner, who would be "freed" of federal supervision. Allotments, held to be untaxable during the trust period, became taxable and could be sold or used as collateral for loans upon expiration of the trust. It was expected that the allottee then would take his or her place as a taxpaying landowner and citizen of the state in which the allotment was located (D. S. Otis, 1973).

The Burke Act of 1906 modified the provisions of the General Allotment Act by tying the expiration of the trust period to the "competence" of the Indian allottee. The secretary of the interior could end the trust period before its expiration for those allottees judged competent to manage their own affairs. For allottees judged not competent at the end of the trust period, the secretary could extend the trust period indefinitely. Thus the Burke Act made possible the extension of federal protection of land, and the associated provision of health and social services, indefinitely for those Indians judged to be "incompetent."

Together, the General Allotment and Burke acts created alternative statuses for American Indians: the incompetent or "ward" Indian, and the competent or "citizen" Indian. In practice, however, many states regarded any Indian as the federal government's responsibility. Problems of landless Indians became serious in the early twentieth century, as much land going out of trust was sold or lost by the Indian owners. To provide authorization for federal health and social services offered to Indians not covered by treaty provisions, Congress passed the Snyder Act in 1921.

The act authorizes the BIA to "expend such monies as Congress may from time to time appropriate, for the benefit, care, and assistance of the Indians throughout the United States." With regard to health care, the act authorizes expenditures "for the relief of distress and the conservation of health of Indians." The authorization for the provision of health and social services to Indians has been held to derive from the Snyder Act and not from treaty obligations. The Supreme Court, in *Morton* v. *Ruiz* (1974), found that the services authorized under the Snyder Act need continue only at the pleasure of the Congress.

The Johnson-O'Malley Act of 1934 authorized the commissioner of Indian affairs to contract with states for the provision of educational, social and health services to reservation Indians. The primary purpose of the act was to integrate Indian children into the public schools; however, provisions for contracting for health and social services were included. States eventually were expected to assume most of the service functions of the Bureau of Indian Affairs (T. W. Taylor, 1983).

Other congressional enactments of the past half-century place the responsibility for providing social and health services to Indians on the states and their subdivisions, often with federal assistance. All Indians were made citizens by the Indian Citizenship Act of 1924. Since Indians are citizens of the states in which they reside, they are entitled to receive services provided by the states to other citizens, such as public schooling and medical assistance to the indigent (Pevar, 1983). The federal government funds some services through intergovernmental grant-in-aid programs; these are theoretically available to American Indians on the same basis as other citizens. However, Indian access to services has sometimes been problematic, because of perceived cultural insensitivity or negative attitudes toward Indians on the part of care givers (Deloria and Lytle, 1983).

The public assistance and social service provisions of the Social Security Act of 1935 have been significant for the Indian elderly for a variety of reasons. Few Indian elderly qualify for old age and survivors insurance (OASI) benefits under the act because of uneven work histories or employment in occupations which were not covered. Since all Indians are citizens, Indians who qualify for categorical assistance cannot be rejected by state or local governments. Nevertheless, in some states with large Indian populations, the Bureau of Public Assistance, the federal agency responsible for implementing the public assistance titles of the Social Security Act, encountered difficulties getting eligible Indians included in public assistance caseloads (S. H. James, 1947).

The Social Security Act and subsequent legislation resulted in the creation of a broad range of service and income programs for which most elderly Indians were technically eligible. Legislation enacted in the year 1965, including the health care amendments to the Social Security Act and the Older Americans Act, was particularly significant. Medicaid was more significant than Medicare for elderly American Indians, since access to Medicare benefits is conditioned on labor force participation. Indians living in different states receive different coverage because Medicaid programs are designed by the states. Significantly, Arizona, a state with a large Indian population, did not participate in Medicaid until the mid–1980s. Provision of health care services for the indigent elderly was in theory a county responsibility in that state. Many counties failed to provide services, and for many indigent elderly American Indians the Indian Health Service (IHS), operating under the broad authorization found in the Snyder Act, provided what health care services were available.

Even after two decades, underutilization of state and locally provided social and health services by American Indians remains a significant problem. Despite the identification of the American Indian and Alaska Native elderly as a *priority group* to receive services funded by the AoA, for example, less than 1 percent of persons served by AoA-funded Title III programs in the early 1980s were Indians or Alaska Natives (National Indian Council on Aging, 1981b). This underutilization was not solely the result of attempts to exclude American Indians. Programs may fail to direct outreach efforts at elderly American Indian populations, or elderly Indians may be reluctant to participate because of cultural insensitivity on the part of program personnel.

This problem is often unrecognized by gerontologists who have little understanding of the Indian elderly. Some attention has been given to the overall lower rates of minority elder participation in some senior citizen programs. Unfortunately, little attention is given to the special barriers that face specific subgroups. The specific barriers differ among minority elderly clusters.

As previously mentioned, the Johnson-O'Malley Act of 1934 looked toward the day when the federal government would disengage from Indian affairs, and services would be provided by the states. After World War II public and congressional sentiment for ending special protections on Indian lands and special services for Indian people was strong. "Termination of federal supervision" of Indians was the slogan of this movement, which was in part a return to the assimilationist thinking of the late nineteenth century and in part an expression of liberal patriotism resulting from the Allied victory over the Axis powers (C. R. Koppes, 1977; L. W. Burt, 1982).

The termination era of the late 1940s and 1950s brought efforts to end federal protection on Indian lands, to dismantle the Bureau of Indian Affairs and distribute its service functions to state and local governments and other federal agencies, and to end special treatment of American Indians on the basis of tribal affiliation or race. Although termination has been repudiated by every president of the United States since Lyndon Johnson, the termination movement has had a significant impact on the provision of services to elderly Indians.

In 1949 the Hoover Commission recommended transferring services, where feasible, from the federal level to the states and private providers (Commission on the Organization of the Executive Branch of the Government [Hoover Commission], 1949). In 1954 Congress transferred the responsibility for providing health care services to American Indians from the BIA to the Public Health Service in the Department of Health, Education, and Welfare, intended as the first step in a total dismantling of the bureau (Taylor, 1983). The legislation authorized a program of contracting with state and local agencies and private providers, similar to Johnson-O'Malley, for the provision of health services to Indian people. The Public Health Service provided Indian health services through a separate division, now known as the Indian Health Service (IHS) (P. Stuart, 1985).

While several tribes were terminated during the 1950s, including the Klamath tribe of Oregon and the Menominee tribe in Wisconsin, attempts to implement the termination policy resulted in a backlash from American Indians. Indians responded to the threat to their separate political identity embodied in the termination policy by lobbying and organizing at the national and state levels. They emphasized Indian identity and attempted to increase the strength of tribal institutions (P. Iverson, 1985). By the late 1960s federal officials had rejected termination; President Richard M. Nixon proclaimed a policy of "self-determination" of Indian tribes and communities (R. M. Nixon, 1971).

The Indian Self-Determination and Education Assistance Act of 1975 provides that, at its request, a tribe can contract with the relevant federal agency to administer the services provided to its members. In such situations, the federal agency's responsibility is simply to monitor the contract. The act envisions the federal government in a funding and advisory role rather than a service provision role. The tribe is intended to be in control. Under the provisions of the act, tribes have contracted to provide a variety of social and health services directly to their members.

ELDER SERVICES AND LONG-TERM CARE

The previous section described the evolution of United States Indian policy. The American Indian elderly of today have lived through some of the various shifts of attitudes about service provision and were often "victimized" by health and social service program fluctuations. No wonder many of the elders have not been eager to participate in programs now targeted for them in later life and promoted as benefits to elderly Indians.

A confusing array of federal agencies controls financing and service provision. The Older Americans Act authorizes the delivery of social and nutritional services to all people 60 and over, with Title VI of the act providing funding for elderly Indians living on reservations. Nonreservation Indians are to be served by general senior citizen aging programs funded under other titles.

An Indian Office on Aging was established in the Administration on Aging to administer the Title VI grants to tribes and to provide technical assistance. During the first year of Title VI grant awards (1980), eighty-five tribal organizations received grants. Eighty-four tribal organizations were funded in 1981. Awards ranged from $65,000 to $100,000 with an average award of $70,500. Despite an encouraging start, Title VI may not significantly improve the provision of services to elderly reservation Indians because of federal financial cuts. Many states with large numbers of American Indian elderly residing in Area Agency on Aging (AAA) service areas have moved to a "targeting" approach, in which American Indian elderly are in direct competition with other high-risk minority elderly. In areas of the Southwest and West where Black and Hispanic elderly co-exist with American Indian elderly, the principle of equity distribution to match greatest risk is difficult to achieve.

Elder advocates charge that the special needs of elderly Indians are not of sufficient priority to the Bureau of Indian Affairs. These critics suggest that the bureau is "organizationally flawed," overly politicized, and inefficient (E. M. Carpenter, 1980; Senate Committee on Indian Affairs, 1982). These criticisms echo long-standing complaints about the administrative competence of the agency (P. Stuart, 1985). Concerns include the lack of specialized services for the elderly, the uncoordinated service delivery pattern, and an overreliance on institutional services for the frail.

The Indian Health Service (IHS) has emphasized the provision of acute care, preventive care, especially in maternal and child health, and public health measures such as sanitation and the improvement of water supplies and waste disposal systems. Preventive care, including both medical and dental care, has emphasized interventions with younger Indians (Office of Technology Assessment [OTA], 1986). IHS provides direct medical care through a system of hospitals and health centers located on reservations and contract medical care for services unavailable at reservation locations. Contract care is increasing. On many smaller reservations contract care is the primary health care provided by IHS. Eligibility for direct care differs from eligibility for contract care. IHS policy has been to provide direct care at IHS facilities to any Indian. Eligibility for contract care, however, has been limited to Indians who are living on reservation lands, to Indian students, and to foster children who are living off-reservation. Since more than half of the Indian population lives in nonreservation areas, with nearly half of all elderly Indians in urban areas, this policy results in significant denials of service.

IHS interprets its role as the health care provider of last resort, thus justifying its restrictions on the provision of contract care to Indians living on reservations. Indigent off-reservation Indians are presumed to be the responsibility of the states. The lack of consistency in the pattern of state service provision under Medicaid leaves some Indian patients vulnerable. Congress attempted to clarify this relationship by making IHS facilities eligible for Medicare and Medicaid reimbursement in the Indian Health Care Improvement Act of 1976. The act articulated the mission of the Indian Health Service as "raising" the health status of American Indians and Alaska Natives to "the highest possible level."

IHS does not regard the provision of long-term care for the Indian elderly as part of its mandate, unless the individual requires skilled nursing home care. Care for other Indians is provided by the Bureau of Indian Affairs. In FY 1983 the number of visits to IHS ambulatory facilities by patients older than 65 accounted for 10 percent of all visits. This group accounted for over 15 percent of all hospitals days provided by IHS (House Committees on Aging and Interior and Insular Affairs, 1985).

As a result of small numbers of elderly at particular reservation locations, problems of securing adequate funding, and the preoccupation of caretakers with the needs of other age cohorts, few community-based or institutional services for the elderly are available on Indian reservations. In 1981 there were only eight Indian-controlled nursing homes on reservations, with a total bed capacity of 410. (See Table 14.7.) Even the Navajo Reservation, the largest in the nation, with an elderly population of 5,000, had only one nursing home, at Chinle, with a bed capacity of 79 (House Committees on Aging and Interior and Insular Affairs, 1985).

The lack of noninstitutional services on many reservations results in a greater likelihood of institutionalization for American Indian elderly. The lack of institutions on reservations means that many elderly American Indians are placed in nursing homes located off their home reservations, frequently a great distance away. In off-reservation nursing homes elderly Indians often feel isolated because of the distance from relatives and the lack of other Indians with whom to converse (R. C. Cooley, D. Ostendorf, and D. Bickerton, 1979). The National Indian Council on Aging estimated that 4,660 persons, 6.2 percent of the elderly American Indian and Alaska Native population, were in nursing homes in 1981 (House Committees on Aging and Interior and Insular Affairs, 1985). Off-reservation placement of the elderly, who provide living contact with traditions, can be a significant problem for small Indian communities. The problem can be serious as well, for elderly Indian people placed in institutions located far away from family and familiar surroundings.

Table 14.7
Indian Nursing Homes—Starting Dates, Bed Capacity, Levels of Care, Percent of Occupancy

Date	Facility	# of Beds	Levels of Care	% of Occupancy
1969	American Indians	96	Skilled, Intermediate, Personal Care, Board and Care	100%
1971	Chinle	79	Skilled	Not answered
1974	Blackfeet	49	Skilled, Intermediate	69-70%
1978	Oneida	50	Skilled, Intermediate, Personal Care, Board and Care	90-92%
1978	Toyei	66	Personal	90-100%
1978	Carl T. Curtis	25	Intermediate	80-85%
1979	White River	20	Personal Care	90% (winter)
1982	Languna-Rainbow	25	Intermediate	100%

Source: Cynthia Mick, "A Profile of American Indian Nursing Homes," in U.S. Congress, House of Representatives, Select Committee on Aging and Committee on Interior and Insular Affairs, *Long-Term Care for the Indian Elderly* (Washington: Government Printing Office, 1985), p. 239.

A change in the congressional mandate to the IHS might well institute steps in the direction of significant expansion and improvement in geriatric care, but the solution to the long-term care problem does not rest with the Indian Health Service alone. Tribes and other federal agencies, including the BIA, the Department of Housing and Urban Development, and the Administration on Aging, must all be involved in planning a comprehensive long-term strategy. The National Indian Council on Aging (n.d., p. 23) recommended that these agencies make elderly American Indians a priority group for services.

CONCLUSION

The preceding sections have discussed the demography of the Indian elderly, the development of federal policy, and current service needs. Solution of the long-term care problem and provision of the other services elderly need will require adequate resources, changes in the relationships among service delivery agencies, and shifts in policies controlling service provision.

An additional variable to consider is the American Indian family. Under close examination one finds a highly diverse institution. Some Indian families are highly vulnerable because of stresses such as poverty, divorce, unemployment, rootlessness, and mental health problems. At the same time there are strong, vital family units that are stable, upwardly mobile, and culturally secure. These families can offer security and fulfillment to members of all generations.

Red Horse (1980) cautions non-Indian helping professionals against stereotyping the American Indian family. Its adaptive capacity, even among families who live in urban areas far removed from reservation roots and kin, is often great. Many families are creating substitute or modified kin networks in new surroundings with nonrelatives. Much of this behavior seems directed toward the significant role of child care socialization, which is a traditional role for elders in many tribal cultures.

Not all Indian families absorb the older generation into meaningful roles as the transmitters of culture, values, language, and religion. Some families, especially those with weakened intergenerational ties, facing problems of poverty and social problems among the younger generation, may not be able to sustain elder care. It seems appropriate to raise cautions about leaving too much of a demand for "elder care giving" to younger generations of Indians without a comprehensive study of what consequences this may yield for the American Indian family. Indian families, while culturally prepared to take on this care giving, are also vulnerable to heavy demands from younger family members. What must be sought are approaches to elder care giving that balance the needs and resources of each generation. The oldest of the old are the immediate victims of inadequate long-term care. A larger population of "young-old" is emerging. That group, now entering the elderly age cohort, is one for which the "old ways" of family life and intergenerational care giving are less strong. They have experienced an alternative socialization, and formulation of national policy toward the American Indian elderly must take into account changes in the life experiences of the new generation of Indian elderly.

Such an approach would require considerable autonomy at the level of the Indian community, whether or not the specific Indian community is located on a reservation. AoA's Title VI programs should be made available to off-reservation Indian communities, even at the expense of creating a parallel service system for the elderly in urban centers with large Indian populations.

Indian families present a significant resource for the Indian elderly. In addition, as keepers of tradition, elderly Indians are a significant resource for the continuation of Indian identity, and hence community survival. Some Indian families will need support in order to assist Indian elders. Federal policy should make such supports available to families in communities requesting such programs. Essential family supports may include funds to purchase respite care, direct financial assistance, employment counseling, training, and placement, among others. The need for a variety of supports is suggested by the wide range of nonmedical social services provided by IHS-funded Urban Indian Health Centers (Office of Technological Assessment, 1986).

Financial support adequate to the task is essential. In the mid–1980s tribes and urban Indian groups are experiencing significant cuts in available funding for a variety of services. The promotion of self-determination, family participation in caregiving, and local autonomy without adequate financial support will do little to resolve the long-term care problem or other problems of the Indian elderly.

REFERENCES

Bureau of Census (1984). *1980 Census of Population. American Indian Areas and Alaska Native Villages: 1980* (Supplementary Report PC80-S1–13). Washington: Government Printing Office.

Bureau of Census (1985). *1980 Census of Population. American Indians, Eskimos, and Aleuts on Identified Reservations and in the Identified Historic Areas of Oklahoma (excluding Urbanized Areas)* (Subject Report PC80–2–1D). Washington: Government Printing Office.

Burke Act of 1906, 36 Stat. 182.

Burt, L. W. (1982). *Tribalism in Crisis: Federal Indian Policy, 1953–1961*. Albuquerque, N.M.: University of New Mexico Press.

Carpenter, E. M. (1980). American Indian Social Services, Policies and Issues. *Social Casework, 61*, 455–461.

Commission on the Organization of the Executive Branch of the Government (Hoover Commission) (1949). *Social Security and Education Indian Affairs: A Report to the Congress*. Washington: Government Printing Office.

Cooley, R. C., Ostendorf, D., and Bickerton, D. (1979). Outreach Services for Elderly Native Americans. *Social Work, 24*, 151–53.

Deloria, Jr., V., ed. (1971). *Of Utmost Good Faith*. San Francisco: Straight Arrow Books.

Deloria, Jr., V., and Lytle, C. (1983). *American Indians, American Justice*. Austin, Tex.: University of Texas Press.

Deloria, Jr., V., and Lytle, C. (1984). *The Nations Within: The Past and Future of American Indian Sovereignty*. New York: Pantheon.

General Allotment Act of 1887, 24 Stat. 388.

House Committees on Aging and Interior and Insular Affairs (1985). *Long-Term Care for the Indian Elderly*, Oversight Hearing. Washington: Government Printing Office.

Indian Appropriations Act of 1871, 16 Stat. 566.

Indian Child Welfare Act of 1978, 92 Stat. 3069.

Indian Citizenship Act of 1924, 43 Stat. 253.

Indian Health Care Improvement Act of 1976, 90 Stat. 1400.

Indian Health Service (1986). *Chart Series Book, April 1986.* Washington: Government Printing Office.

Indian Self-Determination and Education Assistance Act of 1975, 88 Stat. 2203.

Iverson, P. (1985). Building toward Self-Determination: Plains and Southwestern Indians in the 1940s and 1950s. *Western Historical Quarterly, 16,* 163–73.

James, S. H. (1947). Public Responsibility for the American Indian. *Proceedings of the National Conference of Social Work, 74,* 176–84.

Johnson-O'Malley Act of 1934, 48 Stat. 596.

Koppes, C. R. (1977). From New Deal to Termination: Liberalism and Indian Policy. *Pacific Historical Review, 46,* 543–66.

Lowry, I. S. (1982). The science and politics of ethnic enumeration. In W. A. Van Horne, ed., *Ethnicity and Public Policy* (42–61), Milwaukee, Wis.: University of Wisconsin American Ethnic Studies Coordinating Committee.

Morton v. Ruiz, 415 U.S. 199 (1974).

National Indian Council on Aging (1981a). *American Indian Elderly: A National Profile.* Albuquerque, N.M.: National Indian Council on Aging.

National Indian Council on Aging (1981b). *Indian Elderly and Entitlement Programs: An Accessing Demonstration Project.* Albuquerque, N.M.: National Indian Council on Aging.

National Indian Council on Aging (n.d. [1985]). *A National Advocacy Project to Develop Data, Programs and Policies Addressing the Needs of Indian and Alaskan Native Elders.* Albuquerque, N.M.: National Indian Council on Aging.

Nixon, R. M. (1971). Special Message to the Congress on Indian Affairs (July 8, 1970). In *Public Papers of the President of the United States: Richard Nixon, 1970* (564–76), Washington: Government Printing Office.

Office of Technology Assessment (1986). *Indian Health Care* (OTA-H–290). Washington: Government Printing Office.

Older Americans Act of 1965, 79 Stat. 218.

Otis, D. S. (1973). *The Dawes Act and the Allotment of Indian Lands.* Norman, Okla.: University of Oklahoma Press.

Pevar, S. L. (1983). *The Rights of Indians and Tribes.* An American Civil Liberties Union Handbook. New York: Bantam Books.

Red Horse, J. G. (1980). Family Structure and Value Orientation in American Indians. *Social Casework, 61,* 462–67.

Snyder Act of 1921, 42 Stat. 208.

Social Security Act of 1935, 49 Stat. 620.

Stuart, P. (1977). United States Indian Policy: From the Dawes Act to the American Indian Policy Review Commission. *Social Service Review, 51,* 451–63.

Stuart, P. (1985). Administrative Reform in Indian Affairs. *Western Historical Quarterly, 16,* 133–46.

Taylor, T. W. (1983). *American Indian Policy.* Mt. Airy, Md.: Lomond Publications.

SUMMARY

There has been a native self-determination movement in Canada and the United States for the past twenty years. The middle-aged leaders of the movement in the 1960s gave rebirth to the belief that Indians must control their own identity and reestablish their cultural heritage. The young people who were socialized into adulthood during this period of reawakening are now themselves political and social leaders of their tribes. They are giving an important leadership voice to tribal matters, including the welfare of all generations of Native families. Native leaders are working hard to assure that the policies of the Department of Indian Affairs and Northern Development (DIAND) and the Bureau of Indian Affairs (BIA) are serving the best interests and needs of their people.

The degree of direct responsibility that individual tribes can take for direct service provision to their elders depends on such factors as the size of the elderly population on a particular reserve or reservation, the resources the tribe has to actually create special services for elders, and the availability of resources not directly under local authority that can be used to assist the native elderly. In some cases the complexities of federal, provincial/state, and tribal policies become tangled and bureaucratic to the point where there is a lack of clear authority over who shall assume what roles in planning and administering resources.

In both countries greater effort is being made to increase communication among the various tribes around areas of common concern. Certainly the institution of the Indian family is one that must be given greater attention. The white majority needs to recognize the various structural forms in the Native family such as the long-term stable urban dwelling unit, the recently arrived grouping with multiple generations of members closely linked together, the transient family group with movement to and from the reservation, and the highly isolated unit without cultural contact.

These chapters have concentrated to some extent on the characteristics of elderly who have residential connections near reserves or actually reside on reservations. One is left with the impression that a great deal of information is needed to further clarify the variations in situations that face different tribes and groups of tribesmen separated from their social and cultural roots. The research directions needed to increase understanding are:

1. More thorough assessments of social, economic, health and cultural revitalization needs completed by researchers in close cooperation with tribal units and Native scholars;

2. Greater understanding of how white majority aging programs can meet the needs of Native elders in their catchment areas that are beyond the reserve area;

3. Systematic research to understand how preventive programs can be designed and delivered to reach the younger Native groups prior to later life periods.

VIII
CROSS-NATIONAL INTERGENERATIONAL FAMILIES

This section includes two chapters that address the historic and contemporary concerns of variant forms of cross-national families that have connections to French-speaking Canada in the Province of Quebec. Mary Murphy Robertson considers a reverse pattern of immigration of women from the United States who entered into the culture of Quebec within the past three decades and have established their personal lives within the province through marital and nuclear in-law family ties. Peter Woolfson examines the status of the Quebecois who traveled from Canada during multiple waves of immigration into northern New England and Louisiana.

The specific significance of certain social organizations, such as the family and gender roles within the extended intergenerational family, are conceptual bridges between the two distinct but related groups considered in this section. The Franco-American family as a specific cross-national family type has historic ties with the French-Canadian rural farm family. Original patterns of immigration from Canada into northern New England were associated with an intention to establish a better life thought to prevail if the total family group moved to the United States. With these families came the strong religious norms and practices of the Catholic Church in Quebec of an earlier era. The parish, family, and rural life became the interlocking cultural reinforcements for the Franco-Americans that were first-generation American-born, but socialized into the French-Canadian tradition that extended below the United States–Canadian border. Gender roles and family traditions were further reinforced by the establishment of *petits Canadas* once multiple families from Quebec had settled into New England communities. Robertson selected a special subgroup of recent United States immigrants, women who came into Quebec as either single or recently married young women. She correctly states that this group of immigrant women have received little attention, yet they entered into the Quebecois culture at a period of pervasive and rapid social change having great impact on sex roles and female life. Through an in-depth analysis of a small sample of these American-Quebec women, she documents their adaptations into the French-Canadian culture through the available community and spousal family systems. Her theoretical framework for investigating the United States and Canadian kinship networks was modified from contemporary theory on intergenerational kinship networks and aging.

Both authors consider how these cross-national families have dealt with aging family members and multigenerational relationships in their own immediate family. Woolfson considers care-giving traditions as they have been sustained but are now being altered in the Franco-American family. The Louisiana Cajun and New England Franco-American family structure slowly discontinues to reflect the traditions of a tightly committed intergenerational bonding that places responsibility on the younger generations, especially single adult children, to aid and support the eldest generation. In a small percentage of the late middle-aged generation of adult care givers, it is still possible to comprehend vividly how important it once was to avoid nursing home care of the eldest. Loyalties to family within the context of death and dying can be observed in the preservation of some lingering traditions connected to religious practices.

The women that Robertson studied have two dimensions of cross-national family involving older family members. First are their aging family members in the United States, both immediate and extended, who have continued to be part of their lives. Second are their French-Canadian families by marriage, which play significant roles in their lives. The author systematically compares how these women express their attachment behaviors, manage interpersonal conflict, fulfill family maintenance expectations, and offer direct or indirect helping behaviors to older parents and in-laws. Within these five cross-national family systems there are significant differences in behavioral practices, attitudes, and social expectations. The adaptations that these women have made to French-Canadian society display a continued sense of identity with elderly parents rather continuously and delicately balanced with their family and social life in Quebec.

CHAPTER 15

Cross-National Families: The Family Experience of American Women Married to French-Canadian Men

Mary R. Murphy Robertson

INTRODUCTION

Since the American War of Independence, Canada has received Americans as temporary or permanent residents (G. Dirks, 1977). Some of these people were refugees (United Empire Loyalists, fugitive slaves, or men avoiding the draft), while others came for employment or family reasons. During the past twenty years, although Americans have not been the largest immigrant group coming to Canada, they have remained a constant, significant one. For example, in 1979 out of a total of 112,096 immigrants, 9,617 were from the United States, making them 8.6 percent of the total immigrant population (Employment and Immigration, 1979).

American immigrants have settled in all parts of Canada and have generally tended to be male and young (in the 20 to 30 age group). The one exception to this pattern occurred in the mid–1960s when females of this age group dominated the immigration from the United States (A. Green, 1976). The lives of these women have never been studied. Understanding their adaptation patterns could be a useful comparative tool to evaluate the adjustment to Canada of women from other countries. As D. C. Corbett has said about such American women, "The difficulties of their adjustment should not be minimized, but they are a good deal less formidable, in general, than the difficulties faced by people from countries of other languages and cultures" (1957). Insights about their adaption to Canadian culture could be beneficial in formulating immigration programs for women. If these American women have found certain aspects of Canadian life difficult, it can be expected that women from more variant cultures would find these same aspects even more difficult and require substantial help in coping with them.

This chapter contains an overview of American women who immigrated to Canada to the province of Quebec (in particular, the metropolitan Quebec City area) and married French-speaking Quebec men. These women are a specific type of American immigrant because they have retained their American citizenship and identity while becoming very integrated into and acculturated to French-Canadian society. Their adjustment situation has been different from those American women who married into English-Canadian families in Quebec and the rest of Canada, and also different from the adjustment required of American women who migrated to Canada with their American husbands (Corbett, 1957).

A brief outline of Quebec and its unique character in the Canadian and North American mosaic will provide an understanding of the challenges that some of these American women have confronted in their adaptation to the French-Canadian culture while still maintaining relationships with their aging parents in the United States. The chapter describes how American women who have adapted successfully to a new country and culture now perceive their role in relation to their geographically and culturally separated older parents. The demands of two cultural groups and the effects of geographical distance are influential factors in the complex texture of the relationships between adult daughters and their aging parents. This descriptive analysis discusses the adaptation of a pilot sample that may give direction to future research.

THE QUEBEC CULTURE

Since 1960 the social, political, and economic life of the province of Quebec has been reshaped. The much researched and documented *Quiet Revolution* has resulted in many social changes; Quebec has been transformed from a familistic, agrarian, church-oriented and church-dominated society to a more individualistic, urban, and secular one (H. Guindon, 1979; M. Rioux, 1977; K. McRoberts and D. Posgate, 1980). The major social institutions have been reevaluated and their roles redefined.

The Quebec family was the object of a recent provincial government study (Minister of Social Affairs, 1985, Consultation on Family Policy) to examine the current status, definition, and function of the family so that a realistic and coherent family policy could be established. The once prevalent large nuclear family embedded in an extended kin network has been supplanted by the geographically mobile, small, nuclear family housed in a single-family dwelling.

Alteration of gender roles now offers alternatives to men and women. The widespread acceptance of these alternative gender roles is reflected in the new Family Law that recognizes the equality of spouses (An Act Respecting the Legal Capacity of Married Women, Bill 16, 1964, The Code Civil of Quebec, Bill 89, December 1980).

The new family structure has necessitated the involvement of the government in establishing services historically fulfilled by the kin and community networks. For example, new facilities for elderly parents have been built and new policies about coping with this elderly population have been formulated (E. Casseus, 1985). None of these changes are unique to Quebec, but what is unique is the rapidity of the change and the subsequent structural and functional tensions in intergenerational Quebec families.

Anyone arriving to become a member of this fast-evolving society has been met by demanding challenges: a new country, a new language, and a culture that itself is being redefined. Experiences of American women who have married into French-Quebec families warrant special study because these women have not only had to adapt to a different culture, language, and family life but they have also had to adapt to a social institution that was redefining itself. The types of social–emotional pressures these women "de l'extérieure" have faced result from their new family and cultural environments and their American families of orientation. Being enmeshed in a different and changing cultural family system while endeavouring to maintain relationships with one's own family in a native culture is extremely demanding. The extent to which this task has been accomplished is demonstrated in the relationships of American women in Quebec to their parents in the United States as the latter retire and age.

According to the American consulate in Quebec City, there are at present 2,600 Americans registered with them. (This number excludes all those Americans who live in the Montreal/Eastern Townships area.) Among those over age 35, the nature and extent of their contacts with their intergenerational kin in the United States is an intriguing topic. This group faces or will face the situation of aging parents; how they juggle their relationships with these parents is a situation which could be problematic (R. Henderson, 1985).

METHODOLOGY

In-depth investigation is needed to better comprehend international and intergenerational relationships that have Canadian–United States cross-national implications. The detailed case studies summarized in this section of the chapter highlight American women who married into French-Quebec families in Quebec City within the past twenty-five years. The recounting of their experiences provides information and insight into the dynamics of family group management of aging issues that extend across the border of these two countries.

The five families selected for discussion include American women with established French-Quebec families who have retained American citizenship but also have aging family members scattered throughout the United States. They are early-middle-aged, have postsecondary education, tend to be employed out-of-the-home on a parttime basis, have French-Quebec spouses who are senior managers, self-employed professionals, or entrepreneurs, participate in the Catholic Church, and their nuclear families enjoy upper-middle-class status. These illustrative families have multiple children between the ages of 5 and 16, and have one or both of their aging parents alive in the United States. Each has siblings residing in American communities. Their intergenerational aging family network is further expanded by older French-Quebec in-laws living within the Quebec City metropolitan area.

Their Canadian community milieu, Quebec City, is very different from the rest of Canada in that English-speaking people account for only 2.7 percent of the metropolitan population and, in order to live a multifaceted life, use of the French language is essential. The variable of language influences the intragenerational and intergenerational relationships of cross-national families. Different language competencies can affect intergenerational relationships, however, in these families it has not prevented the establishment of bonds between the American wives and their older in-laws. Geographical location is another understudied variable among cross-national families as variations in climate are dramatic. For example, winter temperatures in Quebec can reach $-36°C$ with an average snowfall of 340 cm. Environmental adaptation is yet another challenge associated with settling in Quebec City as Quebec residents, old and young, maintain family lifestyles adapted to these harsh environmental conditions.

Cross-national residence changes in adulthood require shifts in nonfamilial social relationships as well as familial. Intergenerational assistance from native-born in-laws was often very instrumental to these American women. The French-Quebec affinal family members connected to some of these women took direct responsibility for helping them cope with essential adjustment tasks when they entered the new culture. The establishment of friendship relations was also important. Although these women have various levels of involvement with native-born French-Quebec friendship networks, nonnative-born, English-Quebec friendships were highly valued as they facilitated their adjustment to Quebec. The reason for these patterns of relationships is a topic which should be further studied if more insight is to be gained into women's cross-national acculturation processes.

In spite of the initial acculturation difficulties, the women studied have experienced successful adaptation. They have been married over ten years; they have established families, support, and friendship networks in Quebec, and they feel comfortable in their communities. All of them are involved in community activities through their churches, schools, husbands' commitments, and their own interest groups. Some have contemplated becoming Canadian to be eligible to vote. However, none have actually changed citizenship; that decision is associated with the requirement that their children should not lose the option of having American citizenship.

THEORETICAL FRAMEWORK

V. G. Cicirelli in his study, "Adult Children's Attachment and Helping Behavior to Elderly Parents: A Path Model"(1983), established some areas of intergenerational relationships that were used as guidelines in this study to describe and explore critical areas in the relationships of American daughters to their parents in the context of their current Canadian family structure. Feelings of attachment, attachment behaviors, and actual helping behaviors existing among these American women, their parents, and their parents-in-law were investigated. The role geographical location and cultural differences played in the attachment and helping behaviors of these women toward their parents and parents-in-law, regardless of what kind of feelings of attachment were reported, was examined.

The original variables in Cicirelli's model were adapted to make them more relevant to the parameters of this study. For example, present life situations of these daughters were different since they lived in a cross-national context, as compared to Cicirelli's sample where all of his subjects lived in the same city. The adult children were of both genders and all of the parents considered were female. Here only daughters were studied and the American parents in question included mothers and a fewer number of fathers. Furthermore, the scope of this discussion is limited to discussion of attachment feelings and attachment behaviors which generally encompass topics of filial obligation, present parental dependency, and actual helping behaviors.

DATA

Feelings of Attachment to Parents

Questions relating to the daughters' perceived similarities and differences with parents provoked insightful discussions. Discussions around this topic usually evolved into reminiscences about past occurrences where daughters either acted in concert with the parents or reacted in a manner similar to the way they thought the parents would react. Most thought they were probably the closest of their siblings to their parents and felt they were either similar to their parents in approach to life, reactions to children, or how they hoped they reacted to their children. All of them thought very highly of their parents in terms of how well they had managed their lives so far. They appreciated parental acceptance of their marriages to non-American men and the subsequent support. The respondents reported admiration for their mothers whom they viewed as fairly autonomous, secure in their identities, and open to new experiences. Qualified admiration was mentioned by one daughter as her mother experienced increasing dependency on her father because of deteriorating health. In general, mothers provided strong role models with which the women identified. They also indicated feelings of closeness to their fathers, but more emphasis was given to their relationships with their mothers.

Grandparent Relationships

All the women claimed that their children felt "very close" to their maternal grandparents to the point of writing frequent letters as they mature. Even though most mothers have educated their children in French schools, this language difference has not posed a barrier between the children and their grandparents. Having French-speaking grandchildren has apparently been a point of interest, pride, as well as curiosity to their grandparents in the United States. However, as the children reach their teenage years, their mothers have tried to ensure that they are more fluent in English to assure future educational options rather than for improved verbal communication between children and grandparents.

The Attachment Behaviors to Parents

The attachment behaviors were investigated by discussing the frequency and length of visits to parents, the character of the daughters' visits or their parents' visits, the family members who participated in the visits, and the other kinds of contacts such as telephoning and writing letters. Actual or anticipated helping behaviors were examined in relation to contacts.

Contacts

Given the intense feelings of attachment, frequent visits between all of the respondents and their parents were expected, or at least it was expected that they would express deep regret if the visits were not as frequent as the respondents would have wished. The respondents endeavored to visit their parents at least once a year for a period of two weeks or a month. However, travel costs and family and community responsibilities in Quebec were noted as reasons for alterations in the visitation cycle.

Character of Visits of Children to Parents

Some of the visits only include the respondents' children, although the spouses are also included whenever possible, such as at Christmas. The spouses' absences from some of the visits are generally caused by their work commitments or the need to stay at home to look after older children who cannot miss school.

Parental Visits

Parental visitation patterns also vary in frequency, duration, and season. Widowed mothers experience certain limitations, and one older couple has decreased the frequency of visits because of fear of being sick while in Quebec, having to be hospitalized, and not being able to understand hospital personnel because of the different language. One of the mothers has not always been able to fulfill her visiting schedule in the past few years because she is the care giver for some of her older siblings; this decrease has not resulted in her daughter's increasing visits to her mother.

Other Contacts

Although the daughters do not have frequent face-to-face contact with their parents, they maintain involvement with them and their kin network in the United States through the use of telephone calls and communal family letters. These vary in frequency and length as do the phone calls made by elderly parents to daughters. The widowed mothers sometimes phone four times per week, but the other parents only phone on the average of once or twice per month. Perhaps the marital status of parents along with their financial status plays a role in terms of the means and frequency of communication. Regular telephone contacts are not necessarily supplemented with regular letters.

The effects of a cohesive family of orientation and the women's involvement in a larger kin network were seen in three daughters' attitudes and replies to questions about themselves and their status in their families. When these three women return to the United States, they are immediately enmeshed in an interested, supportive kin group with whom they have kept in touch through letters and information from their mothers. Although the other two daughters feel close to their parents and siblings, they do not feel strong ties or support in terms of other kin. One daughter commented about a loss of roots as she had no identifiable kin network on which she could rely when her parents moved to a new community. The other daughter cited the motivation for visits as ensuring parents were "allright" and visiting a few relatives. Being without a cohesive, supportive kin or friendship network in the United States didn't cause her regret, but she indicated that such a state made it hard for her parents whenever they became ill.

Parental Dependency

The daughters were asked about the extent of the parents' current or anticipated dependency on them. This theme always involved an indirect description of the emotional dependency of the parents on the respondents and was expressed in terms of how much the parents looked forward to talking and visiting with them. The need for any immediate concrete assistance was only perceived by one who said she thought her parents really needed her help because of their advancing age and the health problems which her mother was experiencing. Even though she realized that they needed assistance, she accepted the fact that she was unable to help because of the geographical distance. She lacks knowledge about the services available to her parents but she has not attempted to broach the subject of such services with her parents. "They are very proud people and wouldn't be able to accept strangers in to help them" was her conclusion. She seems overwhelmed by the immensity of the problem should either of the parents deteriorate further or should her father die. But she has no immediate plans to implement if a crisis should occur.

Some daughters have tried to discuss the topic of future plans with their parents, but none of them have persisted because their parents seemed unwilling to do so. They also perceive their parents as autonomous individuals who are capable of organizing their own lives. They seem unable to envisage any future situation whereby their parents would be less able to manage and might require direct assistance.

General Issues of Correspondence between Attachment Feelings and Attachment Behaviors

The daughters' attachment feelings are generally manifested in such attachment behaviors as telephone contacts, the reported quality of the visits of the respondents to their parents and vice versa rather than in the frequency or length of visits. The actual presence of the parents seems an unnecessary stimulus for these strong attachment feelings nor is their prolonged presence required to reinforce and maintain these feelings. Perhaps the lifelong positive parental perceptions of these daughters and their relationships are maintained because of their limited face-to-face exposure; that is, they are comfortably distanced from their parents by the telephone and letters and thus not enmeshed in the daily living experiences and interactional systems of their parents.

These middle-aged daughters are able to idealize their relationships with their parents, and they are also able to minimize any difficulties their parents might be encountering as they age. The above observations concur with the findings of M. S. Moss, S. Z. Moss and E. L. Moles (1985) in their research about the effect of geographical separation on family relationships. Geographical distance could thus be seen as a factor in the maintenance of strong attachment feelings between adult daughters and their parents as well as in the persistence of the daughters' positive estimates of their parents' state of health and level of autonomy.

The daughter who had the oldest mother and expressed strong attachment feelings is an example of someone whose attachment behavior, in the form of visits, has not increased even though her mother appears to be deterio-rating. She has not increased her visits because of her family commitments in Quebec, her feelings of helplessness toward her mother's situation, as well as the geographical distance between Quebec and where her mother resides. Telephone contacts have also not been increased perhaps because of this daughter's need to separate herself from a situation in which she feels useless.

The other daughters have parents who are in good health and did not report any necessity to separate themselves because of feelings of sadness or helplessness. They do not visit their parents frequently, citing geograph-ical distance and travel costs as reasons. Is the maintenance of privacy a factor? All daughters' family vacations with their spouses and children in-volve distance and expense. If face-to-face contact with their parents were a priority, perhaps they would substitute these occasions for visits to the United States.

Role of Kin Network

Two daughters with widowed mothers demonstrated the greatest degree of attachment behavior—they communicated the most frequently by tele-phone and had the longest visits with their mothers even though they were reported being enmeshed in a close modified extended family. Perhaps their frequent contacts are used for monitoring their mothers' activities to reassure themselves that the kin group is involved with their mothers. In other words their contacts with their parents inform them about how their proxies are functioning rather than being direct interventions; this indirect investigating allows their mothers to remain autonomous within a secure environment. Another daughter who was also part of a modified extended family did not demonstrate any great attachment behaviors even though she expressed intense feelings of attachment. Perhaps her limited parental contacts are explainable because both parents are alive, in good health, and have daily contact with their large kin network. They are presently very self-sufficient, and she is unable to imagine a future time where her direct assistance will ever be necessary.

DISCUSSION

Any interpretation of the presented case information is speculative, how-ever, it may be used as the basis for more research around the following ideas:

1. The general assumption that strong attachment feelings are manifested in extensive attachment behavior appears to be questionable. In the situa-tions described, geographical distance seems to contribute to the reason why

the regular, warm communication between aging parent and middle-aged daughter does not result in a greater commitment to help the parent or to provide actual concrete assistance.

2. As well, there has been a low degree of increased interaction as the parents age and then, only through more telephone contacts. The fact that this increase has not been exhibited by all the subjects would suggest that more investigation is required into the idea that as parents age children increase their interaction. Perhaps this claim is true given geographical proximity, but not true when children live far from their parents. This may have special significance for cross-national families. Another factor might be that the presence of both parents dilutes feelings of obligation and provides a cushion against the contemplation that assistance from children is necessary.

3. The different roles telephone contacts and face-to-face contacts play should be explored. It would appear that telephone contacts are just as meaningful in the preservation of family bonds as any other type of contact.

4. Some daughters realize that a parental crisis could occur but feel unable to broach the subject with their parents. Others are satisfied to rely on the extended kin network to meet any future needs and claim feelings of content about their parents' situation. This passive response to a potentially volatile or at least unstable situation is cause for concern because if a crisis or greater dependency on the part of the parent occurs, hasty, piecemeal, planning could result in unsatisfactory solutions (A. Montagnes, 1984). The women studied are probably in the most advantageous position concerning access to information about different social services compared with people from other ethnic groups and lower socioeconomic statuses. Reasonable financial security, spousal acceptance, encouragement and involvement in the maintenance of ties with their American kin, and their high level of intellectual, social, and emotional functioning as exemplified by their daily lives—all these factors make their avoidance of the topic of parents' future plans incongruous. The absence of contingency planning could be the result of lack of knowledge about the strategies to use in investigating services for older people, as well as a hesitancy in contemplating possible parental dependency.

Geographical distance, along with cultural and national differences seems to decrease the extent to which adult children can be actively involved in helping their parents as they grow older. These factors appear to limit the options that intergenerational cross-national units have and their desire to risk envisioning many options. None of the women thought that their parents could or would ever come to live in Quebec even if "they were desperate." Although all of their parents enjoyed visiting historical Quebec City, the different climate, language, and culture as well as their ineligibility for government programs if they are not landed immigrants inhibit any permanent residency.

Major obstacles to a relocation option demonstrate the challenges faced by Canadian-American families and point to areas where these and other types of cross-national families should be counseled. Uprooting people from their local neighborhoods and routines is disruptive and contributes to adjustment difficulties. When this factor is combined with the harsh climatic conditions of Quebec, the option of having parents living full-time with their daughters in this setting seems unrealistic. The changes in life-style required by the snowy conditions should be experienced before any decision is made about residency.

The initial adjustment tasks these women faced when they arrived in the province would be magnified for their parents and increase the parental dependency if the parents decided to spend their last years in Quebec City. A simple hospital visit could present a major challenge because most medical personnel do not speak English, most medical prescriptions and reports are written in French, and the government medicare system does not cover non-Canadian residents. The necessity of having translators present during medical consultations and available to translate written instructions would reinforce the loss of autonomy and privacy many people ordinarily experience as they grow older. As well, the expense of maintaining medical insurance to cover any care could be prohibitive. If permanent care were required, there would not be residence facilities for these parents because of the already limited supply of such facilities for English-speaking older Quebec residents.

For the parents under discussion, any consideration of a permanent move to Quebec while there are still options open to them in the United States would seem unrealistic. Nevertheless, there are many ethnic groups in Canada and, in particular, in Quebec, where the parents do not have a choice and have arrived into this new Quebec culture late in life. The support services which such groups require should be investigated, given the difficulties that have been found during this exploratory study.

The official bicultural, bilingual nature of Canada is enhanced by the pluralistic commitment that this country has made. If the recent government program of encouraging immigrants to Canada is continued, then the total family needs of these new arrivals should be attended (L. Diebel, 1986). Some progress has been made by certain ethnic groups in caring for their elderly; these projects should be studied to determine the various models of help that can exist for people in need (E. D. Wangenheim, 1980).

In general, the requirement for eligibility for any medical care or residential care in Canada is that the person should be a Canadian citizen or a landed immigrant. In order to obtain the latter status after the age of 65 years, people have to prove that they are in good health and financially self-sufficient or have a sponsor who will guarantee their independence from government aid. Even if the parents desire to become landed immigrants to Canada and fulfill these requirements, the procedure has to be planned for and accomplished early enough to be successful.

If the decision to live with a child is not reached before the elderly parent deteriorates physically, the difficulties of having the parent admitted to Canada should be realized. Apparently "arrangements can be made," but doing so creates stress and delay in a crisis situation. When residency in Canada seems to be the only option for an older American, the Canadian and American governments should be encouraged to formulate reciprocal financial agreements that would provide for services and facilities to meet the needs of older Americans. Such agreements would eliminate at least one of the barriers faced by American adult daughters living in Canada.

The last ten years have seen the increase in preparatory programs for helping people meet the challenges of certain life stages. Most communities have marriage preparation, family-life, and retirement courses, but they do not have courses to help adult children determine their roles in relation to their elderly parents.

Educational programs and mass media campaigns could be designed to help adult children overcome their hesitancy in selecting appropriate, realistic strategies for helping their parents if the need arises. These programs might decrease the frustration felt by such children by providing them with the support required to realistically assess their role vis-à-vis their parents. Lack of information about choices available and the avoidance of preventive planning can serve to detract from the quality of relationships between parents and their adult children. Children seem either to suffer their anxiety in silence or to view their parents' situation in an unrealistically confident manner. Although planning cannot accommodate every event, it can provide a rough guideline as to what the acceptable solutions might be.

REFERENCES

An Act Respecting the Legal Capacity of Married Women, Bill 16. (1964).

Casseus, E. (1985). Le Travail social en intervention troisième âge. *Intervention*, 72, 69–72.

Cicirelli, V. G. (1983). Adult Children's Attachment and Helping Behavior to Elderly Parents: A Path Model. *Journal of Marriage and the Family*, 45, 815–25.

Code Civil of Quebec, Bill 89 (1980).

Corbett, D. C. (1957). *Canada's Immigration Policy: A Critique*. Toronto: University of Toronto Press.

Diebel, L. (1986, July 26). People Needed, so Canada Eases Entry. *Gazette*, 1.

Dirks, G. (1977), *Canada's Refugee Policy: Indifference or Opportunism*. Montreal: McGill-Queen's University Press.

Employment and Immigration (1979), *Immigration Statistics*. Ottawa: Information Canada.

Green, A. (1976). *Immigration and the Postwar Canadian Economy*. Toronto: MacMillan of Canada.

Guindon, H. (1964), Social Unrest, Social Class, and Quebec's Bureaucratic Revolution. In B. R. Blishen, F. E. Jones, K. D. Naegele and J. Porter, eds., *Canadian Society: Sociological perspectives*. Toronto: MacMillan of Canada.

Henderson, R. (1985, August 28). Grown Children Must Now Care for Parents. *Gazette*, 5.

Ministry of Social Affairs (1985). *Collective Support Demanded for Quebec Families: Report on the Consultation Held on Family Policy*. Ministère des Communications.

McRoberts, K., and Posgate, D. (1980). *Quebec: Social Change and Political Crisis*. Toronto: McClelland & Stewart.

Montagnes, A. (1984, September). When Elderly Parents Need Care. *Châtelaine*, 49, 149–56.

Moss, M. S., Moss, S. Z., and Moles, E. L. (1985). The Quality of Relationships between Elderly Parents and Their Out-of-Town Children. *Gerontologist*, 25, 134–40.

Rioux, M. (1977). *La Question du Québec*. Montreal: Parti Pris.

Wangenheim, E. D. (1980). Ethnicity and Aging—Similarities and Differences. *Multiculturalism*, 4, 3–6.

CHAPTER 16

Cross-Cultural Families: The Franco-Americans

Peter Woolfson

The Franco-Americans are Americans of French descent who live in the United States. For the most part these people are the descendants of the 65,000 French people who remained in Canada after the French government ceded Canada to the English in the Treaty of Paris of 1763. There were two different populations of French people in Canada in what had been known as *New France*: one in Quebec and the other in Nova Scotia; the former became known as *Quebecois*, the latter as *Acadians*. These two major French populations in North America have had quite different histories and display many cultural differences. However, both groups in the Northeast could be considered cousins, while the Acadians of Louisiana, called *Cajuns* are more distant relatives. The Cajuns differ from the Acadians of New England as they are culturally southerners with a whole set of behaviors and attitudes revolving around the large black population of the state.

There are Franco-Americans throughout the United States—from Maine's 292,279 Franco-Americans to California's 1.3 million. In the Southwest Texas has 500,000. Louisiana continues to have its French flavor with close to a million Cajuns and Creoles. The majority of people claiming French ancestry live in the northeastern United States: the seven states comprising New England and New York: 3,158,992 persons in that region reported that they had at least one parent with French-Canadian, Acadian, Cajun, or French-Creole background—some 22 percent of the nation's 13.6 million people claiming some French descent.

In spite of active interest in historical roots, Franco-Americans retain contact with a restricted group of kinspeople. Events like baptism, confirmation, marriage, and death involve participation of multigenerational kin. Grandparents, traditionally, played an important role at the birth of a child. It was often the custom to have the grandparents serve as godparents for a first-born child: paternal grandparents for a boy, maternal grandparents for a girl, although the reverse occurs as well. Siblings and cousins form the backbone of the network of relatives who share informal and intimate events: it is this group from which, in most cases, friendship choices develop (P. Woolfson, 1983).

The most important social unit for the French-Canadians and Franco-Americans is the household: a man, his wife, his children, and any other close relatives who happen to live with them—his parents, younger siblings, perhaps a maiden aunt. In farming communities, when a man retired, the son who had been designated as heir to the farm moved downstairs to indicate symbolically the change in status to head of household. Arrangements were often made for parents to move upstairs: the father continued to work on the farm as long as he was able and the mother helped the daughter-in-law with the household. As the pareents aged, they might decide to move into a local village in order to be closer to the church for more regular attendance. Younger siblings often stayed with their brother to help with the farm work until the farmers' sons were old enough to shoulder much of the responsibilities of farm duties.

Franco-Americans, if they are financially independent, tend to marry earlier than their French-Canadian counterparts. This is true in both Louisianan Cajun and New England Franco-American society. Financial independence is not, however, the major issue, in the multigenerational farm families described above since resources continue to be shared. Traditionally mature daughters, even those with full-time jobs, were expected to remain at home with their parents well into their middle twenties or so long as they were not married.

Similar to the tradition of Irish-Americans, one of the unmarried daughters was expected to stay at home, unmarried, to take care of incapacitated or elderly parents. The Franco-Americans in New England and the Louisiana Cajuns both felt very strongly about the responsibility of relatives to care for the frail and elderly (M. R. Esman, 1985). Placement of elders in nursing homes is opposed unless absolutely necessary. If there were no daughters available, unmarried sons might choose to remain living at home to care for the parents. The elderly siblings may also join in care-giving roles. For example, an elderly nun came from Quebec to Vermont to assist her sister-in-law and niece with the care of her convalescing brother. This situation, temporary or long-term, illustrates how some multigenerational families continue to extend assistance across the national border when there is a family need.

Marriage is still performed in the parish of the bride and like other events concludes with the celebration of the Mass. Employed wives continue to work at their jobs after marriage. But there is the tendency not to delay having children. Some opt to quit work in order to take care of their small children. This is becoming more common, given maternity leave benefits.

Wives who go back to work tend to rely on their mothers to help them with child care. Louisianan grandmothers feel a strong obligation to help their daughters take care of their grandchildren. They firmly believe that families can offer better child care than that provided by strangers (Esman, 1985). Likewise, Franco-American grandmothers feel strongly about helping their daughters. They often raise questions about the quality of care available in day care centers and show concern about daughters having to leave their infants in the care of others while working, but they are largely resigned to their daughter's financial realities of trying to live on the son-in-law's income.

Children today are more mobile than their parents and are choosing where they live on the basis of job opportunities rather than on proximity to their families. Consequently daughters often live too far from their mothers to involve them in child care. Except for vacations, often for the Christmas holidays, families stay in touch by telephone rather than by visiting. Older Franco-Americans, if they can afford to, are spending the winter months in Florida. It has been suggested that there are as many as 250,000 French-Canadians who spend six months or more in that state. One retired Franco-American felt that the ideal retirement life would include a trailer in Vermont for the spring and summer and a trailer in Florida for the fall and winter. This mobility also limits the amount of time mothers and fathers can spend with their children and grandchildren and offer concrete assistance.

Old age brings few changes in living arrangements for those fortunate to be in reasonably good health and to have a family support system at hand. Fifty years residency in the same house is not uncommon. However, other Franco-American elderly, like their nonethnic counterparts, find it impossible to continue this pattern. Winooski, Vermont, has a very large concentration of Franco-Americans who have retired from working in local mills. Fanny Allen Hospital, their personally identified health center, has instituted a system where monitors are placed in the home so that help can be summoned at the touch of a button. Many Franco-American elderly express great relief at having this system. They have faith in this small community hospital: it is still operated by an order of nuns originally from Canada, who continue to use personalized approaches, as compared to the more bureaucratic professional approach at the local university medical center. There are also some nursing homes that have a substantial Franco-American patient population who are very aged, largely alone, without families, and incapacitated.

In Louisianan Cajun and Franco-American communities, old people are treated with respect. This pattern is especially strong for elderly priests and nuns who remain in the local area. Respect is further displayed in fiftieth wedding anniversaries that are very important in the Franco-American tradition. Children and extended family often make elaborate parties for their parents in catering halls following the celebration of a special Mass to honor the occasion. In the Poutre home in Beecher Falls, Vermont, for example, there is a special scroll on the wall carefully calligraphied and ornately decorated to honor the occasion. It was a gift from the nuns who teach at the parish school.

After retirement, men and women do more things together than they did when working. Women, however, spend more time in social activities than their husbands. At La Société des deux Mondes, a Franco-American group in Burlington, Vermont, most of the activities are planned by women: dances, potluck suppers, quilting bees, and special events like talks on I.R.A.s and gardening. The men often find themselves volunteering to set up chairs and tables for banquets or cleaning up after events. It should be noted, however, that for much of its history, the president of the association was a man (Woolfson, 1983).

Death by tradition occurs two hours after a person has been declared dead by a medical authority. When someone is on the verge of death, if it is possible, a priest is called to administer the rites of Extreme Unction. A 60-year-old man in Burlington, Vermont, who recently had a massive stroke and is now recovering, reports that the priest was called in. Because the doctors believed death was imminent, the family allowed the priest to give only a brief benediction. The family during this crisis debated whether to bury him in Vermont or the family plot in Quebec. This decision illustrates the continued attachment that some French families living in the United States still have to Quebec.

After death the body is laid out, most likely for three nights in a funeral home. Frequently the coffin remains open; the body, if male, is dressed in a dark suit with tie; the hands are folded over the chest and clasping a rosary. When Louis Beaudoin, a well-known Franco-American fiddler died, his family surrounded his coffin on the first night and sang hymns, an indication of the importance of music in the lives of Franco-Americans. Often photographs are taken of the deceased while they are lying in their coffins, and the photos kept in the ubiquitous family album. If the person was an American veteran, those participating in the funeral salute the body with rifle fire and the body is draped in an American flag. After the burial the participants go back to the local American Legion Hall to drink to the deceased (L. French, 1980).

There are many activities of a folk or quasi-religious nature which many Franco-Americans practice. An important manifestation of the relationship between health and religion are the miraculous cures. An older Franco-American woman recalls that when she was a child, her knees were deformed and she could not walk correctly. Her doctors put her in a cast from the waist down in order to minimize further deterioration, but they held out little hope for her condition to improve. Given the hopelessness of the case, her father decided to take her to the famous French-Canadian healer, Frère

André at St. Joseph's Oratory in Montreal. She remembers that her father walked on his knees up the steps of the basilica, carrying her on his shoulders and saying a Hail Mary on each step. After Frère André touched her, she was taken to the hospital and her cast removed—she was completely cured.

TRADITIONAL VALUES AND ORIENTATIONS

Within the French-Canadian system of values, two themes appear to be central: *la survivance* and *l'indépendence*. Although both themes appear as national goals—i.e., the preservation of the French language, the moral values of the faith, the culture, and the protection of the group from the interference of foreigners (*les étrangers*), these themes have most relevance within the family household. The survival of the family and its protection from outside harm becomes a central theme that influenced the move from Canada to the United States. Sometimes groups of families came together, or younger members would follow older siblings. Cultural values about family, marriage, and responsibility to children were central to these families. (P. Chasse, 1975).

Of the cultural values considered most important to maintain was what Hughes (1963) called the *individualism of the family*. That is, although strictly personal interests that do not affect other members of the family are given due respect, the individual is expected to subordinate his or her personal interests for the good of the family as a whole.

Chasse (1975) and J. Searles (1982), who have studied the contemporary Franco-American family, report on the struggle to maintain traditional values, especially the value of individual sacrifice for the family. This value competes directly with more current values of economic and social independence from the family. Franco-American mill families, often living eight or nine in a small apartment a few decades ago, required a spirit of cooperation and interdependence that reinforced Quebec farm family values (Woolfson, 1982). That pattern reinforced family bonding. Respect for authority was also part of this familial tradition, with fathers and grandfathers serving as the model for this pattern of behavior.

However, authority is not always adhered to slavishly. J. Ducharme (1980) writes about the intense individuality of the Franco-American, "who is after all a Frenchman. You know the Frenchman is perfectly content with authority so long as he feels that he can be independent of it any time he wants" (1980, p. 259). With their orientation to familial and parochial models for interpersonal relationships, it is not surprising that many Franco-Americans feel uncomfortable in dealing with bureaucracies and impersonal social agencies.

Both men and women take pride in work. Elderly women saw their primary vocations as wives and mothers: they took pride in having well-fed, well-clothed children and a spotless home. Traditionally the French-

Canadian housewife took her home apart every spring for the *grand ménage* (spring cleaning). H. Miner (1937) comments that all women of the family cleaned the house a room at a time. Everything was removed and wooden walls, ceiling, and floor were all scrubbed. It required several weeks for the women to complete the ménage (1937, p. 146).

Men took pride in doing their job well—working hard, producing prodigiously, and doing it with craftsmanlike skills. D. Hendrickson (1980) writes about the attitudes held by the men who worked as weavers in the mills and took meaning and pride in their tasks. In the era of the 1920s Franco-American men of the working class did not give education priority. They frequently left school to start work, for example, at age fourteen to earn eleven dollars a week.

Working-class Franco-American parents saved their money without the expectation that it would be used to further their children's postsecondary education. L. French (1980) notes that these families avoided long-term loans and mortgages. Money was saved by renting and avoiding purchase of expensive unnecessary items and did not the families traditionally indebt themselves by spending money on their children in a prolonged adolescence. Even though working-class Franco-Americans did not put a high value on education, Franco-Americans as a group have been very active in founding 264 colleges, high schools, and primary schools.

ACCULTURATION

Elderly Franco-Americans are products of cultural contacts between the French-Canadian culture and its American counterpart. As an immigrant group, their lives and intergenerational families have been affected through confrontation with differences in language, political structure, and the reorganization of familiar religion. Language usage is probably the most powerful acculturation force. In the 1970 census only 9.5 percent of Vermont's population claimed to have French as their major language, but in the 1980 census only 5 percent reported using French in the home.

Many of the elders experienced the battle between the use of English and French in their own parishes. As early as 1934 the religious life of those attending St. Joseph's Church in Burlington, Vermont, was confronted with the bilingual realities when their priest was given permission by the bishop to deliver a sermon in both French and English (Woolfson, 1979).

The eldest generation of Franco-Americans who did not develop English-speaking skills encountered many barriers. Some became estranged in their own religious life because French was no longer used in the local parishes because of the unavailability of French-speaking priests. They found themselves unable to participate fully in intimate daily family life because their grandchildren spoke only English and the parents reinforced this pattern for young children in the home. French-speaking elders also encountered ever greater numbers of English-speaking and fewer numbers of bilingual people in their neighborhoods and communities.

Some community agencies, where there is still a concentration of Franco-American elderly with very limited or no English, attempt to maintain a bilingual nonprofessional staff, but this is far from ideal when communicating with some aged. This language problem is especially evident when these elders must receive medical care. Sometimes nonprofessional people must be brought in to translate into French medical or counseling vocabularies foreign to them. The professional practitioners, speaking only English, are forced to rely on third-party translators; this results in an unsatisfactory rapport. Practitioners working in institutions and community programs having contact with this segment of the aging community recognize their own difficulties when attempting to evaluate dementia and aphasia or other basic life needs not easily communicated in any language.

The social life of some older Franco-Americans centered on the Franco-American societies. As mentioned earlier, coupled with family and church these organizations were sources of cultural and social stimulation. The societies have always varied in membership and continuity. The Fédération Féminine Franco-Americaine established in 1951 now unites 14,000 women throughout New England (R. Chasse, 1975). It continues to be a resource for older women; at the local level groups such as the La Société des deux Mondes in Burlington, Vermont continue even though younger people consider them organizational relics.

The economic life of the Franco-Americans who owned farms on the American side, particularly along the border and in nearby rural communities, has been affected by the changes in farm and family life. Data from the 1930s indicated that Canadian French in Vermont had an average family size of nine children, but by the 1970 census the average family size was four. Many of these older modest farmers were not able to handle the trends of agribusiness that began in the 1950s. When family farms were sold outside the family, there was a significant social displacement for the older farmer and his wife. In some cases when a son continued to own the farm, the elderly parents remained, but under somewhat different arrangements. J. Albert (1979) reports that for Acadian families with a farm inheritance a contract was drawn up between parents and son and daughter-in-law that specified terms of intergenerational obligations extending into directives for matters such as burial instruction. These conditions were taken seriously by adult children.

Economic, social, and cultural impacts were felt by the older Franco-Americans when the cotton and woolen mills throughout northern New England began to close, never to reopen. For some workers it created a form of involuntary preretirement. For others it was the loss of a mill work environment that had always offered much reinforcement for the traditional Franco-American community since French was spoken in the shops. After the mill closings both men and women found themselves in unemployment lines; many had to leave their *petits Canadas* to find work farther afield. This cast them into the melting pot of work. Yet for the older Franco-American mill workers the mill has remained a focal point even in very recent years. Searles (1982) reports that it was a common reference point in homes for the aged with Franco-American residents. If these older residents were not fortunate enough to find other Franco-Americans to share their cultural bond and memories about the textile mills, they could easily experience social isolation (D. Hendrickson, 1980). As a group, older Franco-Americans have struggled under changing circumstances and, even in the face of advanced age, they have always sought to maintain independence (T. Harven and R. Langenbach, 1980).

Smaller families and the dispersal of family members far away from their parents and grandparents has affected family life and traditional activities. One student describes the historical importance of gatherings in his own farm family, especially during festive periods from Christmas to Lent. In rural Vermont as in other areas, families had designated holidays filled with personal traditions, religious observations, reminiscences, food, and festivity. Cultural events such as rites of intensification which strengthened family ties are increasingly rare, as is the family farm that housed these gatherings.

The older Franco-American woman feels strongly the ending of her traditional role as matriarch of a large clan. French (1980) writes that if both grandparents survived, it was the female who held the higher status. To the extent that their higher status was linked to traditional roles, most of these aging women can not expect to now plan the large *soirées* and *veillées* that were so important in their past. Their household traditions, such as the *grand ménage*, are no longer practiced to any extent as a result of poor health. This is a common reason for giving up the home and moving into retirement. Widowed mothers maintain close associations with their children if they live closeby. Otherwise, travel including throughout the region and into Canada, can be very expensive and difficult.

Historically the only social agency of any consequence to this group has been the Catholic Church. Parishes that continue to have some elderly Franco-Americans in their congregations serve this community through offering senior citizen programs. They offer parish outreach through community visitations by the priests and younger congregation members. That form of contemporary ministry has many traditional elements, such as visitation to the homebound and sick and support to families in times of crisis or death. Churches sometimes offer trips to special healing shrines such as Ste. Anne de Beaupré in Quebec, and these are still popular with the elderly.

The attitudes Franco-Americans hold about Social Security benefits are generally receptive, as they believe this is their due as former workers in America, but many remain distrustful of governmental services. That reservation is most apparent among the rural Franco-American aged. Their values require expected help to come from very interpersonal relationships, and they feel uncomfortable and stigmatized when encountering large impersonal service sources.

Overall the extent of the acculturation process, as experienced by any elderly individual, is dependent upon where he or she was raised—in Quebec or the United States—the ties maintained to the French language and culture, and the connections with family still in Canada. Intergenerational and multigenerational visitation patterns among these cross-national families help reinforce French-Canadian cultural aspects. The lack of contact—sometimes due to a loss of fluency in French, to self-consciousness on seeing relatives, or to a general mistrust of the highly urbanized Quebec society—weakens those connections.

THE FUTURE

The population of the United States is aging and the Franco-American population is aging with it. However, the generation of elderly that is most traditionally French-Canadian is dying out. Acculturation of Franco-Americans had its greatest impact in the years following World War II. The labor shortages of the war offered a way for Franco-Americans, like other ethnic groups, to become prosperous. With prosperity, growing ambitions, and changes in mass media, there has been a growing dependence on television for information and entertainment. This is especially the case since access to French broadcasting is limited in much of New England and New York.

The future need to deal with the older Franco-American as a special linguistic and cultural problem is limited. One can look ahead to a time— perhaps only twenty years from now—when French-dominant, culturally distinct Franco-Americans will not require services distinctive to their group. Even now, few people in the health and social services industries are aware of the special needs of the Franco-American patients and clients; they blend into the background so well.

Since the 1970s there has been a resurgence of interest in ethnicity in the United States, reinforced by the surge of patriotism at America's bicentennial in 1976. The Franco-Americans are no exception to other ethnic groups in this country. Searles (1982) documents some of the major interest in reviving the Franco-American heritage that has been facilitated by federal and state funding. Programs offering bilingual education, Franco-American festivals, special public television programs, and university-based Franco-American and Canadian Studies programs (sometimes in English and sometimes in French) are all having some impact on a resurgence of interest and knowledge.

These kinds of activities have been duplicated throughout New England, New York, and Louisiana. While there is little chance to recreate the *petits Canadas*, the resurgence of interest in Franco-American traditions has led to a change in status for the older Franco-American—from rejected cultural baggage to respected cultural resource. One student in a high-school project that used members of a Franco-American Senior Citizens Group in Augusta, Maine, discovered how useful talking to older people can be:

Raissa St. Pierre, a junior from Massachusetts, summed up the feeling of our class:

The French-Canadians went out on a limb, moving to another country and not knowing what to expect. I didn't understand how or what kept them going. After listening to their stories, I wanted to find that kind of confidence and faith in myself (Searles, 1982, viii).

REFERENCES

Albert, J. (1979). The Acadians of Maine. In R. Albert (Ed.), *The Franco-American Overview*. Volume 1 (pp. 151–215). Manchester: Nation Materials Development Center for French.

Chasse, P. (1975). *The Family*. Worcester: Franco-American Ethnic Heritage Studies Program. Assumption College.

Ducharme, J. (1980). The Shadows of the Trees: Religion and Language. In M. Gigue (Ed.), *The Franco-American Overview*. Volume 2 (pp. 255–260). Manchester: National Materials Development Center for French.

Esman, M. R. (1985). *Henderson, Louisiana: Cultural Adaptation in a Cajun Community*. New York: Holt, Rinehart and Winston.

French, L. (1980). The Franco-American Working Class Family. In M. Gigue (Ed.), *The Franco-American Overview*. Volume 2 (pp. 173–190). Manchester: National Materials Development Center for French.

Harevan, T., & Langenbach, R. (1980). *Amoskeag*. New York: Pantheon Books.

Hendrickson, D. (1980). *Quiet Presence*. Maine: Gannet Publishing.

Hughes, E. C. (1963). *French Canada in Transition*. Chicago: University of Chicago Press.

Miner, H. (1939). *St. Denis: A French Canadian Parish*. Chicago: Phoenix.

Searles, J. (1982). *Immigrants From the North*. Bath, Maine: The Hyde School.

Woolfson, P. (1979). The Rapid Assimilation of Canadian French in Northern Vermont. In R. Albert (Ed.), *The Franco-American Overview*, Volume 1 (pp. 211–215). Manchester: National Materials Development Center for French.

Woolfson, P. (1982). The Rural Franco-American in Vermont. *Vermont History*, 50, (pp. 151–162.

Woolfson, P. (1983). The Franco-Americans of Northern Vermont: Cultural Factors for Consideration by Health and Social Service Providers. In P. Woolfson and S. J. Senecal (Eds.), *The French in Vermont: Some Current Views. Occasional Paper 6*, (pp. 1–26). Burlington: University of Vermont.

SUMMARY

Acculturation is reflected differently in these two groups of cross-national families. The United States family with Franco-American background is quickly losing or has lost its ties with French-Canada. This pattern is even present when geographic distance between the branches of the extended family is less than fifty miles across the border. Language barriers represent one major intergenerational isolator. The Canadians from Quebec may never have learned English, and they are very culturally remote from those United States relatives that speak no French. The French-Canadian sectors of these family groups have continued to maintain their rurality. For some members there is sufficient detachment from English-speaking Canada to prevent them from travel anywhere beyond the boundaries of rural Quebec. It is also typical that many of the United States relations are bewildered and resentful about some of the major cultural and political changes within Quebec over the past several decades.

The acculturation process experienced by the women in Robertson's chapter is also relevant and significant in its reversed pattern. Lasting marriages to French-speaking Quebec men have brought them, to varying degrees, into the French-Canadian community. The in-law network has been one consistent acculturation factor, even though the degrees of intimate relationship are not equal among the women. Their ties to older parents in the United States are an important aspect of their personal and family identity, but those connections have far less impact on their daily life or on their children. Robertson found little or no indication that the likelihood of parental frailty would lead to the relocation of either parents or their daughters and nuclear families. Since the parents are United States citizens, they are not covered by the long-term care benefits extended by the Canadian federal or provincial government structures.

In conclusion, this unit has offered interesting evidence to suggest that there is a history of cross-national intergenerational family relationships between the United States and Canada through the extended kinship systems. While this section highlights French-Canadian and Franco-American samples, somewhat similar issues are raised across the borders of Canada and the United States from coast to coast. Some of the patterns described are more characteristic of the French-Canadian sector for which the different language usage has become a factor even when great geographical distance is not a reality. For some families the sense of cross-national connections has long faded, and for others it is still a factor to be managed in the face of no clear socialization guidelines or international cooperative social welfare policies that cover the conditions of cross-national family aging.

IX
CONCLUSION

CHAPTER 17

Future Cross-National Developments

Eloise Rathbone-McCuan and Betty Havens

Throughout this book the reader has been presented with numerous points of congruence in the aging issues facing Canada and the United States. Demographic trends show the rapid expansion of the aging population and a predictable unequal sex ratio between older men and women that widens dramatically with each emerging older cohort. The two countries espouse the aim that the extension of life should equal an extention of the quality of existence. But scientific advances to remove serious and sustained dysfunctionality from chronic conditions has been marginal. Admeasurement of publicly contributed and governmentally distributed benefits to the older population has created a financial stability for many Canadian and United States elderly. Yet economic retirement pension policies have not eliminated poverty, especially for very old women and minority groups.

Millions of elderly citizens live in the rural sections of both countries. Yet neither nation has determined comprehensive strategies for assuring service availability and accessibility. Philosophically the two countries are committed to the principle of noninstitutionalization of the frail elderly. However, a range of barriers prohibits shifting the necessary proportion and amount of budgetary resources from institutional to community care; formal service reimbursement to informal care; and acute care to prevention and rehabilitation services. Until these shifts are reflected in federal, provincial/state, and local policies, unnecessary risks of institutionalization will remain high for aged persons.

Chronic mentally ill patients discharged from hospitals are now a very visible part of the aged in rural and urban communities. Their quality of life ranges from satisfactory to deplorable with few effective reforms in near sight. The bureaucracies charged to provide service for older veterans are marginally prepared for the emerging care demands. These systems appear oblivious to the widows of the elderly male veteran cohorts and to aging female veterans.

Native elders have experienced displacement within their bands and tribal cultures. Native communities lack resources, both political and economic, to advocate needed services of all forms for the aged. Long-term care is among the most urgent. Cross-national families in their many and varied forms are confronted by governmental policies that preclude the portability of health and pension benefits between the United States and Canada. This renders it difficult for families to sustain the care of their relocated elders.

These are but a few of the common problems revealed in the book. There has been little initiative to pursue the joint research needed or problem solving and problem prevention. Our governments can cooperate to resolve problems of acid rain, internationally disadvantageous foreign trade rules, terrorism of the citizenry, and safe affordable energy. Why is it not possible for them to engage in cooperative actions that address social problems?

The point of this text is to initiate the conceptualization of a North American gerontology that addresses the "whitening of the region." If that condition had resulted from a shifting of the Arctic Ice Cap, the two nations would be quick to mobilize the best scientists to cooperatively reduce the environmental threat. The "whitening" phenomenon in this context is the aging of both populations. Aging population structures create significant social issues that demand scientific and practitioner attention. That expertise can be mobilized if the countries give these problems sufficient priority.

ADVANCING CROSS-NATIONAL EFFORTS IN GERONTOLOGY

There are diverse ways to encourage and facilitate cross-national gerontological activities. Three approaches seem especially relevant to the advancement of research, education, practice and policy. First is the process of technological data transfer. It involves developing information exchange systems that can quickly and comprehensively move between the two countries information about model programs and their outcome evaluations. Such a system could be designed for access through information and data bases that are already accessible between the countries or can be easily programmed for cross-national retrieval.

The second method would be to increase programs for scholar and practitioner exchange. These would be financed by government and private sources and administered through the national gerontological organizations, universities, and service centers. It is exciting to contemplate a two-way participation of "observe, demonstrate, and share" about what is working in each country and why. A third approach is through parallel collaborative projects designed and implemented within each country under a cooperative cross-national authority or an active consultation. Projects would evaluate service delivery processes and assess the outcomes. Such endeavors would be linked to the policy design and decision-making arenas with ongoing feedback to and from both countries.

The foundation for a cross-national gerontology must encompass issues of practice, research, and education. Under optimal circumstances these functions would be fully integrated. But such is rarely the case. In part, these tasks are not fully integrated because there are separate policy directives controlling their conduct and completion. A basic shift is needed to uncomplicate the pathways to policy reform. Restructured policy should enable all of these functions to be integrated, especially around priority issues. Policies authorizing larger multidimensional projects should be consolidated within single administrative units that can unify rather than fragment education, practice, and research tasks.

These conditions are necessary for research and demonstration projects with cross-national applications in Canada and the United States. During a period of decreased funds for training and for basic and applied research, much is being lost. It is short-sighted to divert monies from longitudinal projects that help refine practice techniques, outcome measures, and programmatic designs. Sometimes this funding diversion occurs to finance unique and isolated projects of narrow scope and limited application. While there is merit to considering very specialized problems, in times of limited resources these projects must be weighed with the application value of other competing projects.

For example, a study of patients suffering from a combination of depression, cancer, and Alzheimer's disease may be very limited in focus if the criterion variable is the cancer condition. Such a variable priority may obscure the more essential study of the longitudinal patterns of geriatric depression as it is masked by or coexists with Alzheimer's disease during various stages. Projects that combine the examination of depression risks within large samples of care-giving families might offer key findings of immediate application in many social programs, for example, programs designed to lessen caregiver burden for the families of those suffering with Alzheimer's disease. This problem merely illustrates the type of project that is critical to practitioners in both countries. Therefore, it might be considered very important to cross-national gerontological concerns. A criterion for selecting cross-national projects should be their mutual importance to the needs of the two countries.

No major advances can be made in gerontological research without the benefit of longitudinal studies. The scientific community has long struggled to find ways to maintain the few longitudinal data bases established in each country. If we can continue to maintain these longitudinal projects within each country according to proper standards of data base management, such projects will enrich and expand our intra- and cross-national knowledge.

Program evaluation research also has important cross-national implications. These projects will have greatest application within each nation at the regional level. Even at the regional level, such projects require cooperative planning and continued integration throughout the implementation, data collection, analysis, and reporting phases. To maximize the value of evaluation research for national and cross-national comparisons, several factors must be operative: (a) there must be a reduction of "turfism," which can be accomplished by greater cooperation among the units that have a shared investment in study outcomes; (b) practitioners and policymakers should be engaged in a partnership from start to finish of the project; and (c) appropriate research questions must be matched with methodologically realistic designs. To discard research and demonstration activities is counterproductive when data on programmatic and clinical intervention effectiveness are so badly needed in the United States and Canada.

At the core of any cross-national research strategy are comparative macrolevel projects that engage the interest of scholars and practitioners and receive governmental funding commitments. Large-scale research is often so costly that no single governmental unit may be able independently to justify its costs over the long term. Because of cost there needs to be alternative funding strategies. Cooperative long-term agreements need to be established and adhered to, even if political leaders change and party priorities shift. These conditions help to assure that research can be conducted under better conditions.

It is evident that only a small proportion of Canadian and U.S. researchers and practitioners have been trained in the design and conduct of longitudinal studies. Most researchers seldom outlive their subjects and therefore rarely realize the larger pay-off for answering difficult questions that cannot be adequately addressed through any other methodological approach. Furthermore, most researchers and practitioners lack preparation for undertaking secondary analyses. The processes of research using secondary data are not understood because methodological training is dominated by teaching primary data collection and analysis techniques. This is a current barrier to comparative cross-national collaboration that could be changed by shifting research instruction objectives and priorities.

Cross-national gerontological studies would be recognized as having greater value if individual scholars and practitioners from each country were better equipped with skills in longitudinal projects. Especially is this the case in the area of configuring subsets of data that can be used with secondary analyses to answer more applied and immediate programmatic questions. This research activity requires training with access to and information selection from large data sets. The benefits of invested time, money, and energy to glean this information from large data sets are often not understood, and thus they are often passed over in a preference for other designs that have far less potential to answer questions about national policy and service provision.

QUESTIONS APPLICABLE TO CROSS-NATIONAL GERONTOLOGY

Many questions raised in the units and chapters of this text can be appropriately explored through a cross-national perspective. Questions regarding the structure and function of family systems engaged in long-term care giving are numerous and complex. What is the long-range cost-effectiveness of investing in a comprehensive system that affords financial benefits and service supports to the informal care-giving system? Over time, how do family systems gain or lose functionality as the result of sustained care for their frail elderly members? When and under what conditions does the elderly female care giver experience increased risks of impairment? What are the epidemiological charcteristics and risks of impairment? What are the epidemiological characteristics and risks of the young, middle-aged, and older women who are also the major providers of care in the formal system? What are the intervening cultural variables that help to moderate the caregiving burden? There is every reason to believe that these types of questions can be answered more adequately through various types of cross-national research efforts between United States and Canadian gerontologists, and that the issues of cross-national families can only be addressed in this way.

Specific populations have gender-related issues to consider in the planning of long-term care strategies. The demographic data presented in the second chapter points to the common trend of an increasing proportion and number of older women living into advanced old age without a spouse. Both countries have to take additional steps to guarantee that the benefit and pension structures are expanded to adequately cover cohorts of old women. Long-term care policies must be modified to assure equity between elderly men and women. Service delivery patterns must be sensitive to rural realities in both countries.

While longevity patterns of aging cohorts of the chronic mentally ill have not been systematically studied, there is clearly a gender and longevity issue to be considered. The greatest number of this subgroup likely to live into very advanced age are females. Their earlier life histories often involved living in institutions from which they were removed. Follow-up studies of these women as they reach the stages of altered mental and physical functioning would be useful. We need to understand their advanced aging processes and socialization experiences to better serve them in both countries.

The veteran service bureaucracy in each country is embroiled in a search for better ways to care for aging veteran cohorts, but attention is being given almost exclusively to male veterans. Both countries should devote attention to the elderly care-giving spouses and widows of male veterans and to female veterans who are reaching advanced ages.

The area of long-term care delivery and its similarities and variations in both countries illustrates another example of how cross-national research can be profitable. It is the responsibility of higher educational institutions to expand boundaries to include cross-national perspectives in professional training programs. Intellectual isolationism is not productive, whether in Canada or the United States.

This book is a preliminary effort to gather and organize information of cross-national value. The topics selected should be the initial areas of investigation that foster cross-national exchanges. In both countries, there are institutions and organizations that can readily redirect gerontological interest into the realm of Canadian and United States comparative efforts. It is a realistic agenda that first requires a priority for cross-national research and then a commitment to implement United States and Canadian collaboration for the benefit of all North American elderly persons—now and in the future.

Bibliography

No other text provides similar comprehensive analyses of the major aging issues in Canada and the United States on the basis of independent contributions from the leading gerontologists in both countries. All the contributing experts have presented the most current statistical, policy, and social program information on the gerontological facts and trends in their respective countries. Immediate and future societal problems and possibilities related to the aging population in North America represent a distinct knowledge base for cross-national understanding. However, there are other cross-national books in the fields of gerontology, health, and human services that provide additional information comparing Canada and/or the United States to other industrial nations with large aging populations. A few of the more readily available and relevant works of cross-national interest are listed below in alphabetical order by the authors' last names.

Brocklehurst, J.C. (1975). *Geriatric Care in Advanced Societies.* Baltimore, Md.: University Park Press.

Carboni, D.K. (1982). *Geriatric Medicine in the United States and Great Britain.* Westport, Conn.: Greenwood Press.

Corr, C.A. and Corr, D.M., eds. (1983). *Hospice Care: Principles and Practice.* New York: Springer Publishing Co.

Cowgill, D. O. and Holmes, L. D. (1972). *Aging and Modernization.* New York: Appleton-Century-Crofts.

Dean, K., Hickey, T., and Holstein, B.E., eds. (1986). *Self-Care and Health in Old Age: Health Behavior Implications for Policy and Practice.* London: Croom Helm.

Doran, C.F., and Sigler, J.H., eds. (1985). *Canada and the United States: Enduring Friendship, Persistent Stress.* Englewood Cliff, N.J.: Prentice-Hall.

Doyle, K. (1983). *Pensions around the World.* London: Witherby and Company.

Fay, C.L. (1981). *Dimensions: Aging, Culture and Health.* New York: Praeger.

Glendenning F., ed. (1985). *Educational Gerontology: International Perspectives.* New York: St. Martin's Press.

Gurland, B., Copeland, J., Rurinshy, J., Kelleher, M., and Dean, L.L. (1983). *The Mind and Mood of Aging: Mental Health Problems of the Community Elderly in New York and London.* New York: Haworth Press.

Guillemard, A.M. (1983). *Old Age and the Welfare State.* Beverly Hills, Calif.: Sage Publications.

Hatch, G.H. (1981). *Universal Free Health Care in Canada, 1947–1977.* Washington: Government Printing Office.

Kane, R.L. and Kane, R.A. (1985). *A Will and a Way. What the United States Can Learn from Canada about Caring for the Elderly.* New York: Columbia University Press.

Kayser-Jones, J.S. (1981). *Old, Alone and Neglected: Care of the Aged in Scotland and the United States.* Berkeley, Calif.: University of California Press.

Landsberger, B.H. (1985). *Long-Term Care for the Elderly: A Comparative View of Layers of Care.* New York: St. Martin's Press.

Myles, J. (1985). *Old Age in the Welfare State: The Political Economy of Public Pensions.* Boston: Little, Brown.

Soderstrom, L. (1978). *The Canadian Health System.* London: Croom Helm.

Sokolovsky, J. (1983). *Growing Old in Different Societies: Cross-Cultural Perspectives.* Belmont, Calif.: Wadsworth Publishing.

Streib, G.F. (1984). *Old Homes—New Families: Shared Living for the Elderly.* New York: Columbia University Press.

Teicher, M., Thursz, D., and Vigilante, J.L. (1979). *Reaching the Aged: Social Services in Forty-Four Countries.* Beverly Hills, Calif.: Sage Publications.

Index

Contributors

A. MARGERY BOYCE, special advisor on gerontology, Department of Veterans Affairs.

LAURENCE G. BRANCH, Ph.D., Chief, Health Service Section, Boston University, School of Public Health.

NEENA L. CHAPPELL, Ph.D., Director, Centre on Aging, University of Manitoba.

RAYMOND T. COWARD, Ph.D., Social Work Program, University of Vermont.

SUSAN FLETCHER, Office on Aging, Health and Welfare, Canada.

ELLEN M. GEE, Ph.D., Department of Sociology and Gerontology Research Centre, Simon Fraser University.

JOAN HASHIMI, Ph.D., Social Work Department, University of Missouri–St. Louis.

BETTY HAVENS, Provincial Gerontologist, Manitoba Department of Health.

NANCY HERMAN, Ph.D., Department of Sociology, McMaster University.

ROBERT HUDSON, Ph.D., School of Social Work, Boston University.

ANNE MARTIN MATTHEWS, Ph.D., Director, Centre on Aging, University of Guelph.

ALLAN R. MEYERS, Ph.D., School of Public Health, Boston University School of Medicine.

JOHN MYLES, Ph.D., Department of Sociology, Carleton University.

ELOISE RATHBONE-MCCUAN, Ph.D., Social Work Program, University of Vermont.

MARY R. MURPHY ROBERTSON, Professor, Champlain Regional College, St. Lawrence Campus.

COLIN M. SMITH, M.D., Psychiatric Services Branch, Saskatchewan Health.

LEROY O. STONE, Ph.D., Director, Population Studies Division, Statistics Canada.

PAUL STUART, Ph.D., School of Social Work, University of Alabama.

ROSAMOND M. VANDERBURGH, Ph.D., Anthropology Department, Erindale Campus, University of Toronto in Mississauga.

PHILIP G. WEILER, M.D., Department of Community Health, University of California-Davis.

PETER WOOLFSON, Ph.D., Department of Anthropology, University of Vermont.